The
best preparation for

LISTENING

2
Level

The best preparation for Listening Level 2

Published by Nexus Co., Ltd.
5 Jimok-ro, Paju-si, Gyeonggi-do 10880, Korea
www.nexusEDU.kr

Authors: Nexus Contents Development Team, Miran Hong
Publisher: Sangjin Lim
ISBN: 978-89-6790-703-7 54740 ⓔ⑪
      978-89-6790-701-3 (SET)
Copyright ⓒ 2022 Nexus Co., Ltd.

Printed in Korea

The best preparation for LISTENING

Nexus Contents Development Team · Miran Hong

2 Level

NEXUS Edu

How do we improve listening skills?

According to Asher (1974) and Hughes (1992), the four skills of language (speaking, listening, reading, and writing) are fundamentally intertwined. Then improving one language skill facilitates improvement in the other three language skills. In order to reflect this perspective during the development process of this new listening textbook, we designed tasks that give learners opportunities to relate their understanding of the sound-based messages to tasks that require speaking, reading and writing. There are several ways in which this listening series offers benefits to language learners.

Language learners need to be aware of variations in expression. We present listening information in different forms, such as in paraphrases and summaries, in order to help learners improve their awareness of how language structures are manipulated. Carefully chosen tasks encourage learners to compare, contrast, and analyze information received in different forms and to produce language appropriate to the different forms. Learners can notice the variety of language structures that reflect the way English is actually used. Sharing information in a real-life language interaction is not, after all, mostly contained in one structure.

Language learners need a variety of interesting contexts in order to make the learning experience memorable. The dialogs and passages in our listening series are in themselves interesting and offer a variety of information and ideas that add to the learner's store of general knowledge. As language learners work within these interesting contexts, they also gain awareness of differences in spoken and written discourse.

We encourage language learners to take advantage of the chances offered by this textbook to improve their listening skills in a more effective way, not only through sound-based comprehension drills, but also through our integrated skill-based tasks and structurally manipulated linguistic tasks such as summarizing and paraphrasing.

 Contents

Preface

Contents

Unit Preview

Answers

Unit Preview

Getting Ready

Students are introduced to the unit's topic. Key expressions of the unit are presented through simple exercises.

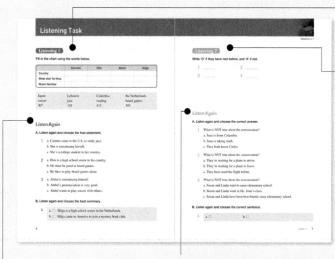

Listening Task

Listening 1 · 2

Students listen to four or five short listening scripts commonly used in everyday speech. The exercises check general comprehension of the listening material.

Listen Again

Students listen to each passage one more time.

A These multiple-choice exercises check specific level of comprehension of the listening material.

B These simple exercises require students to analyze and summarize the text-based information.

Review

Students review, by dictation,
the unit's key vocabulary and expressions.

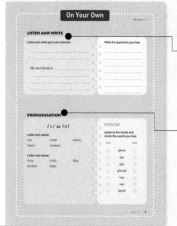

On Your Own

Listen & Write

Students identify the topic
and relate it in their own lives.

Pronunciation

Basic pronunciation rules are
reinforced for better listening
comprehension.

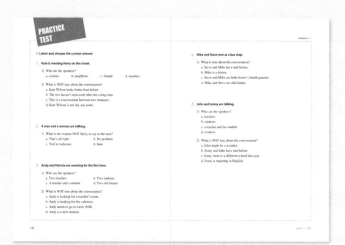

Practice Test

These multiple-choice exercises test
students on material from the entire
unit.

Dictation

Students can check their
ability to write precisely what
they hear.

Answers & Translations

The answers and translations for each unit are found in this section. Students can match their answers with the help of the answer key.

Vocabulary Test

Available via download from **www.nexusEDU.kr,** each unit's vocabulary test enables accurate assessment of student's retention of key vocabulary.

UNIT
1

I don't think we've met.

Answers p. 2

GETTING READY

1 Write 'S' if the expression is for strangers, and 'F' for friends.

I don't think we've met.   _____

What's up?   _____

How have you been doing?   _____

Don't I know you from somewhere?   _____

How's it going?   _____

Nice to meet you.   _____

Haven't we met before?   _____

My name is Will Smith.   _____

Nice to see you again.   _____

What are you up to?   _____

2 Match the expressions with the responses.

1. Haven't we met before?   •   • a. Nothing much.

2. What's up?   •   • b. Hi, my name is Sue Grant.

3. I don't think we've met. I'm Brad. • • c. No, I don't think so.

4. How have you been doing?   •   • d. Pretty good.

5. What are you up to?   •   • e. I'm going to see the doctor.

6. Why are you here?   •   • f. I'm here to get a degree in chemistry.

Listening Task

Listening 1

Fill in the chart using the words below.

	Carmen	Hiro	Abdul	Hilga
Country				
What she/ he likes				
Room Number				

Japan	Lebanon	Columbia	the Netherlands
soccer	jazz	reading	board games
307	102	415	305

Listen Again

A. Listen again and choose the true statement.

1   a. Carmen came to the U.S. to study jazz.

      b. She is introducing herself.

      c. She's a college student in her country.

2   a. Hiro is a high school senior in his country.

      b. He must be good at board games.

      c. He likes to play board games alone.

3   a. Abdul is introducing himself.

      b. Abdul's pronunciation is very good.

      c. Abdul wants to play soccer with others.

B. Listen again and choose the best summary.

4   a. ☐ Hilga is a high school senior in the Netherlands.

      b. ☐ Hilga came to America to join a mystery book club.

Listening 2

Write 'O' if they have met before, and 'X' if not.

1 _____ 2 _____

3 _____ 4 _____

Listen Again

A. Listen again and choose the correct answer.

1 What is NOT true about the conversation?

a. Juan is from Columbia.

b. Juan is taking math.

c. They both know Carlos.

2 What is NOT true about the conversation?

a. They're waiting for a plane to arrive.

b. They're waiting for a plane to leave.

c. They have used the flight before.

3 What is NOT true about the conversation?

a. Susan and Linda went to the same elementary school.

b. Susan and Linda were in Ms. Jone's class.

c. Susan and Linda have been best friends since elementary school.

B. Listen again and choose the correct sentence.

4 a. ☐ b. ☐

Review

❋ Listen and fill in the blanks.

1

John   I don't think we've _____. My name is John Smith.

Jim   Hi! I am Jim Brown. _____ to meet you.

John   Glad to _____ you, too.

2   Hi! I am Kenji Junko _____ Japan. I am a high school _____ in Japan. I am here to _____ English. I like to _____ baseball. Oh, my room number is _____.

3

W   Don't I _____ you from _____?

M   Well, I don't think so.

W   _____ you go to Green Hill high school?

M   No, I didn't.

W   I'm sorry. I was mistaken.

4   Good _____ everyone. _____ my best friend Mario. Mario _____ in Mexico but he grew up in the U.S. He _____ English and Spanish. He _____ to teach Spanish to other students.

5

Nancy   Which floor are you going to?

Cathy   10th. Thank you.

Nancy   You look _____ to me. _____ you just _____?

Cathy   Yes, just a week ago, to 1003.

Nancy   I live in 506. Hi, _____ Nancy Brown. _____.

Cathy   Hi, Cathy Johnson. _____.

8

On Your Own

Answers p. 4

LISTEN AND WRITE

Listen and write your own answers.

- _____

- _____

- My best friend is _____ .

  _____

  _____

  _____

Write the questions you hear.

_____

_____

_____

_____

_____

_____

_____

PRONUNCIATION

$/ \Lambda /$ vs $/ \partial /$

Listen and repeat.

son	come	money
lunch	summer	

Listen and repeat.

Asia	extra	idea
madam	papa	

EXERCISE

Listen to the words and check the sound you hear.

$/ \Lambda /$		$/ \partial /$
☐	about	☐
☐	run	☐
☐	ago	☐
☐	abroad	☐
☐	was	☐
☐	sun	☐
☐	lunch	☐

✳ **Listen and choose the correct answer.**

1 **Kate is meeting Harry on the street.**

1) Who are the speakers?

    a. cousins   b. neighbors   c. friends   d. teachers

2) What is NOT true about the conversation?

    a. Kate Wilson looks better than before.

    b. The two haven't seen each other for a long time.

    c. This is a conversation between two strangers.

    d. Kate Wilson is not shy any more.

2 **A man and a woman are talking.**

1) What is the woman NOT likely to say to the man?

    a. That's all right.   b. No problem.

    c. You're welcome.   d. Sure.

3 **Andy and Patricia are meeting for the first time.**

1) Who are the speakers?

    a. Two teachers   b. Two students

    c. A teacher and a student   d. Two old friends

2) What is NOT true about the conversation?

    a. Andy is looking for a teacher's room.

    b. Andy is looking for the cafeteria.

    c. Andy needs to go to room 104B.

    d. Andy is a new student.

4   **Mike and Steve met at a bus stop.**

1) What is true about the conversation?
   a. Steve and Mike have met before.
   b. Mike is a doctor.
   c. Steve and Mike are Dr. Smith's patients.
   d. Mike and Steve are old friends.

5   **John and Jenny are talking.**

1) Who are the speakers?
   a. teachers
   b. students
   c. a teacher and his student
   d. workers

2) What is NOT true about the conversation?
   a. John might be a scientist.
   b. Jenny and John have met before.
   c. Jenny went to a different school last year.
   d. Jenny is majoring in English.

Dictation
Listen and fill in the blanks.

1

W Excuse me. Harry? Harry Finn?

M Yes... And...

W It's me. Kate, Kate Wilson.

M _____ I don't think I remember you.

W _____ you do! I'm the girl who always _____ .

M Oh, the shy girl in Ms. Hill's class. Now I _____ you.

W So how are you, Harry?

M I'm doing okay. And you? You _____ _____ .

W Oh, do I? I'm the class president now. I'm not shy any more.

M All right.

2

M Haven't we _____ ?

W Well, I don't know.

M Don't you work in the _____ ?

W No, I don't.

M Oh, I'm sorry. I was _____ .

3

M Excuse me. Where is Mr. White's room?

W It's 104B. It's right _____ the cafeteria.

M Thanks a lot.

W _____ ?

M Yes, this is my second day in this school.

W Where are you _____ ?

M California.

W Oh, hi, I am Patricia Davis.

M I am Andy Wang. _____ you, Patricia.

W Nice to meet you too, Andy.

4

Mike Don't I know you from _____ ?

Steve No, I don't think so.

Mike Oh, wait! You came to see _____ Smith last week.

Steve _____ . My name is Steve West.

Mike Hi, I'm Mike Green. I'm doctor Smith's nurse.

Steve Oh, I remember you now.

Mike So, when are you _____ to see the doctor?

Steve Next Friday.

Mike See you _____ . Bye.

Steve Bye.

5

M Haven't we met _____ ?

W No, I don't think so.

M _____ ?

W Yes, because I was at another school last year.

M Well, I'm John. I'm here to get a degree in chemistry.

W Hi, I'm Jenny. _____ to get a degree in English.

UNIT

2

What name and city?

GETTING READY

1 Fill in the blanks with the words in the box below.

area code	connect	operator	press	hold	hang

1. A(n) _____ helps you with phone calls.
2. The _____ for Chicago is 901.
3. Please _____ . I'll put you through.
4. Don't _____ up. An assistant will serve you soon.
5. If you want to make a reservation, _____ 1 now.
6. Could you _____ me to Room 408 please?

2 Match the questions with the answers.

1. What name and city?   •   • a. Yes, Peter called a couple of
                                              hours ago.

2. Could you connect me to   •   • b. Brown, David. Seattle.
   Room 201 please?

3. Were there any calls for me? •   • c. Yes, please ask Jane to call
                                              me back.

4. May I take a message?   •   • d. Please hold. I'll put you
                                              through.

Listening Task

Listen to the telephone messages and choose the correct answer.

1 Who left the message?
a. Susan   b. Shirley   c. Nancy

2 Who is the message left for?
a. a dentist   b. Jeff   c. Dr. Gray

3 Where is the message from?
a. a movie theater   b. a hotel   c. an airline company

4 Who made this message?
a. a home owner   b. a company   c. a restaurant

Listen Again

A. Listen again and choose the correct answer.

1 What is true about the message?
a. Nancy is going to call again.
b. Susan is expected to call Nancy to her home number.
c. Nancy is inviting Susan.

2 What is true about the message?
a. Jeff is supposed to call back.
b. They will call Jeff again tomorrow morning.
c. The original appointment was for Friday.

3 You have to press _____ to change your reservation.
a. 2   b. 3   c. 4

B. Listen again and choose the best summary.

4 a. ☐ All the assistants are busy.
   b. ☐ People who call need to wait all the time.

14

Listening 2

Listen and choose the correct word to fill in the blank.

1 The woman is calling a(n) _____.
   a. directory assistant   b. airlinec. hospital

2 Amy is _____ right now.
   a. angry   b. in a hurry   c. excited

3 The man is calling to _____.
   a. make a reservation   b. speak to someone   c. ask for information

4 The call from Simon was a(n) _____ call.
   a. local   b. long-distance   c. international

Listen Again

A. Listen again and choose the true statement.

1 a. The woman needs to know Michael McDowell's phone number.
   b. The woman needs to know Michael McDowell's address.
   c. The woman needs to know Michael McDowell's city.

2 a. Amy cannot come to the phone right now.
   b. Amy has to hang up the phone.
   c. Amy will take a message.

3 a. The person he is calling for is out.
   b. He has the wrong number.
   c. He is leaving a message.

B. Listen again and choose the correct sentence.

4   a. ☐   b. ☐

Review

Answers p. 9

✳ **Listen and fill in the blanks.**

1

W   What name and _____?

M   Kenjo, Baltimore.

W   Could you _____ the name please?

M   It's K-_____-N-_____-O.

W   Okay. The number is _____ code 401-725-_____.

M   401-725-_____. Thank you.

2   You have _____ Park View Insurance, Co. All our assistants are _____ right now. Please _____. Our next available assistant will _____ you in a few minutes.

3

M   Hello, could you _____ me to Room 701, please?

W   Certainly. Please _____ while I _____ you through.

M   Sure.

W   There is no one in right now. May I _____ a message?

4   Thanks for _____ AT&T. If you have any questions about your telephone bill, _____ 1 now. If you have problems with your phone, _____ on the line. Our staff member will be with you shortly.

5

M   Were there any _____ for me?

W   Yes. Mary called a few _____ ago.

M   Did she _____ any messages?

W   No, she said she would call _____.

On Your Own

Answers p. 9

LISTEN AND WRITE

Listen to the questions and write your own answers.

- I dialed _____
- Yes, _____ called _____

  No, _____

- Yes, _____

  No, _____

Write the questions you hear.

_____

_____

_____

_____

PRONUNCIATION

/ θ / vs / s /

Listen and repeat.

| think | thing | thick |
| path | math | |

Listen and repeat.

| sink | sing | sick |
| pass | mass | |

Listen carefully and notice the difference.

think / sink	thing / sing
thick / sick	path / pass
math / mass	

EXERCISE

Listen and check the words you hear.

☐ think	☐ sink
☐ thing	☐ sing
☐ thick	☐ sick
☐ path	☐ pass
☐ math	☐ mass

❋ Listen and choose the correct answer.

1 **A man is talking with an operator on the phone.**

   1) What is NOT true about the conversation?
      a. The caller is asking for directory assistance.
      b. Jacob lives in San Francisco.
      c. There may be more than one Jacob Simpson.
      d. The operator gave the caller the wrong number.

   2) The caller couldn't reach Jacob because he _____.
      a. has the wrong number
      b. dialed the wrong number
      c. forgot the number

2 **Mr. Williams is leaving a message for Jeff.**

   1) Who is the caller?
      a. friend   b. teacher   c. father   d. doctor

   2) What is true about the message?
      a. Jeff is supposed to call back.
      b. Jeff is working for school newspaper.
      c. Jeff can see Mr. Williams in the morning.
      d. The newspaper has already come out.

3 **Susan and Mary are talking.**

   1) What is NOT true about the conversation?
      a. Mary is waiting for an important phone call.
      b. Susan will answer the phone for Mary.
      c. Susan will give James Mary's home phone number.
      d. Susan will take messages from James.

4   **Mr. Brown is talking to the operator.**

1)   What did the operator NOT need in the conversation?
     a. the number
     b. the country
     c. the zip code
     d. the city

2)   What number is Mr. Brown calling?
     a. 81-902-3678
     b. 81-902-3687
     c. 81-902-6378
     d. 81-920-3678

5   **Kim and Ben are talking.**

1)   What is the woman looking for?
     a. Nina's work number
     b. Directory assistance
     c. Nina's new phone number
     d. Ben's number

2)   What is true about Nina's phone number?
     a. The new number is not available in directory assistance.
     b. The new number is her home number.
     c. The new number is her work number.
     d. The work number is not available in directory assistance.

1

Operator What _____ and city?

Man Simpson, Jacob. San Francisco.

Operator _____ on Lakeside Ave.?

Man Yes.

Operator Okay. The _____ is area code 301-672-0253.

Man Thanks. ......(dialing)

Man Hello, can I speak to Jacob, please?

Woman What number did you _____?

Man Isn't this 301-672-0253?

Woman This is 301-672-2253. I think you dialed the _____ number.

Man Oh, I'm sorry.

Woman _____.

2

Hello, Jeff. This is Mr. Williams. I'm _____ the school newspaper this month. _____? You must know that the paper should be out by 25th. If you need my help, please drop by my room anytime _____ and 4 p.m. See you!

3

Mary Susan, can you _____ my phone while I'm gone? I am waiting for an important call _____ James.

Susan No problem. I will take his _____.

Mary If James calls, could you give him my cell phone number?

Susan _____.

4

Mr. Brown Hello, operator?

Operator This is the _____. How can I help you?

Mr. Brown I want to _____ an international call.

Operator What number, city and _____?

Mr. Brown Could you connect me to 81-902-3678 in Tokyo, Japan?

Operator _____, please... Please hold... I'll put you through, now. _____, please.

Mr. Brown Thank you.

5

Kim What is Nina's new cell phone number?

Ben I _____ it, Kim. Don't you know it?

Kim No, Ben. I called her home and she's _____. I'll have to call her on her new cell phone.

Ben Just ask for _____ assistance.

Kim They don't tell you cell phone numbers.

Ben OK, call and get her work number. Maybe, you can _____ there.

Kim You're right.

UNIT
3

She is too messy.

Answers p. 11

GETTING READY

1 Fill in the blanks with the letters of the words in the box below.

a. forgetful	b. messy	c. generous	d. dirty
e. pushy	f. bossy	g. mean	

1. He wants to do everything in his own way. _____

2. He forgets our date. _____

3. He breaks my things and doesn't say sorry. _____

4. She keeps telling me to work harder. _____

5. She forgives my small mistakes. _____

6. He doesn't pick up his things off the floor. _____

7. He doesn't brush his teeth. _____

2 Match the questions with the answers.

1. Didn't you notice any difference? •   • a. Yes, a lot better.

2. What is she like? •   • b. He is too bossy.

3. Is this one better? •   • c. Yes, I did. He has changed a lot.

4. How do you like your boyfriend? •   • d. She is nice and friendly.

Listening Task

Teens are talking on a radio show. Choose the correct word to fill in the blank.

1   Her boyfriend is too _____.
    a. shy   b. bossy   c. quiet

2   His mother is too _____.
    a. pushy   b. messy   c. mean

3   His friend is too _____.
    a. noisy   b. forgetful   c. bossy

4   Her brother is too _____.
    a. messy   b. mean   c. noisy

Listen Again

A. Listen again and choose the false statement.

1   a. Her boyfriend always gives her presents.
    b. Her boyfriend doesn't care her feelings.
    c. Her boyfriend never takes her home.

2   a. His mother thinks he is not smart.
    b. His mother thinks he doesn't work hard.
    c. His mother hurts his feelings.

3   a. His friend forgets their appointment.
    b. His friend never says sorry.
    c. His friend has been his best friend for a long time.

B. Listen again and choose the best summary.

4   a. ☐ She cannot stand her brother because he is too mean.
    b. ☐ She cannot stand her brother because he is too young.

Listening 2

Are the changes good or bad? Check one.

1   a. ☐ good   b. ☐ bad

2   a. ☐ good   b. ☐ bad

3   a. ☐ good   b. ☐ bad

4   a. ☐ good   b. ☐ bad

Listen Again

A. Listen again and choose the correct answer.

1   What made Karen change?

     a. her friends

     b. her boyfriend

     c. her family

2   What is NOT true about the new teacher?

     a. She is generous.

     b. She is different from the last teacher.

     c. She is pretty and smart.

3   What is NOT true about Peter?

     a. He washes his clothes.

     b. He hangs his clothes.

     c. He makes his bed.

B. Listen again and choose the correct sentence.

4   a. ☐   b. ☐

Review

Answers p. 14

✳ Listen and fill in the blanks.

1

W Have you _____ Ken lately?

M Yes, why?

W Didn't you _____ any difference?

M Yes, I did. He is totally _____!

2 I don't like Alex. She is very _____. She never says "thank you" or "sorry."

She is also very _____. She wants to do everything in her own _____.

She thinks she is the smartest in our school. I like Terry better for school president.

3

M What is your new roommate _____?

W She is really _____.

M You must _____ the last one.

W I do. She was nice and _____.

4 I really like my new teacher. She is not very _____, but she is very _____

and _____. She is _____ than the last one. I am really

happy to be in her class.

5

M I don't want to go to school.

W What's the problem?

M My teacher is too _____. She gives too much homework. And she is
not very _____.

24

LISTEN AND WRITE

Listen and write your own answers.

• My mom is _____

_____

• She / He is _____

_____

• I think she(he) is _____

_____

Write the questions you hear.

_____

_____

_____

_____

_____

PRONUNCIATION

/ tʃ / vs / dʒ /

Listen and repeat.

chair   change   choose
match   watch

Listen and repeat.

Janet   juice   jug
bridge   village

EXERCISE

Listen to the words and check the sound you hear.

/ tʃ /		/ dʒ /
☐	jug	☐
☐	cheap	☐
☐	cheep	☐
☐	jeep	☐
☐	much	☐
☐	college	☐
☐	Mitch	☐

✳ Listen and choose the correct answer.

1 Two friends are talking about their boyfriends.

1) Why is Amy's boyfriend NOT perfect?
   a. He is too generous.   b. He is too messy.
   c. He is too forgetful.   d. He is too gentle.

2) What does he forget?
   a. He forgets their date.
   b. He forgets her birthday.
   c. He forgets her phone number.
   d. He forgets to give her flowers.

2 Sam is talking about Chris at school.

1) Chris is running for _____.
   a. school president   b. club president
   c. class president   d. company president

2) What is NOT true about Chris?
   a. hard-working   b. helpful
   c. polite   d. hard to others

3 Jeff and Mrs. Brown are talking.

1) What does Jeff NOT say about Tim's mother?
   a. She is very nice.
   b. She is very generous.
   c. She doesn't do Tim's homework.
   d. She gives Tim lots of money.

2) What is Tim like in Mrs. Brown's opinion?
   a. generous   b. nice   c. friendly   d. careless

4 **John and Sue are talking.**

1) What was Gail like before?
   a. She was always on time.
   b. She always forgot to meet John.
   c. She played loud music all the time.
   d. She was dirty.

2) What is NOT true about Sue's boyfriend?
   a. He is noisy.
   b. He is dirty.
   c. He plays loud music.
   d. He is always late for everything.

5 **A college student is talking to her grandmother on the telephone.**

1) What was her boyfriend like before?
   a. sorry   b. forgiving
   c. nice   d. forgetful

2) What is the mood of the conversation?
   a. relaxed   b. angry
   c. afraid   d. impatient

Answers p. 16

1

Mary _____ your boyfriend _____, Amy?

Amy He is nice and gentle. He is very _____. He gives me flowers all the time.

Mary He is _____, isn't he?

Amy Well, _____.

Mary Why not?

Amy He is very _____. He forgets our date and doesn't show up. I am very upset with him sometimes.

Mary But he is better than my boyfriend. Mine is _____.

2

Chris is a wonderful person. He _____ _____. He helps others a lot. _____ on himself but generous to others. He is smart and _____. He doesn't talk much but listens. He can do a lot for our class and _____. I think he will make the perfect class president.

3

M Mom, Tim's mother is very nice.

W _____?

M She is never angry. She _____ doing Tim's homework.

W Really? Tim must like her very much.

M _____. And she is very generous. She gives Tim a lot of pocket money.

W Oh, _____ Tim is rude, _____ and messy.

4

M Hey, Sue. _____ from Gail?

W No, why, John?

M _____, again.

W But she is always on time!

M I know! But, she has really _____.

W How?

M She often forgets to meet me. She plays loud music _____ and doesn't brush her teeth.

W That's too bad. My boyfriend is like that, _____ he's always on time.

5

Hi, Grandmother! I'm fine. My boyfriend? He is doing _____, too. Of course, I still like him. Yes, he used to forget our dates, _____, and not say he was sorry. But, Grandmother! He has changed a lot. _____, now? He is nice and friendly and forgives my small mistakes.

Put the coin in first!

Answers p. 16

GETTING READY

1 Fill in the blanks with the correct words in the box below.

| insert | pick | press | click | turn | enter | raise | mix | add | point |

1. _____ the button on the screen.
2. _____ on the computer.
3. _____ your ID and password.
4. _____ on the icon with the mouse.
5. _____ your arms and _____ them straight out.
6. _____ some salt and _____ the all the ingredients well.
7. _____ up the receiver and _____ coins.

2 Following are directions on how to cook rice. Put them in the right order.

a. Can you tell me how to do it?

b. Sure, come on. I'll show you how.

c. Next, put the washed rice in a pot.

d. Add three cups of water into the rice.

e. First, wash two cups of rice.

f. And then cook it for 10 minutes on a high heat.

g. Finally, turn down the heat and cook another 5 minutes on a low heat.

_____ ➡ _____ ➡ _____ ➡ _____ ➡ _____ ➡ _____ ➡ _____

Listening Task

There are two sets of instructions. Listen and number the pictures.

1

2

Listen Again

Listen again and choose the correct word. (Don't look at the pictures above.)

1 1) You should raise your (legs / arms).

2) You should point your arms (out / forward).

3) You shouldn't bend your (arms / knees).

4) You should touch your hands to your (shoulders / feet).

2 1) You need (two / three) eggs.

2) You add some (oil / salt).

3) Let the bag of eggs stay in the boiling water for (twenty / fifteen) minutes.

4) You need a (dish / pot).

Listening 2

What are the directions about? Listen and choose the correct answer.

1   a. how to turn on the computer
   b. how to enter a password
   c. how to access to the Internet

2   a. how to use a vending machine
   b. how to drink canned soda
   c. how to change a bill for coins in the machine

3   a. how to buy pictures from the Internet
   b. how to upload pictures to an on-line album
   c. how to upload to an Internet site

4   a. how to make a long-distance call
   b. how to get help from the operator
   c. how to use a pay phone

Listen Again

A. Listen again and choose the correct answer.

1   What do you first see on the screen?
   a. server home page   b. icons

2   What do you do first?
   a. get the change   b. take out your drink

3   What do you do first?
   a. hit the "Upload Image"   b. click the 'Browse'

B. Listen again and choose the correct sentence.

4   a. ☐   b. ☐

Answers p. 18

✳ **Listen and fill in the blanks.**

1

M Can you _____ me how to _____ the pay phone?

W First, _____ up the receiver. _____ 35 cents in the slot.

M I hear the _____ .

W Now you _____ the number. That's it.

2 Here's your warm-up exercise. Everybody, _____ up straight. _____ your arms. _____ your left foot with your right hand.

3

W How can I access the Internet?

M _____ on the computer.

W I see the start menu.

M _____ on the icon 'Internet Explorer' on the _____ .

W I see the server home page.

M _____ your ID and password.

4 This is how to make scrambled eggs. First, _____ two eggs into a bowl. _____ a little salt and pepper. _____ them well. Pour the mixture onto the _____ . Now cook it and enjoy it.

5

M Hey, I will show you how to _____ your pictures. First, _____ the 'Browse' button.

W Okay.

M Now _____ the picture you want and hit the '_____' button and wait. In a few seconds, you will have the _____ on your _____ album.

On Your Own

LISTEN AND WRITE

Listen and write your own answers.

• First, _____

_____

_____

• _____

_____

• _____

_____

Write the questions you hear.

_____

_____

_____

_____

_____

_____

PRONUNCIATION

/ m / vs / n /

Listen and repeat.

mail	moon	mine
sum	gum	

Listen and repeat.

nail	noon	nine
sun	gun	

Listen carefully and notice the difference.

mail / nail   moon / noon

mine / nine   sum / sun

gum / gun

EXERCISE

Listen and check the words you hear.

☐ mail   ☐ nail

☐ moon   ☐ noon

☐ mine   ☐ nine

☐ sum   ☐ sun

☐ gum   ☐ gun

PRACTICE TEST

✲ Listen and choose the correct answer.

1 **Minsu is using a pay phone for the first time.**

1) What is NOT true about the conversation?
   a. It's about how to use a pay phone.
   b. It's about how to make a long-distance call.
   c. It's about how to make a local call.

2) Which action comes first?
   a. pick up the receiver b. put coins in c. talk to the operator

2 **The following are the directions to make scrambled eggs.**

1) Listen and number the pictures in the order you hear.

2) What do you NOT need to make scrambled eggs?
   a. milk b. pan c. bowl d. sugar

3 **A man is using an ATM machine for the first time.**

1) What is the man trying to do?
   a. send money b. take out money c. deposit money

2) Which action comes first?
   a. touch the button on the screen
   b. enter your password
   c. take your receipt

4 A mother and her son are talking.

1) Which one comes last?
   a. wash the rice
   b. wash the potatoes
   c. mix the rice and potatoes
   d. peel the potatoes

2) What do you NOT need to make the soup?
   a. rice   b. potatoes
   c. sack   d. water

5 An elderly woman is talking to a group.

1) Who is the speaker?
   a. student   b. teacher
   c. parent   d. principal

2) What is NOT true about the talk?
   a. It's about how to use a word processing program.
   b. It's about how to write a thank-you note to parents.
   c. It's about how to thank teachers.
   d. It's about how to use new computers.

1

M   Can you tell me _____ this
    phone please?

w   Is it a _____ call?

M   No, it's a long-distance call.

w   Then pick up the _____.

M   Okay.

w   Now dial the number. Be sure to dial 1
    first. Now the operator will tell you how
    much money you need to put in.

M   She says it's $1.75.

w   Put the money _____. That's it.

M   Thanks a lot.

w   No _____.

2

1. _____ two eggs into a bowl.

2. _____ some milk and salt.

3. Mix everything together.

4. Pour the mixture onto a pan and heat it.

5. Stir the eggs until they are _____.

6. Now _____ the heat and enjoy it.

3

M   How can I use this machine? I want to
    _____ some money.

w   Put your card in the slot.

M   Now what? There is a menu on the screen.

w   Touch the 'withdraw' button on the screen.

M   Now I need to enter my _____.

w   Yes, _____. And enter the
    amount of money you want to take out.

M   Oh, here comes my money. Thank you.

w   _____.

4

w   Let's make soup.

M   Can you _____ how to do it?

w   Sure. What kind of soup do you want?

M   _____ potato and rice soup.
    I'll get the potatoes.

w   Okay. Get five potatoes from the sack.
    Then _____ and peel them. I'll
    wash and prepare the rice. Two cups of
    rice in three cups of water. Then, heat
    _____ on high.

M   I want to mix them together.

w   Okay.

5

_____ your computers and enter
your IDs and passwords. Click on the icon
with the mouse and double click here.
Very good! _____ your mouse at the
folder and click _____. This is your
word processing program. Now, everyone
_____ a thank-you note and e-mail it
to _____ for these new school
computers.

UNIT

5

The steak is too cold!

Answers p. 20

1 What are the following descriptions about? Write the correct letters in the box below.

| a. service | b. food | c. location | d. price | e. atmosphere |

1. The restaurant is hard to find. _____
2. The waiters and waitresses are really nice and friendly. _____
3. It is fresh and delicious. _____
4. It is cozy. The music is great, too. _____
5. They charge too much. _____
6. The chef knows how to cook. _____
7. The waitresses don't care about their customers. _____
8. You will feel at home. _____

2 Match the expressions with the responses.

1. How did you like the place? •   • a. Me too. I'm stuffed.
2. Have you tried Mexican food? •   • b. Yes, it was great.
3. I'm full. I can't eat one more bite. •   • c. No, I haven't. Have you?
4. Did you enjoy your meal, sir? •   • d. It was good. I liked the food.
5. How much longer do we have   • • e. Seems like it will take forever.
   to wait to eat?

Listening Task

Listening 1

Which place is the best for each situation? Write the correct number.

· When you want to eat seafood.   _____

· When you want to eat spicy food.   _____

· When you don't have time to cook or eat out.   _____

· When you want to eat something light and unusual.   _____

Listen Again

A. Listen again and choose the true statement.

1 a. It is an Asian restaurant.

   b. The food is good, but the service is better.

   c. You can eat Chinese food there.

2 a. It is a Vietnamese restaurant.

   b. They serve mostly meat.

   c. You can enjoy Thai culture there.

3 a. It is an Italian restaurant.

   b. The food is fresh and delicious.

   c. They have a special price all the time.

B. Listen again and choose the best summary.

4 a. ☐ Quick Cuisine offers hot American meals in 30 minutes.

   b. ☐ Quick Cuisine delivers for free.

Listening 2

What do speakers like about each eating place? Choose the correct answer.

1   a. location   b. service   c. food

2   a. price   b. service   c. food

3   a. service   b. location   c. atmosphere

4   a. price   b. food   c. atmosphere

Listen Again

A. Listen again and choose the correct answer.

1   What is the problem of the place?
    a. It is not easy to find.
    b. It is too small.
    c. The chef is not experienced.

2   What is the problem of the place?
    a. The service is too slow.
    b. The waitresses are too noisy.
    c. It is too crowded.

3   What is the problem of the place?
    a. The meal is too expensive.
    b. Their service charge is too high.
    c. The meal is not good enough.

B. Listen again and choose the correct sentence.

4   a. ☐   b. ☐

Review

Answers p. 22

✳ **Listen and fill in the blanks.**

1

W Did you _____ your meal?

M Yes, it was really good. I really liked your place.

W Thank you. Here's your _____.

2 If you like Mexican food, you should _____ the new Mexican restaurant. It is easy to _____. You can also listen to Mexican music and _____ traditional Mexican culture there. The waitresses _____ in traditional Mexican dresses.

3

M I am _____. I can't eat another _____.

W The food is excellent.

M But the _____ is poor. It is too _____.

4 You are _____ of hamburgers and pizza and you feel like something _____ and unusual. How about _____ noodle soup? Please call at _____ - _____ - 204 - 2354. We are a new Thai restaurant _____. You can get a delicious Tai _____ in 30 minutes.

5

W Have you _____ the new Chinese restaurant?

M No, is it good?

W Yes, the _____ is excellent. But what I like best is you can _____ some live music there.

LISTEN AND WRITE

Listen and write your own answers.

Write the questions you hear.

- Yes, I _____

  No, I _____

- The restaurant _____

  _____

- Yes, I _____

  No, I _____

_____

_____

_____

_____

_____

_____

PRONUNCIATION

How to Pronounce -ed

/ id / *vs* / t /

Listen and repeat.

wanted   ended

Listen and repeat.

liked   watched   hoped

laughed   washed

EXERCISE

Listen and write each word in the correct column.

started, missed, worked
waited, needed, baked

/ id /	/ t /
_____	_____
_____	_____
_____	_____

✳ Listen and choose the correct answer.

1 **Two people are talking about what to eat.**

1) What are they NOT going to eat tonight?
   a. steaks   b. Korean food
   c. something light   d. something different

2) What is NOT true about Korean food according to the speakers?
   a. It is light.   b. It is healthy.
   c. It is mostly vegetables and grains.   d. It is healthy but not tasty.

2 **A man is talking about a restaurant.**

1) What is the problem with the place?
   a. food   b. location   c. service   d. atmosphere

2) What is NOT true about the place?
   a. The service is fast.
   b. The waiters are nice.
   c. It is a little expensive.
   d. It is hard to find.

3 **Two people are talking about what to eat.**

1) What is true about the conversation?
   a. They will eat out.
   b. They will eat something in the refrigerator.
   c. They will order something home.
   d. They will eat pizza.

2) What is NOT true about the food?
   a. popular   b. nice
   c. a little expensive   d. cold

4 **Tim is talking to Kelly.**

1) Where is the conversation taking place?
   a. in Mexico
   b. in the Mexican restaurant
   c. in the Market
   d. in the Hot spa

2) What is NOT true about the conversation?
   a. Kelly has eaten Mexican food before.
   b. The chef cooks hot and strange food.
   c. Tim likes rice.
   d. The chef makes delicious meals.

5 **A woman is talking.**

1) The woman is talking about _____.
   a. the restaurant where she works
   b. food and service
   c. the restaurant where she eats every day
   d. her favorite restaurant

2) What is NOT one of the restaurant's problems?
   a. the customers
   b. the location
   c. the amount of food
   d. the price

Answers p. 25

1

M Let's have dinner _____ tonight.

W Sure. Where would you like to go?

M _____ some Asian food? I'd like something light and different. _____ burgers and fries.

W Me, too.

M Let's go to the Korean restaurant _____.

W Is it good?

M Oh, yes. The food there is mostly vegetables and grains. My friend Sandy is _____ bibimbap there. She says it's really tasty and _____, too.

2

It's my _____ restaurant. _____ _____, the food is fresh and delicious. Second, the service is excellent. It is _____ slow. You never have to wait more than twenty minutes to eat. The waiters and waitresses are _____. And it is _____. The only problem is the location. It is hard to _____.

3

M Let's _____ this evening.

W I don't want to.

M But there's nothing to eat in the refrigerator. _____ something nice and hot.

W Why don't we _____ something at home?

M Like what? Pizza? No way.

W There's a food delivery chain. I have the phone number here. _____. Everybody says the food is nice and hot, even though it's a little expensive.

M _____.

4

M Kelly, have you tried Mexican food before?

W Yes, it was great! Haven't you ever _____ it, Tim?

M No, I think it might be _____ and strange for me.

W Oh, this chef knows _____ it right. The food is fresh and delicious with lots of rice.

M Rice! I would _____ that meal!

5

My favorite restaurant has some _____. It's hard to find and it's a little expensive to eat there. And _____, they serve too much food. However, I go there almost every weekend because of the great food and service. The food is really _____ and the waitresses are really nice and friendly. They really _____ their customers.

44

I want a refund.

Answers p. 25

GETTING READY

1 Write 'CL' if it is said by a store clerk, and 'CU' if it is said by a customer.

1. I'd like a refund on this. _____

2. Where is the customer service? _____

3. It looks good on you. _____

4. When does the sale end? _____

5. Can I exchange this for a different one? _____

6. We can give you an extra 5% off. _____

7. Do you have the receipt with you? _____

2 Match the expressions with the responses.

1. Did you pay by cash or by card? •   • a. No, but we can order one
                                             for you.

2. I'd like to get a refund on this. •   • b. No, it's already on sale.

3. Can you give me a discount? •   • c. You look great.

4. Do you have this one size smaller? •   • d. What's the problem?

5. How do I look? •   • e. By cash.

Listening Task

Choose the correct clothing item each speaker is talking about.

1   a. spring blouse   b. summer blouse   c. spring dress

2   a. wool coat   b. suit   c. fur coat

3   a. shoes   b. jacket   c. hat

4   a. suit   b. shoes   c. sweater

Listen Again

A. Listen again and choose the false statement.

1   a. The item is green.

    b. The price is good.

    c. It's too long for the customer.

2   a. It is quite expensive.

    b. The customer has not been here before.

    c. The item is already on sale.

3   a. She likes the material of the item.

    b. She likes the style of the item.

    c. She wants a bigger size.

B. Listen again and choose the best summary.

4   a. ☐ The items in the store are 50% off.

    b. ☐ It's the first sale of the year.

46

Listening 2

People are in a store. Listen and choose the correct answer.

1　The customer is _____.
　a. making a payment　　　b. getting a refund　　　c. exchanging an item

2　The customer is _____.
　a. looking for something to buy　　　　　b. exchanging an item
　c. asking for information about the store

3　The customer will _____.
　a. have a radio of different brand　　　　b. have his money back
　c. buy something different

4　The customer is _____.
　a. correcting a bill　　　b. making a complaint　　　c. getting a refund

Listen Again

A. Listen again and choose the true statement.

1　a. She needs to have the receipt with her.
　b. She paid by credit card.
　c. She brought the item because she didn't like the color.

2　a. The item was too small.
　b. He wants a refund on the item.
　c. The customer service will take care of this.

3　a. He has to show the receipt.
　b. He has to fill out a form.
　c. He has to fix it himself.

B. Listen again and choose the correct sentence.

4　　a. ☐　　　　　　　　　　b. ☐

Review

Answers p. 27

❄ Listen and fill in the blanks.

1

W   I'd like a _____ on this hat.

M   Do you have the _____ with you?

W   Yes, here it is.

M   Did you pay by _____ or card?

2   The coat looks good _____ you. I like the _____ and style. Pink is very

_____ this year. Besides, it's not too expensive. It is _____,

40% off the original price.

3

W   Can I _____ this shirt for a new one?

M   What was the problem with it?

W   It has a small _____ in it.

M   Oh, sorry about that. Sure. Take _____.

4   I think these pants look great _____ me. Also it was buy one _____ one free. It

was a good _____ to get these great pants at half the price. The sale _____

today and it is the last sale of the year. Maybe I should _____ another pair.

5

W   Do you have this one _____ smaller? This is a little big for me. I
_____ a size 6 1/2.

M   Sorry, we don't have the size right now. But we can _____ one for you.

W   How long will it take?

M   Less than three days.

On Your Own

Answers p. 27

LISTEN AND WRITE

Listen and write your own answers.

- I bought _____
- Yes, _____
- I think _____
- Yes, it was _____

  No, It _____

Write the questions you hear.

_____

_____

_____

_____

_____

PRONUNCIATION

Intonation
↗ vs ↘

Listen and repeat these questions.

Is Amy home?

Do I go straight ahead?

Is it on the right?

Listen and repeat these questions.

How do you make an apple pie?

Where can I put my bag?

When can I go home?

EXERCISE

Listen to the questions and check up(↗) or down(↘).

          ↗ ↘

Do I turn left? ☐ ☐

What are you doing on Friday? ☐ ☐

Can I call you later? ☐ ☐

How are you doing? ☐ ☐

* Yes/no questions usually have a rising intonation.

* Wh- and how questions usually have a falling intonation.

✳ **Listen and choose the correct answer.**

1   A man is talking to a clerk.

1) The man is trying to _____.
   a. exchange the item   b. get the item repaired
   c. refund on the item   d. correct the bill

2) What is true about the conversation?
   a. The item has a hole in the screen.
   b. The man has to take the item to the customer service.
   c. The customer service is far from the door.
   d. The item is a VCR.

2   A woman is talking.

1) The woman doesn't like the _____ of the dress.
   a. color   b. style   c. material   d. price

2) What is true about the talk?
   a. She wants a refund on her dress.
   b. She wants a cheaper one.
   c. She wants to exchange the dress.
   d. She wants to get a discount.

3   Jeff and his friend are talking.

1) What's the problem with the computer?
   a. It is broken.
   b. It doesn't work.
   c. It doesn't start at all.
   d. It makes noise.

2) What is true about the conversation?

    a. She can't get a refund on the computer.

    b. She bought it almost three months ago.

    c. She wants to get it fixed.

    d. She will take it to the store to get a refund.

4 A girl is shopping.

1) Who are the speakers?

    a. two customers

    b. two store clerks

    c. dad and daughter

    d. a store clerk and a girl

2) What will the girl probably do, next?

    a. buy the hat

    b. leave the store

    c. put on the hat

    d. get a different hat

5 A woman is in a store.

1) What is true about the conversation?

    a. Her skirt was too large.

    b. The amount on the receipt was too small.

    c. She bought the last skirt in the store.

    d. She got a different skirt.

2) The woman will get _____.

    a. one size smaller   b. an exchange

    c. a discount   d. a refund

1

M I'd like to _____ on this TV.

W Is there a problem?

M Yes, the screen is cracked.

W You _____ to take it to customer service. They will take care of it.

M Where is _____?

W It's _____ the hall next to the other door.

M Thanks a lot.

W _____.

2

This dress is beautiful. I like the color. Pink is my favorite color. I like the _____, too. It's not too long and _____. It's cute. I also like the soft silky material. The problem is the _____. It's too _____. It's on sale, but it still costs too much money. Can you give me a _____?

3

M What's wrong with the computer? It doesn't work.

W Yes. The problem _____ yesterday. When it happens, I have to start it all _____.

M When did you buy it?

W In June.

M _____ take it to the store right now. You can get a refund within three months after you buy it.

W I think _____.

4

M You'll look great in this hat!

W No, I'll try on a different one. How about this one?

M Yes, that looks good on you. You should get that one.

W Do you have this one size _____ in blue?

M Don't worry! _____.

W I won't have any _____ until Saturday. When does the sale end?

M On Sunday.

5

W Can I exchange this skirt for a different one?

M What's the problem?

W It's too _____.

M Do you have the receipt with you?

W Yes, but _____ one size smaller?

M No, yours is the only one.

W Then, I'd like to get a refund.

M Don't you want to _____ it for another item?

W No, thanks. I just want my _____.

I'd like to make a reservation.

Answers p. 30

GETTING READY

1 Write 'CL' if it is said by a clerk, and 'CU' by a customer.

1. I'd like to reserve a table for two. _____

2. I'd like a room for two nights, please. _____

3. Have you made a reservation? _____

4. I have to cancel my reservation. _____

5. Is a back row seat okay with you? _____

6. I'm calling to confirm my reservation. _____

7. I'm afraid you have to wait for 30 minutes. _____

8. I made a reservation under the name of John Smith. _____

9. Are there any tickets available? _____

2 Match the expressions with the responses.

1. Are there any seats left? • • a. By the window.

2. Where would you prefer to sit? • • b. At 8 p.m.

3. Smoking or non-smoking? • • c. Sure. What's your name, please?

4. What time are you arriving? • • d. Not right now.

5. I have to cancel my reservation. • • e. Non-smoking, please.

6. How long will you be staying? • • f. For three nights.

Listening Task

People are leaving messages on the phone. Choose the correct answer.

1 The message is to reserve a _____.
   a. table at a restaurant   b. hotel room   c. seat at a concert

2 The message is left for a _____.
   a. teacher   b. doctor   c. dentist

3 The person called a _____.
   a. restaurant   b. hotel   c. theater

4 The person called a(n) _____.
   a. airline company   b. restaurant   c. doctor's office

Listen Again

A. Listen again and choose the true statement.

1 a. The woman wants the smoking section.
   b. There is a lake by the restaurant.
   c. The woman will be with a big group of people.

2 a. She wants to change her appointment.
   b. Her daughter has a toothache.
   c. She wants an appointment as soon as possible.

3 a. He wants a double room.
   b. He will stay in the hotel for 2 days.
   c. He will call again later.

B. Listen again and choose the best summary.

4 a. ☐ He wants to have the return call today.
   b. ☐ He is going to New York with a friend.

Listening 2

Where is the conversation taking place? Choose the correct answer.

1 a. restaurant b. hotel c. travel agency

2 a. movie theater b. concert hall c. airline company

3 a. hotel b. movie theater c. restaurant

4 a. airline company b. hotel c. restaurant

Listen Again

A. Listen again and choose the correct answer.

1 What is NOT true about the conversation?
   a. He is going to travel in India.
   b. The trip is scheduled for this month.
   c. He hasn't made a reservation yet.

2 What is true about the conversation?
   a. The woman will watch the show on the back row.
   b. The woman will not watch the show.
   c. The woman will watch the show on the front row.

3 What is true about the conversation?
   a. He is alone here.
   b. He will wait for some time.
   c. He will go to another place to eat.

B. Listen again and choose the correct sentence.

4   a. ☐ b. ☐

Review

Answers p. 32

✳ Listen and fill in the blanks.

1
> W I'd like to _____ a table for four.
>
> M Sure. For when?
>
> W Friday at 6:30 p.m.
>
> M Would you _____ smoking or non-smoking?
>
> W Non-smoking, by the window, please.

2
I'd like to make a _____ for the flight to L.A. this Friday afternoon. I'll be _____ and I'd prefer a _____ seat.

3
> M I'm calling to _____ my reservation.
>
> W Can I have your name, please?
>
> M Brian Nelson.
>
> W Your reservation for flight 605 to L.A. has been _____.

4
Hello. I'm afraid I have to _____ my reservation for flight #342 to Chicago. My name is Jane Pond, and the time is _____ the 12th at 7:00. Please give me a _____ and let me know if it is possible. My _____ number is 715-254-_____.

5
> M I think there's a _____ on my reservation.
>
> W What do you mean, sir?
>
> M I reserved a _____ room, not single.
>
> W Let me check the record. You're right. We're very sorry. But we have some double rooms _____ right now. Would you like one?

On Your Own

Answers p. 32

LISTEN AND WRITE

Listen and write your own answers.

- Yes, I _____
- No, I _____
- _____
  _____
- _____
  _____

Write the questions you hear.

_____

_____

_____

_____

_____

PRONUNCIATION

Stress
beginning *vs* end

Listen and repeat.

pílot	déntist	clínic
óffice	dríver	

Listen and repeat.

guitár	befóre	Japán
Taiwán	routíne	

EXERCISE

Listen and write "b" if the stress is at the beginning and "e" if the stress is at the end.

airline _____

honest _____

yourself _____

CD _____

Monday _____

below _____

✳ Listen and choose the correct answer.

1 **A man is talking on the phone.**

1) What is the phone call for?
   a. to reserve a table at a restaurant
   b. to reserve a seat at a concert
   c. to reserve a room at a hotel
   d. to reserve a seat at a flight

2) What is NOT true about the conversation?
   a. He is going to stay for one night.
   b. He reserved one double room.
   c. He is staying in the hotel this week.
   d. They don't have any double rooms available.

2 **A man is talking on the phone.**

1) What is the man making the reservation for?
   a. a bus ticket   b. a train ticket
   c. a plane ticket   d. a concert ticket

2) What is NOT true about the reservation?
   a. It is for a one-way ticket.   b. It for a first-class seat.
   c. It is for May.   d. It is to Boston.

3 **A woman is talking on the phone.**

1) What is the woman doing?
   a. She is making a reservation.
   b. She is canceling the reservation.
   c. She is changing her reservation.
   d. She is confirming a reservation.

2) What is NOT true about the conversation?

   a. The woman's name is Karen Johnson.

   b. She is calling a restaurant.

   c. She will go there with two other people.

   d. It is not Tuesday yet.

4 The following is a phone conversation.

1) Where is the man calling to?

   a. train station

   b. travel agency

   c. hotel

   d. apartment rental office

2) What does the man NOT want?

   a. a quiet room

   b. a view of the lake

   c. a room for two nights

   d. a smoking room

5 The following is a phone conversation.

1) What is NOT true about the woman's reservations?

   a. She will take a flight.

   b. She and two others are confirmed.

   c. She arrives at 11 p.m.

   d. She leaves on Saturday.

2) The woman will NOT sit _____.

   a. by the window

   b. on the back row

   c. with two others

Dictation
Listen and fill in the blanks.

1

M Hello, I'd like to _____ a room for coming Saturday.

W Certainly. How long will you be staying?

M _____.

W Would you like a single or _____ _____?

M A double room, please.

W _____ we don't have any double rooms available.

M Then make it two single rooms please.

W _____, sir. Two single rooms for Saturday the 5th.

2

M Hello, can I reserve a train ticket _____ _____?

W Certainly.

M I'd like to reserve a _____ from Boston to Chicago.

W Which date will you be _____?

M May 28.

W Which class would you like?

M First class, please.

W Okay. Can I have the name for the _____?

M Please _____ Nick Wilson.

3

W _____ change my reservation.

M Sure. Can I have your name and the time of reservation, please?

W It's under my name Karen Johnson, Tuesday at 8:00 p.m.

M _____ to change it?

W Please make it a _____ for six, not two.

M Okay. Anything else?

W No, _____ is the same.

4

W Park Lake Inn! How can I help you?

M I'd like to make a reservation for a room, please.

W Certainly! _____ are you going to stay?

M _____.

W Do you prefer smoking or _____?

M Non-smoking, please. Quiet with a view of the lake, if _____!

W Sure! What's your name, please?

5

W I'm calling to _____ my flight on Saturday.

M Certainly.

W I made the reservations under the name of Jenny Smith.

M Yes, _____ are you arriving?

W At 11 a.m. Are there _____ left by the window?

M Not right now. But would back row seats be _____?

W Sure.

M All three of you are confirmed.

60

UNIT

8

What's going on?

Answers p. 34

GETTING READY

1 Fill in the blanks with the words in the box below.

| upstairs | stains | neighborhood | floor | story | rent | view |

1. There are so many stores in my _____.

2. The walls are covered with _____. They're so dirty.

3. The house is old and dirty, so the _____ is very low.

4. My room is _____ right under the attic.

5. My apartment is on the tenth _____ of that building.

6. It has a great _____.

7. My home is a two-_____ house.

2 Match the expressions with the responses.

1. There is a leak in the sink.   •
2. How long have you been living here?   •
3. What color will the room be?   •
4. Are you moving out of town?   •

• a. Since I was four.
• b. It will be green.
• c. We have to call a plumber.
• d. No, in the same neighborhood.

Listening Task

People are talking about their homes. Choose the correct picture.

1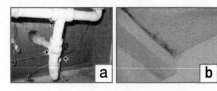

2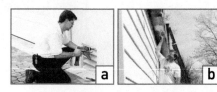

3

4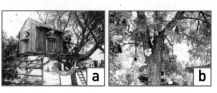

Listen Again

A. Listen again and choose the false statement.

1   a. Jeff has new roller-blades.

     b. Jeff is home alone now.

     c. A plumber is going to fix the sink today.

2   a. The house is very messy now.

     b. Jeff's room will be painted blue.

     c. The whole house will be painted blue.

3   a. A garage sale is going on.

     b. The garage is very dusty.

     c. Amy is cleaning the garage.

B. Listen again and choose the best summary.

4   a. ☐   She has been living in the house for 12 years.

     b. ☐   She played and fell from the tree house.

Listening 2

Four children are talking about their homes. Number the pictures.

Listen Again

A. Listen again and choose correct answer.

1   What is true about the place?

     a. The apartment has a good view.

     b. It doesn't have any sports facilities.

     c. There is a lake nearby.

2   What is NOT true about the place?

     a. It is not quiet.

     b. It is close to the public transportation.

     c. All his family members like the house.

3   What is NOT true about the place?

     a. The rent is low.

     b. The walls shake when wind blows.

     c. Her mom likes it.

B. Listen again and choose the correct sentence.

4   a. ☐   b. ☐

Review

Answers p. 36

❋ **Listen and fill in the blanks.**

1

w What's _____ on here?

m We're painting the _____ house.

w What _____ will the living room be?

m It will be light green.

2 My home is a two-_____ house. It is _____ from public transportation, but it is safe and _____ . I have been living here _____ I was born. I have a lot of memories around the house.

3

m Do you like your new home?

w Yes. It is on the fifteenth _____ of a high-rise apartment building. It has a great _____ . I can see the whole town from my room.

m How is the _____ ?

w It is good, only $1,500 a month.

4 My family has just moved into a house. I didn't like my old _____ because it was so _____ . Now I am relaxed. It is in a good _____ , nice and quiet.

5

m What are you doing up there?

w I am _____ the attic. There are so many things piled up.

m What are you going to do with all the stuff?

w I'm going to have a _____ .

Answers p. 37

LISTEN AND WRITE

Listen and write your own answers.

Write the questions you hear.

- I live in _____

  _____

- My house is _____

  _____

- _____

_____

_____

_____

_____

PRONUNCIATION

/ e / vs / æ /

Listen and repeat.

bet   head   merry

said   set

Listen and repeat.

bat   had   marry

sad   sat

Listen carefully and notice the difference.

bet / bat   head / had

merry / marry   said / sad

set / sat

EXERCISE

Listen and check the words you hear.

☐ bet   ☐ bat

☐ head   ☐ had

☐ merry   ☐ marry

☐ said   ☐ sad

☐ set   ☐ sat

✳ Listen and choose the correct answer.

1 **Amy and Jane are talking.**

1) What is NOT true about the conversation?
   a. Jane is moving out of town.
   b. Jane is excited about moving.
   c. Her new home is bigger and newer.
   d. It has more than one story.

2) Jane's new room _____.
   a. is downstairs   b. has a good view
   c. is not so big   d. will have posters on the wall

2 **A girl is talking about her house.**

1) According to the girl, what is NOT the problem of the house?
   a. It is too noisy.   b. It is too dirty.
   c. It is too far from her school.   d. It is too old.

3 **Mrs. Brown and Jeff are talking about their house.**

1) What is the problem of the house?
   a. It is too small.   b. It is too noisy.
   c. It is too old.   d. It is not safe.

2) What's true about the conversation?
   a. Mrs. Brown wants to move out of the house.
   b. Jeff thinks he can fix all the problems.
   c. It is far from the town center.
   d. The house has many things to take care of.

4 **Jim and Pete are talking.**

1) What is true about the conversation?
   a. Orange and brown are Jim's favorite colors.
   b. Jim is a painter.
   c. Pete and Jim are painting the house together.
   d. Pete is going to paint his two-story house.

2) Where are the speakers?
   a. inside the house
   b. outside the house
   c. in a paint store
   d. in a painting store

5 **A woman is talking about her neighborhood.**

1) The woman's neighborhood _____.
   a. is nice
   b. is closed
   c. has new apartments
   d. is far from public transportation

2) How does the woman feel?
   a. strange   b. excited
   c. patient   d. bored

1

Jane _____ next month.

Amy Are you moving _____?

Jane No, in the same neighborhood.

Amy So you can still go to school with me.

Jane Sure.

Amy Why are you moving?

Jane My mom thinks this house is _____ _____ and old. In the new house my room is upstairs and it has a great view. It is bigger too. I'll _____ my favorite pictures on the wall. I can't wait to _____ to you.

2

Look, Mom. I can't study with the _____ open. It is too _____ outside. I can hear all the cars and people from the street and the market. And this house is too old. The doors and windows _____ when wind blows. There are stains all _____. I can't bring my friends home. Let's _____ of here. Please, Mom.

3

W The sink is leaking. The floors are squeaking. The paint is fading. I don't know _____ with.

M Why don't we _____ this house and move?

W I don't want to. I like this _____. It's safe and _____. Besides it is in the walking distance from the town center.

M I'll help you, Mom. _____ I can paint my room.

4

Jim Hey, up there! What's going on, Pete?

Pete We're _____ the whole two-story house.

Jim Oh, what color will the house be?

Pete Yes, this outside color _____ blue.

Jim _____ your room will be blue?

Pete No, you know me! It will be _____ and brown. My two favorite colors.

5

I have lived in my neighborhood _____. The houses used to be nice. Now, they are old and dirty, so the rent is low. They are _____ public transportation, and many shops have closed. I am moving out of here, _____. I can't wait to _____ my new apartment. It has a great _____!

UNIT

9

Where to, sir?

Answers p. 39

GETTING READY

1 Where might you hear these expressions? Write 'B' for bus, 'T' for taxi, 'S' for subway, and 'A' for airplane.

1. Fares, please! _____

2. Where to, sir? _____

3. Take line one to Museum Station. _____

4. Do I check in here for United Airlines to Chicago? _____

5. May I see your passport? _____

6. Exact change only. _____

7. Take me to City Hall, please. _____

8. Change to the blue line at Union Station. _____

2 Match the questions with the answers.

1. How can I get to the mall from here? •   • a. Sure. Here it is.

2. May I see your passport? •   • b. It's $3.50.

3. What is the fare to City Hall Station? •   • c. It's $70.

4. How much is a round-trip ticket? •   • d. Take a bus over there.

5. How long does it take to get there? •   • e. Use the subway.

6. What is the best way to get there? •   • f. About 40 minutes.

Listening Task

People are going to use public transportation. Where are they now?
Number the pictures.

Listen Again

A. Listen again and choose the correct answer.

1 The limousine bus runs _____.
   a. every hour
   b. every twenty minutes
   c. every half hour

2 You can save _____ dollars if you get the round trip ticket.
   a. about 40   b. about 10   c. about 18

3 You have to put _____ in the fare box.
   a. 55 cents   b. a token   c. one dollar bill

B. Listen again and choose the best summary.

4 a. ☐ She wants to go to the bus terminal in 10 minutes.

   b. ☐ She needs to get to the bus terminal in 30 minutes.

70

Listening 2

People are going to take different types of transportation. What are they?

1 a. subway   b. bus   c. taxi

2 a. taxi   b. bus   c. subway

3 a. bus   b. taxi   c. subway

4 a. bus   b. airplane   c. train

Listen Again

A. Listen again and choose the correct answer.

1 What is true about the conversation?

   a. The bus runs every ten minutes.

   b. Different-colored buses take different routes.

   c. The bus stop is nearby.

2 Where is the place?

   a. It's next to City Hall.

   b. It's across from the Tower Hotel.

   c. The driver doesn't know where it is.

3 The person is heading to _____.

   a. a music hall   b. a museum   c. the National Gallery

B. Listen again and choose the correct sentence.

4 a. ☐   b. ☐

Review

✳ Listen and fill in the blanks.

1

W How can I _____ to the train station from here?

M You can take the bus or _____.

W Where is the bus _____?

M Over there at the end of the next block.

2

Put 55 cents in the _____ box, please. Exact _____ only. Can you see the _____ over there? I don't _____ change.

3

W How much is a _____ to Baltimore?

M Forty-two fifty for one-way, eighty for the _____-trip.

W One one-way ticket.

M _____ you are.

4

Please _____ to General Hospital. My wife is very sick. _____ do you think it will _____? We need to get there as soon as possible. I will give you the money you ask for. Please _____!

5

W Do I _____ here for United Airlines to Chicago?

M Yes. May I see your _____?

W _____ you go.

M Can you put your _____ up here, please?

On Your Own

Answers p. 41

LISTEN AND WRITE

Listen and write your own answers.

Write the questions you hear.

- _____

  _____

- The best way _____

  _____

  _____

- _____

_____

_____

_____

_____

_____

PRONUNCIATION

/ ʌ / vs / ʌr /

Listen and repeat.

bust	gull	hut
shut	ton	

Listen and repeat.

burst	girl	hurt
shirt	turn	

Listen carefully and notice the difference.

bust / burst	gull / girl
hut / hurt	shut / shirt
ton / turn	

EXERCISE

Listen and check the words you hear.

☐ bust	☐ burst
☐ gull	☐ girl
☐ hut	☐ hurt
☐ shut	☐ shirt
☐ ton	☐ turn

✳ **Listen and choose the correct answer.**

1 Susan is calling for a taxi.

1) The taxi company doesn't ask _____.
    a. Susan's address
    b. Susan's phone number
    c. Where Susan wants to go
    d. Susan's name

2) What is NOT true about the conversation?
    a. Susan will have the taxi in five to ten minutes.
    b. Susan wants to go to a hospital.
    c. Susan is heading to Lincoln Ave.
    d. The taxi company's name is City Cab.

2 Mr. Brown is buying a ticket.

1) Mr. Brown is at _____.
    a. a train station
    b. a bus terminal
    c. an airline ticket counter
    d. a subway station

2) What is true about the conversation?
    a. He is paying by cash.
    b. He is buying a round-trip ticket.
    c. He is going to New York.
    d. There is no tax for an airplane ticket.

3 **Two people are asking for and giving directions.**

1) The person has to take Line (1 / 3) first and change for Line (3 / 1).

2) He takes the subway at (Central Station / City Hall Station) and changes at (City Hall Station / Market Street).

3) He has to get off at the (fourth / fifth) stop after he changes the line.

4) His friend will be waiting for him at Exit (3 / 5).

4 **A woman is going to London from Seoul.**

1) Where is the conversation taking place?
   a. at the train station   b. in a taxi
   c. on a bus   d. on the subway

2) What is NOT true about this conversation?
   a. She will fly to more than one airport.
   b. There are two airports around Seoul.
   c. She has to check in at the airport.
   d. The man will help with her bags.

5 **A woman is talking about her experience in L.A.**

1) What is NOT true about the talk?
   a. She used the bus.
   b. She used the subway.
   c. She didn't have the exact change.
   d. She changed from the bus to the subway.

1

M City Cab. Where are you _____?

W Lakeside _____.

M Where are you now?

W 256 Lincoln Ave.

M What's your _____?

W It's 301-245-7890.

M A taxi will _____ in five to ten _____.

2

M Hi. What time is your next _____ to New York?

W 3:45 p.m. There are some _____ _____.

M What's the _____ fare?

W It's $249.80 with _____.

M Okay. _____. Put it on my card, please.

W All right. Just a _____.

3

M What is _____ to get to your house?

W _____ the subway. Line number 3. Where are you coming from?

M I _____ Line one, at Central Station.

W Then you can change for Line three at City Hall Station. _____ at Market Street. It's the _____ stop from there. I'll be _____ for you at Exit 5.

4

M I'll take your _____. Now, _____, Ma'am?

W The Airport, please. I'm flying _____ to London.

M Which one?

W Do you have _____ one airport?

M Yes. May I see your ticket?

W Sure. Here it is.

M Oh, you want Incheon Airport. I'll help you with your bags and _____ you right to the _____ check-in desk.

W Wonderful!

5

I went to L.A. last year. Once, I _____ _____ because I wanted to _____ all forms of public transportation over there. However, I didn't see a _____ that said to pay the driver with exact _____ only. The driver made a gesture toward the sign. I had to _____ _____ the bus and use the _____.

10

I'd like to open an account.

Answers p. 43

GETTING READY

1 Write the letter of the word group next to the name of each place where you can hear them.

>   a. package, zip code, air mail, surface mail, stamp
>   b. room service, check in, check out, double room, health club the Internet connection
>   c. battery, engine, unleaded, oil check
>   d. boarding, flight, passenger, ticket
>   e. dry-clean, iron, sew, stains
>   f. check, cash, savings account, checking account

1. airport _____   2. bank _____

3. post office _____   4. hotel _____

5. gas station _____   6. dry-cleaner's _____

2 Match the expressions with the responses.

1. I'd like to send this package, please. •   • a. It's 81009.

2. I'd like to open an account.   •   • b. Okay, air mail or surface mail?

3. What is the zip code for Pueblo, Colorado?   •   • c. Here it is.

4. I'd like to pick up my laundry.   •   • d. Sure. What kind of account, please?

Listening Task

Where can you hear the following? Choose the correct picture.

1

2

3

4

Listen Again

A. Listen again and choose the true statement.

1   a. The flight is bound for Chicago.

     b. All the passengers are now boarding.

     c. There will be another announcement before boarding.

2   a. The pants have a small ink spot.

     b. The pants have a missing button.

     c. He wants the laundry back on Friday.

3   a. The address is wrong.

     b. There is no zip code.

     c. There is no sender's name.

B. Listen again and choose the best summary.

4   a. ☐ She wants to change rooms because it's noisy.

     b. ☐ She wants the room because it has an Internet connection.

Listening 2

People are in different places. Where are they? Choose the correct answer.

1   a. at a car wash   b. at a gas station   c. at a supermarket

2   a. at a discount store   b. at a drugstore   c. at a bank

3   a. at a music store   b. at a radio station   c. at a bookstore

4   a. at a service station   b. at a gas station   c. at a drugstore

Listen Again

A. Listen again and choose the true statement.

1   a. The woman wants super unleaded oil.

     b. The woman wants to get the oil checked.

     c. The woman has to get out of the car.

2   a. The check is $100.

     b. The man wants all his money in ten dollar bills.

     c. He has to sign it before he can get the money.

3   a. The album doesn't come as a cassette.

     b. The clerk doesn't know about the album.

     c. The album is very popular.

B. Listen again and choose the correct sentence.

4   a. ☐   b. ☐

Review

Answers p. 45

✽ **Listen and fill in the blanks.**

1

M I'd like to _____ this check, please.

W Sure. It's $60. _____ would you like the money?

M One twenty and four _____.

2

I need this shirt dry-cleaned and _____. There's a button missing.

Can you _____ the button back on?

And please take out the ink _____ on the back. I need it back before Tuesday.

3

W _____ it up, please!

M Regular unleaded or super?

W Regular unleaded. And _____ the oil, please.

4

Attention passengers.

This is the last _____ call for Flight 324 to Miami.

The flight will be _____ in 5 _____.

5

W Oh, you put the _____ in the wrong place.

M Really? Where should it be?

W The sender's address should go _____ here, not on the _____.
And are you sending this _____ or surface mail?

On Your Own

Answers p. 46

LISTEN AND WRITE

Listen and write your own answers.

- _____
  _____
- I want _____
  _____
- _____
- _____

Write the questions you hear.

_____

_____

_____

_____

_____

PRONUNCIATION

/ s / vs / ʃ /

Listen and repeat.

same	save	sip
seen	sell	class

Listen and repeat.

shame	shave	ship
sheen	shell	clash

Listen carefully and notice the difference.

same / shame	save / shave
sip / ship	seen / sheen
sell / shell	class / clash

EXERCISE

Listen and check the words you hear.

☐ same	☐ shame
☐ save	☐ shave
☐ sip	☐ ship
☐ seen	☐ sheen
☐ sell	☐ shell
☐ class	☐ clash

✳ **Listen and choose the correct answer.**

1 **Jeff is at the post office.**

1) Jeff is sending a (letter / package).

2) It is going to be (air mail / surface mail).

2 **Mrs. Brown is at the bank.**

1) What is Mrs. Brown doing?
   a. cashing a check   b. taking out money
   c. putting in money   d. sending money

2) What is true about the conversation?
   a. The bank clerk filled out the form for Mrs. Brown.
   b. Mrs. Brown is using an ATM machine.
   c. Mrs. Brown will get the money all in hundred-dollar bills.
   d. Mrs. Brown is taking out money from her savings account.

3 **Mr. Brown is at a dry-cleaner's.**

1) What is Mr. Brown doing?
   a. leaving his laundry
   b. making a complaint
   c. getting his laundry back
   d. asking for information about the cleaner's

2) What is true about the conversation?
   a. The cleaner couldn't take some stains out.
   b. Mr. Brown is satisfied with their job.
   c. Mr. Brown paid more than 20 dollars.
   d. The cleaner didn't know there were stains.

4 **A woman is at a hair salon.**

1) What did the woman decide?
   a. the color of her hair
   b. the length of her hair
   c. how much to spend today
   d. which hair salon to go

2) The woman's haircut will NOT be _____.
   a. longer than before
   b. simpler than before
   c. easier to care for
   d. more colorful

5 **Two people are talking.**

1) Where is the conversation taking place?
   a. gas station
   b. market
   c. bank
   d. post office

2) What is NOT true about the conversation?
   a. The man is opening a bank account.
   b. The woman works at the bank.
   c. The man is saving some money.
   d. The woman is asking for his photo ID.

1

M Hi! I'd like to _____ this _____ to Los Angeles.

W Sure. What's in it?

M Some _____ .

W Let's see. It's 8 pounds, so you can send it by air mail or by _____ mail. Which way would you like?

M How much is it by air?

W Let me check... $16.80.

M I'll send it _____ .

2

W I want to _____ $300 from my _____ .

M Sure. Could you fill out this _____ ?

W Okay. Here you go.

M How would you like your money?

W Two _____ and five _____ , please.

3

M I'd like to _____ my laundry. Here's my claim ticket.

W Here it is. That _____ to eighteen dollars.

M Oh, my jacket is not _____ yet. Look! The _____ are still there.

W Sorry, but we couldn't get them out. That's the _____ we could do.

M I see. Thanks anyway. Here's the money.

4

M How would you like your _____ , today?

W I'd like to have simple style that's easy to _____ .

M Would you like it the same _____ ?

W No, a little shorter.

M Sure. What kind of _____ ?

W I'd like to see some samples, please.

M Okay. Mine are beautiful.

W How much is color?

M Only $25 _____ .

W Oh!

5

M I'd like to open an _____ .

W Sure. Savings or checking?

M A _____ account, please.

W I need you to _____ this form and I need to get a photo ID.

M OK. Here is my driver's license.

W Sign at the _____ of the form, please.

M Here?

W Right. Well, we are all _____ .

84

Which house appliance?

Answers p. 48

GETTING READY

1 Fill in the blanks with the letters of the appliances in the box below.

a. TV set	b. refrigerator	c. cassette player
d. washing machine	e. sewing machine	f. oven

1. The tape is stuck inside. It won't come out. _____

2. It doesn't keep food fresh any more, and it leaks. _____

3. I have lots of laundry with heavy stains. _____

4. I want to make my own clothes. _____

5. I only watch it for the news and weather. _____

6. It bakes, grills and roasts. _____

2 Match the questions with the responses.

1. Does it wash well? •   • a. The tape is stuck inside.

2. When can I get it? •   • b. It'll take three days to deliver.

3. What happened to the •   • c. Sure, it will get out any stains.
   cassette player?

4. How fast is it? •   • d. It prints 25 pages in one minute.

Listening Task

Listening 1

Which items are the people talking about? Choose the correct picture.

1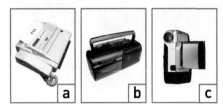

2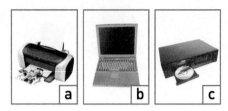

3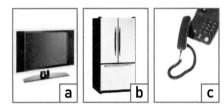

4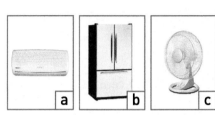

Listen Again

A. Listen again and choose the true statement.

1   a. This is the first time the problem happened.

    b. It has happened several times.

    c. The person can fix it.

2   a. The person likes the machine.

    b. The person is busy.

    c. Now the ink has run out.

3   a. The person dropped it in the water.

    b. It is not working at all.

    c. It makes noise.

B. Listen again and choose the best summary.

4   a. ☐ It leaks and makes noise but it still keeps food fresh.

    b. ☐ It only makes noise that is really irritating at night.

Listening 2

What are they going to buy? Choose the correct answer.

1   a. a stereo   b. a TV set   c. a video camera

2   a. a rice cooker   b. a toaster   c. an oven

3   a. a dryer   b. a washing machine   c. a dishwasher

4   a. a sewing machine   b. a VCR   c. an iron

Listen Again

A. Listen again and choose the true statement.

1   a. They like the model on sale.
       b. 20 inch model is the only one on sale.
       c. They don't like the big one.

2   a. It is a new model.
       b. It takes fifty minutes to clean it.
       c. The woman is worried because she doesn't know how to cook.

3   a. She can get it home today.
       b. They give a free repair service for ten months.
       c. The same model is on a TV commercial.

B. Listen again and choose the correct sentence.

4   a. ☐   b. ☐

Review

Answers p. 50

❊ Listen and fill in the blanks.

1

W It's too big. I'd like a _____ one.

M Sorry, but this is the only model on _____ .

W How about the twenty-inch model? Is it a good _____ ?

M Sure. It has a ten-year warranty. It's a very good brand. But it's not on sale.

2

I don't know what _____ . The tape is _____ inside and I can't get it out. Do you think you can _____ it?

3

M What's the problem?

W It _____ . Water keeps coming out.

M Does it _____ food fresh?

W No, it doesn't.

M Maybe you should _____ it away then.

4

I hear a buzzing _____ all the time. Sometimes the lines get _____ and I can hear other people talking. Other times it just doesn't _____ and there is no sound at all.

5

W Does it _____ well?

M Sure. It is a very _____ model.

W When can I get it?

M It'll take a week to _____ .

LISTEN AND WRITE

Listen and write your own answers.

- It's _____

  _____

- It _____

  _____

- It's _____

  _____

Write the questions you hear.

_____

_____

_____

_____

_____

_____

PRONUNCIATION

/ n / *vs* / ŋ /

Listen and repeat.

| ban | tan | sin |
| thin | ton | sun |

Listen and repeat.

| bang | tang | sing |
| thing | tongue | sung |

Listen carefully and notice the difference.

ban / bang	tan / tang
sin / sing	thin / thing
ton / tongue	sun / sung

EXERCISE

Listen and check the words you hear.

☐ ban	☐ bang
☐ tan	☐ tang
☐ sin	☐ sing
☐ thin	☐ thing
☐ ton	☐ tongue
☐ sun	☐ sung

✳ **Listen and choose the correct answer.**

1　**A man is shopping.**

　　1)　The man (is / isn't) looking for a specific brand.

　　2)　He thinks the model is too (heavy / big).

　　3)　The model is cheaper than a smaller one because of its (age / brand).

　　4)　It is (one / two) year[s] old.

2　**A customer is shopping at a store.**

　　1)　What house appliance are they talking about?
　　　　a. a washing machine
　　　　b. a refrigerator
　　　　c. a printer
　　　　d. a video camera

　　2)　What is NOT true about the conversation?
　　　　a. It works fast.
　　　　b. They are a customer and a clerk.
　　　　c. The person doesn't like it very much.
　　　　d. It's new.

3　**The following is about a piece of electronic equipment.**

　　1)　What is the item NOT used for?
　　　　a. a telephone　　　　　　b. a computer
　　　　c. a TV　　　　　　　　　d. a pocket

2) What is NOT true about the item?

    a. You can do many things with it.

    b. You can check your e-mail with it.

    c. With it you can watch TV on the subway.

    d. It is small but heavy.

4 Johnny is talking to his mom.

1) What is the best response that can follow?

    a. No, thanks.

    b. Sure, it will just take some time.

    c. Yes, I know.

    d. Yes, he will try.

5 Paul is talking about his new oven.

1) What is NOT true of the appliance?

    a. It must be ordered.

    b. It arrives overnight.

    c. It requires a phone number to order.

    d. It is fantastic.

2) What does it NOT do?

    a. bake   b. grill   c. roast   d. keep food fresh

Answers p. 52

1

W May I help you?

M Yes, I'm _____ for a refrigerator.

W Do you have a certain _____ in mind?

M No, not really.

W How about this one?

M It's too _____ .

W It's big but it's _____ . It is _____ than this smaller one.

M Why is it so cheap?

W It's an _____ . But it's not so old, only one year old.

2

M This one is _____ . It works really well.

W How _____ is it?

M It prints 25 pages a minute.

W That is fast.

M And the image is very _____ and _____ . Look! What do you think?

W That is impressive! _____ .

3

TV, _____ , computer, and telephone are all in one. You can _____ TV while chatting with your friend in a foreign country. You can check your e-mail on the subway while _____ to some good music. You have the world right in your hand. It is _____ and _____ .
You can carry even it in your pocket. It is still very _____ but it's worth it.

4

M Mom! I need help.

W Oh, really? What's _____ ?

M Yes, something _____ to my cassette player.

W Again? Oh, my! The tape is _____ inside, and it won't _____ . This will take some work to _____ .

M Can you _____ it?

5

M I have a new wonderful oven that _____ everything!

W Really?

M Yes, it _____ , grills, and _____ !

W Sounds like it's really a good oven.

M I think with this new oven I'm going to become a chef soon.

W I like to cook, too. Where can I _____ one?

M Here is the number. It'll take several days to deliver _____ .

Did you see the news last night?

Answers p. 52

1   The following are from newspaper articles. Write the letter of the section in the blank.

a. sports	b. business and economy	c. weather
d. news	e. science and technology	f. entertainment

1. The Lakers lost to the Bulls 78 to 79.   _____

2. The temperature will be in the low 30's to high 40's.   _____

3. Top stars Tim Brown and Nicole White announced they're
    going to get married.   _____

4. A plane crashed in the woods near L.A.   _____

5. Microsoft developed a new software program.   _____

6. Bill Gates earned the most in the U.S. last year.   _____

2   Match the expressions with the responses.

1. Any interesting news?   •   •   a. Yes, I did.

2. What will the weather be   •   •   b. There's a heavy rain in India.
    like tomorrow?

3. Oh, no. They were beaten again.   •   •   c. By whom this time?

4. Did you see the news last night?   •   •   d. It will be hot and sunny.

Listening Task

Listen to the news and number the headlines.

Tom Crane and Cindy Hoffer to Wed _____

Dog Saves His Owner _____

Hundreds Killed in a Plane Crash _____

China Hit Hard by Heavy Rains _____

Listen Again

A. Listen again and choose the false statement.

1 a. The plane was heading to New York.

   b. No one on the plane survived.

   c. The black box has been found.

2 a. The rain has killed thousands of people already.

   b. It continued for a week.

   c. This happened in China.

3 a. The couple are both film stars.

   b. They are now on their honeymoon.

   c. The wedding is scheduled for May.

B. Listen again and choose the best summary.

4 a. ☐ A brave dog saved his owner when their house caught fire.

   b. ☐ A house caught fire and a dog and his owner were killed.

Listening 2

What are people talking about? Choose the correct answer.

1 a. a new software program
   b. a new computer company
   c. handicapped people

2 a. a painting   b. a robbery   c. a robber

3 a. weather   b. a football game   c. a picnic

4 a. a TV sports program   b. a basketball player   c. basketball shoes

Listen Again

A. Listen again and choose the false statement.

1 a. People with no hands can use the program.
   b. Blind people can use the program.
   c. It is made for handicapped people.

2 a. Paintings were stolen.
   b. The robbers have been caught.
   c. The robbers were videotaped.

3 a. He can play football tomorrow.
   b. It will be cold and cloudy.
   c. It will be sunny but windy.

B. Listen again and choose the correct sentence.

4   a. ☐   b. ☐

Review

Answers p. 54

✳ **Listen and fill in the blanks.**

1

M Any _____ news?

W Yes. A typhoon hit Japan and _____ hundreds of people.

M Oh, not again. These days _____ creates more and more problems.

2

A French airplane _____ in the woods near Chicago.

All the passengers and crew members _____.

The people are _____ the black box in the woods.

There have been three plane _____ only this year.

3

W _____ that Bill Jones announced a new _____?

M He did? _____.

W And they say he will win a Grammy Award this year.

M Where did you hear that?

W It was in today's _____.

4

Good morning, this is John Watson with the 8 o'clock _____ from BBS.

Our _____ this morning: British Air Flight 405 has crashed in a

_____ neighborhood near _____. Everyone on board seems to be dead.

The police are still _____ for survivors.

5

M The bank robbers were _____ yesterday morning.

W _____.

M But they _____ last night.

W That's bad.

On Your Own

Answers p. 55

LISTEN AND WRITE

Listen and write your own answers.

• Yes, I _____

  No, I _____

• _____

  _____

• Yes, today _____

  No, I didn't _____

  _____

Write the questions you hear.

_____

_____

_____

_____

_____

_____

PRONUNCIATION

/ t / *vs* / θ /

Listen and repeat.

tank	tin	team
bat	mat	

Listen and repeat.

thank	thin	theme
bath	math	

Listen carefully and notice the difference.

tank / thank	tin / thin
team / theme	bat / bath
mat / math	

EXERCISE

Listen and check the words you hear.

☐ tank   ☐ thank

☐ tin   ☐ thin

☐ team   ☐ theme

☐ bat   ☐ bath

☐ mat   ☐ math

✳ Listen and choose the correct answer.

1 **The following is 9 o'clock News.**

   1) Listen and choose the correct statement.
     a. The robbery took place in Chicago.
     b. There have been no bank robberies in Chicago this year.
     c. The security system worked but it couldn't stop them.
     d. The robbers have been caught.

   2) Listen and choose the correct statement.
     a. The boy is from a rich family.
     b. The boy got the highest SAT score this year.
     c. The boy is under thirteen.
     d. The boy is a Korean-American.

2 **Two people are talking about the news.**

   1) What is true about the conversation?
     a. Bill Gates earned the most money in the world.
     b. He earned $30 million last year.
     c. The man is not surprised at the news.
     d. This is the first time he earned the most money in the U.S.

3 **Two people are talking about the news.**

   1) What is the conversation about?
     a. A cell phone
     b. Samsung
     c. The biggest company in the world
     d. A new software program

2) What is true about the conversation?

a. Samsung sold the most TV sets last year.

b. Samsung is one of the world's top ten companies.

c. The speakers are amazed about the news.

d. Samsung has developed a new computer.

4 **Two co-workers are talking.**

1) What is true NOT about the conversation?

a. A tornado damaged Oklahoma City last night.

b. A tornado killed some people.

c. The man read about a tornado.

d. Oklahoma City had another tornado last week.

2) What is the mood of the speakers?

a. glad   b. annoyed

c. happy   d. upset

5 **The following is news.**

1) What is the news about?

a. medical news

b. science and technology

c. weather

d. entertainment

2) What is true about the news?

a. There are 21 actors competing for the best actor award.

b. Mexican actress Salma Hayek is a Festival jury member.

c. The Cannes film festival will continue until next Wednesday.

d. The festival jury members will pick the winners for 6 awards.

Dictation

Listen and fill in the blanks.

Answers p. 57

1

M Our _____ tonight. A National Bank in downtown Chicago was _____ yesterday. There was a security system but it was not _____. This is Chicago's _____ bank robbery this year.

W Next story. A _____ boy has entered one of the best universities in the U.S. He scored the _____ highest on this year's SAT. He is a Chinese-American and his father _____ a small restaurant in L.A.'s China Town.

2

M _____?

W Bill Gates _____ the most money in the U.S. last year.

M That's not new. How much did he earn _____?

W About $13 million.

M $30 million?

W No. _____.

3

W Samsung _____ the most cell phones last year!

M Yes, it's _____. It seems that the company develops a new model almost every month.

W I heard it is one of the world's top 100 _____.

M It is. Samsung is now an international brand. I _____ them.

4

M Did you read the _____ this morning?

W No. Did you find anything _____?

M I'll say! There was _____ in Oklahoma City last night.

W Really? Did many people _____?

M Some people are dead and many houses have been _____.

W _____. I think they had another tornado some years ago, didn't they?

M You're right. They had a bad tornado _____.

5

The 58th International Cannes film festival _____ at Le Palais de Festival on Wednesday. 21 films are competing _____. Festival jury _____ including German director Fatih Akin, Mexican _____ Salma Hayek and Spanish actor Javier Bardem will pick the _____ of the Palme d'Or as well as six other awards. The festival continues _____ May 22.

100

I work part time.

Answers p. 57

GETTING READY

1 Fill in the blank with the letter of the correct job in the box.

a. carpenter	b. bank clerk	c. factory worker
d. actor	e. store clerk	f. travel agent
g. hotel receptionist	h. professional baseball player	

1. I have made tables and chairs all my life. _____

2. Do you want to open a checking account? _____

3. This package trip to Malaysia is great. _____

4. What kind are you looking for? _____

5. I work in a factory all day. _____

6. I have been in twelve movies. _____

7. I hope they enjoy their stay in our hotel. _____

8. I have hit 200 home-runs. _____

2 Match the expressions with the responses.

1. Could I have your name please? • • a. It's Joseph Kennedy.

2. How long does it take to get there? • • b. He fell off his bike.

3. How did this happen? • • c. As much as $100.

4. How much can you spend? • • d. It takes two and a half hours.

Listening Task

What is his job? Choose the correct answer.

1 a. hotel manager   b. train conductor   c. flight attendant

2 a. cashier   b. bank clerk   c. hotel receptionist

3 a. telephone operator   b. store clerk   c. travel agent

4 a. pharmacist   b. doctor   c. lifeguard

Listen Again

A. Listen again and choose the correct answer.

1 What's going on?
   a. The passenger lost her ticket.
   b. She didn't buy the ticket.
   c. She had misplaced the ticket.

2 What does he need to know?
   a. The person's phone number
   b. The person's address
   c. The person's size

3 What is true about the conversation?
   a. The fight is to Ankara.
   b. It takes thirteen hours to get there.
   c. The plane will drop by several places.

B. Listen again and choose the best summary.

4 a. ☐ The boy was riding a bicycle when he got hurt.
   b. ☐ The boy is bleeding a lot.

Listening 2

Listen and choose the correct word to fill in the blank.

1 His grandfather's first job was a _____.
   a. professional swimmer   b. lifeguard   c. swimming instructor

2 Her mother's first job was a _____.
   a. traveler   b. writer   c. tour guide

3 His uncle's first job was a(n) _____.
   a. actor   b. doctor   c. singer

4 Her grandfather's first job was a _____.
   a. miner   b. woodworker   c. construction worker

Listen Again

A. Listen again and choose the true statement.

1 a. He became a lifeguard after marriage.
  b. He is still saving lives on the beach.
  c. He was a swimming champion in his school days.

2 a. She traveled all around the country.
  b. She wrote more than one book.
  c. She is still working as a tour guide.

3 a. He changed his job in his thirties.
  b. His dream did come true.
  c. Now he works as a doctor.

B. Listen again and choose the correct sentence.

4   a. ☐   b. ☐

Review

Answers p. 59

✷ Listen and fill in the blanks.

1

M I need to see your _____ , please.

W Oh, I can't find it. I seem to have _____ it.

M _____ your time. I'll be back _____ .

2

My mother was a _____ guide.

She _____ thousands of people to _____ of the world.

Now she is not _____ , but she helps people with her _____ from work.

3

W I'd like to open a checking _____ .

M Certainly. Could you _____ out this form, please?

W Sure. _____ .

M Thank you. Now just _____ here, and we're all set.

4

My brother is an _____ .

He was a _____ and he _____ his job in his late thirties.

Now _____ because his childhood dream has _____ .

5

M How did this _____ ?

W He tripped and _____ in the playground.

M I have to _____ the blood first.

LISTEN AND WRITE

Listen and write your own answers.

- Sure, _____

- Yes, my name _____

- As much as _____

- She is _____

Write the questions you hear.

_____

_____

_____

_____

PRONUNCIATION

/ t / vs / tʃ /

Listen and repeat.

| tin | top | time |
| cat | it | mat |

Listen and repeat.

| chin | chop | chime |
| catch | itch | match |

Listen carefully and notice the difference.

tin / chin	top / chop
time / chime	cat / catch
it / itch	mat / match

EXERCISE

Listen and check the words you hear.

☐ tin	☐ chin
☐ top	☐ chop
☐ time	☐ chime
☐ cat	☐ catch
☐ it	☐ itch
☐ mat	☐ match

✳ Listen and choose the correct answer.

1　People are talking about their jobs. What are their jobs?

1) What is his job?
    a. artist　　　　　b. singer　　　　　c. actor　　　　　d. musician

2) What is her job?
    a. tour guide　　　b. pilot　　　　　c. travel agent　　d. hotel manager

2　Two people are talking.

1) Fill in the blank.

    He is a professional _____ _____.

2) What's NOT true about the conversation?
    a. He makes money by playing baseball.
    b. He is a batter.
    c. He has been in this job less than 10 years.
    d. He hits 250 home-runs a year.

3　John is at work.

1) What does he do?
    a. cashier　　　　b. waiter　　　　　c. store clerk　　　d. photographer

2) What is true about the conversation?
    a. The customer is looking for a video camera.
    b. The customer doesn't like the model the clerk is showing.
    c. The customer can't spend more than $200.
    d. The customer doesn't like the model because it is old.

4   **Two people are talking.**

1) What is the best response that could follow?
   a. OK. I will take it.
   b. No, it's too far.
   c. OK, let's go together.
   d. No, it takes too long.

2) Who are the speakers?
   a. a travel agent and a carpenter
   b. a hotel receptionist and a factory worker
   c. a factory worker and a travel agent
   d. a store clerk and a driver

5   **Two people are talking.**

1) What is true about the conversation?
   a. Tim is famous.
   b. Tim needs the woman's name.
   c. Tim signed the woman ticket.
   d. It was news that Tim lost the race.

2) What does Tim Sutton do?
   a. He is a newsman.
   b. He makes sports clothing.
   c. He is a professional bike racer.
   d. He is a doctor.

Listen and fill in the blanks.

Answers p. 62

1

M _____ what my _____ is. I make people laugh and cry. I make them excited and scared. I _____ a different person in different times and places. It's fun, because _____ many different lives. I have been in dozens of _____, but I can remember _____.

W I help people to plan their _____. There are a lot of things to _____. I help them plan their _____, what to see, where to stay, and so on. I give them _____ about various places around the _____. These days more _____ are going to Asia.

2

W What do you do _____?

M I play baseball.

W How long have you been _____?

M For eight years.

W _____ on the team? I mean do you hit, pitch, or catch?

M I hit. _____. I'm even batting in my _____.

W How many home runs have you _____?

M 250.

3

W Can you _____ some digital cameras, please?

M _____, ma'am. Do you have any particular brand _____?

W I'd prefer Canon.

M _____ this one? It's the _____ model.

W _____, but it's more than I can afford.

M How much can you _____?

W Around $200.

4

M I have _____ cars and trucks all _____ _____. Now, I want to see the world.

W This package to Asia is perfect for you.

M Oh, _____ does it take? I only have _____.

W It leaves Thursday and _____ two weeks.

M Perfect! And _____ is the package?

W Only $3,300.

5

W Could I have your _____ and _____, please?

M Here. It's Tim Sutton.

W Oh, are you the Tim Sutton that _____ the news?

M Yes.

W You _____ your _____ in Stage Five, and lost time.

M Well, _____ the blood coming from my _____.

W But you won, anyway. Could I have you _____ my shirt for my son?

M Sure.

How was the trip?

Answers p. 62

GETTING READY

1 Choose the right group of words from the box and write the letter in the blank.

> a. roller coaster, water slide, bumper cars
> b. sand, clear sky, cruise, island
> c. museums, temples, tombs, churches, wall paintings, city tour
> d. rafting, campfire, river, woods

1. a beach   _____

2. a mountain   _____

3. an amusement park   _____

4. a historic site   _____

2 Match the questions with the answers.

1. How was the trip? •   • a. Absolutely. Very much.

2. When did you come back from vacation? •   • b. I liked France best.

3. Did you like Europe? •   • c. Last week.

4. Was this picture taken on the trip? •   • d. Yes, it was.

5. What country did you like best? •   • e. It was awful.

Listening Task

Where are/were they? Listen and choose the correct answer.

1   a. amusement park   b. mountain   c. beach

2   a. amusement park   b. historic site   c. island

3   a. mountain   b. beach   c. amusement park

4   a. mountain   b. lake   c. beach

Listen Again

A. Listen again and choose the correct answer.

1   What is NOT true about the place?

a. It is quiet.

b. It is crowded.

c. It is nice.

2   What is NOT true about the vacation?

a. She sees many natural things.

b. She sees many cultural items.

c. She sees many old things.

3   What is NOT true about the place?

a. The place is not very crowded.

b. There are many things to ride.

c. Children like the place better than adults.

B. Listen again and choose the best summary.

4   a. ☐ She enjoyed rafting and camping out.

b. ☐ She got off the raft because she was scared.

Listening 2

Where have the speakers been to? Choose the correct answer.

1   a. Africa   b. Asia   c. Europe

2   a. sea   b. woods   c. amusement park

3   a. island   b. woods   c. beach

4   a. cousin's place   b. friend's place   c. grandparents' place

Listen Again

A. Listen again and choose the correct answer.

1   What is true about the vacation?

    a. She traveled to only one country.

    b. She liked things from the past.

    c. She was back on Friday.

2   What is true about the vacation?

    a. He traveled by ship.

    b. He visited many places.

    c. He stayed in the room because he was sick.

3   What is NOT true about the vacation?

    a. She stayed in a big hotel.

    b. She stayed close to nature.

    c. She touched some animals.

B. Listen again and choose the correct sentence.

4   a. ☐   b. ☐

Review

Answers p. 64

✳ Listen and fill in the blanks.

1

W How was the _____ ?

M It was _____ . I got _____ and couldn't eat anything on the first day. For the next two days the _____ was so bad, and we couldn't go _____ .

2

My kids are having a lot of _____ . They _____ everything over and over again. But I am so _____ . There are so many people. We have to _____ for everything.

3

M When were you _____ from your vacation?

W On Tuesday.

M _____ was it?

W Amazing! The sky was blue. The water was crystal _____ . The wind was _____ and cool. _____ lying on the _____ .

4

Listen up! We are having a _____ today. We'll see the old _____ . We will visit a famous _____ . And if we _____ enough time, we'll go to the riverside _____ to watch the fire works that you all wanted to see.

5

M So did you like rafting?

W Yes, it was _____ . I screamed all the way.

M Did you sleep in a hotel?

W No. We _____ out. We saw stars and _____ around a _____ .

On Your Own

Answers p. 64

LISTEN AND WRITE

Listen and write your own answers.

Write the questions you hear.

• I came back _____

_____

_____

• Yes, it was _____

No, _____

_____

_____

_____

_____

PRONUNCIATION

/ h / vs / f /

Listen and repeat.

| hat | hall | hear |
| heel | hold | |

Listen and repeat.

| fat | fall | fear |
| feel | fold | |

Listen carefully and notice the difference.

hat / fat	hall / fall
hear / fear	heel / feel
hold / fold	

EXERCISE

Listen and check the words you hear.

☐ hat	☐ fat
☐ hall	☐ fall
☐ hear	☐ fear
☐ heel	☐ feel
☐ hold	☐ fold

✳ Listen and choose the correct answer.

1 **People are talking during a vacation trip.**

1) Where are they now?
   - a. at an amusement park
   - b. at a beach
   - c. at a historic site
   - d. in the woods

2) What's NOT true about the conversation?
   - a. They don't like the weather.
   - b. They have already seen the old temples.
   - c. They have not seen the museum yet.
   - d. There are not many tourists in the place.

2 **A woman is talking about her vacation.**

1) Where has she been?

  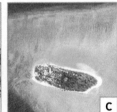 

2) What's NOT true about her vacation?
   - a. She enjoyed the trip very much.
   - b. She was driving an unusual car.
   - c. She could touch some animals there.
   - d. The animals were not scared of people.

3 **Jeff and John are talking about John's vacation trip.**

1) Where has he NOT been?
   - a. big cities
   - b. small towns
   - c. countryside
   - d. beach

2) What's NOT true about the trip?

    a. He liked the countryside best.

    b. He has been to many places.

    c. He had a hot-air balloon ride.

    d. He has pictures taken during the trip.

4 **A man and a woman meet, and one sees that the other has a photo.**

1) What is true about the conversation?

    a. Gail went to England this year.

    b. Jenny went to England and Germany.

    c. Mark went to Germany recently.

    d. Jenny went to England with Gail.

2) What is the mood of the speakers?

    a. excited   b. sad   c. angry   d. surprised

5 **A teacher is talking to her students.**

1) Which one does the speaker NOT want the listeners to do?

    a. Explain what they expected to see at the historic site.

    b. Explain why they chose the historic site.

    c. Explain what they didn't see at the historic site.

    d. Pick one historic site.

2) Which historic sites did the speaker and listeners tour?

    a. two churches

    b. the New City tour

    c. a park

    d. three museums

1

M Look at those _____ and tombs. They are _____.

W And look at those wall paintings. They look so _____.

M It's _____.

W By the way, what are we doing tomorrow?

M I think we are going to the museum.

W I only hope the weather is _____. It's so hot here.

M I hope there are less people in the _____. It's crowded everywhere.

2

The _____ was full of animals and plants. There were no such things as tall buildings or cars. We _____ on the _____ with birds and turtles all around. They didn't _____ from us. I even touched them. Some animals looked very _____. I felt like I was part of the place. It was a special _____.

3

Jeff Where have you been, John?

John Many _____. Big cities, small _____ and countryside.

Jeff What did you enjoy most?

John It's _____ one thing. But I liked the hot-air balloon riding best. It was _____. I will never forget it.

Jeff Do you have any _____ of it?

John Sure. _____.

4

W _____ back, Mark!

M Thanks, Jenny!

W _____?

M Absolutely!

W Was this picture _____ on the _____?

M Yes, it was! We stayed in this _____ castle for a week!

W I like _____! Especially ancient ones! Gail went to England last year and _____. I liked the English castles in her pictures, too!

5

W Finally, write about what _____ you liked best and why? We saw three museums, _____, four parks, a _____, and the Old City _____. What did you think about the site before you went? What about when you were _____? You have one week to finish and _____.

116

What's on TV tonight?

Answers p. 66

GETTING READY

1 Write the words in the correct column.

too violent   disappointing   exciting   ridiculous   excellent   touching

Programs He Likes

news, sports

movies, documentaries

Programs He Doesn't Like

talk shows, quiz shows

reality shows, music

The reason he likes them

_____

_____

_____

The reason he dislikes them

_____

_____

_____

2 Match the questions with the answers.

1. What's on TV tonight? •   • a. No, not until the game is over.

2. Can I change to channel 12? •   • b. There are some movies and quiz shows.

3. Did you see the news last night? • • c. It's on Friday.

4. What day is it on? •   • d. No, I didn't. Did you?

Listening Task

What kind of programs are people talking about?

1 a. news   b. talk show   c. variety show

2 a. drama   b. movie   c. documentary

3 a. sports   b. reality show   c. game show

4 a. quiz show   b. news   c. documentary

Listen Again

A. Listen again and choose the false statement.

1 a. It will be about dieting.

   b. It will be about the talk show host.

   c. It will be about her life secrets.

2 a. The program is useful.

   b. It's about a giant whale.

   c. It's about an animal discovered in the ice.

3 a. There are pets to choose.

   b. There are a rich man and many women.

   c. It is popular.

B. Listen again and choose the best summary.

4 a. ☐ The woman won a million dollars because she was smart and lucky.

   b. ☐ The woman won a million dollars because the questions were too easy.

Answers p. 67

Listening 2

Can the first speaker watch the show he or she likes? Write 'O' if yes and 'X' if not.

1 _____

2 _____

3 _____

4 _____

Listen Again

A. Listen again and choose the false statement.

1 a. The game show is not on today.
   b. Today is Thursday.
   c. He is not going to watch TV tonight.

2 a. Jeff needs to see the program for homework.
   b. The program is on too late.
   c. Jeff and his mom will see the program together.

3 a. Amy's dad likes to watch the football game.
   b. Amy wants to turn down the TV.
   c. Amy wants to change the channel.

B. Listen again and choose the correct sentence.

4 a. ☐   b. ☐

Review

Answers p. 69

❋ **Listen and fill in the blanks.**

1
W What's _____ TV tonight?

M _____ and some documentaries.

W But no _____?

M Yes, there are, but no _____ movies you like.

2   That reality show is just _____. A rich man dates twenty different

women and _____ one for his girlfriend. That is _____! I don't

understand why it is so _____.

3
M Did you see the _____ show last night?

W I wanted to, but I didn't know what time _____.

M On _____ at 9, on _____ 9.

4   The _____ on Channel 7 last Friday was really good. It was not

just good. It was _____. It showed a mammoth discovered in the ice. A

mammoth from _____ of years ago. It was _____!

5
W The quiz show is not _____ any more.

M Why did they _____ such a popular program?

W They started a _____ to attract more young viewers.

M That was my favorite. It's not _____.

On Your Own

LISTEN AND WRITE

Listen and write your own answers.

- It's _____

  _____

  _____

- Yes, I _____

  No, I _____

Write the questions you hear.

_____

_____

_____

_____

PRONUNCIATION

/ æ / vs / a /

Listen and repeat.

cat   hat   lack
map   black

Listen and repeat.

cot   hot   lock
mop   block

Listen carefully and notice the difference.

cat / cot   hat / hot
lack / lock   map / mop
black / block

EXERCISE

Listen and check the words you hear.

☐ cat   ☐ cot
☐ hat   ☐ hot
☐ lack   ☐ lock
☐ map   ☐ mop
☐ black   ☐ block

✳ Listen and choose the correct answer.

1 **A woman is talking about a TV program. Listen and check T(True) or F(False).**

	T	F
1) The program is a talk show.	☐	☐
2) The show's host is a woman.	☐	☐
3) There are always famous people on the show.	☐	☐
4) The show is always disappointing.	☐	☐
5) The show is popular because of famous guests.	☐	☐
6) The show's host makes people feel at home.	☐	☐
7) Last week the host told about her diet program.	☐	☐

2 **Susan and Brian are talking about a TV program.**

1) The show is a _____.
   a. drama   b. variety show   c. documentary   d. reality show

2) What's true about the conversation?
   a. The woman doesn't like the show because it is too realistic.
   b. The man likes the show because it is violent.
   c. The show is very popular.
   d. The man is going to change the channel.

3 **Jeff is talking with his mother.**

1) What is NOT true about the program?
   a. It is a quiz program.   b. It is on Channel 11.
   c. It is at 6:30.   d. It's Jeff's favorite.

2) What is true about the conversation?

    a. Jeff's friend will show up on the program.

    b. Two contestants compete on the show.

    c. Jeff watches the show very often.

    d. Jeff is sure that his teacher will win easily.

4 Mike is talking to Karen.

1) What are the speakers talking about?

    a. some baseball players

    b. a TV documentary

    c. the woman's husband

    d. a baseball game

2) What is NOT true about the conversation?

    a. The woman missed seeing the documentary.

    b. The documentary will be shown again on Tuesday.

    c. The woman's husband plays baseball.

    d. The woman's husband doesn't like baseball.

5 A girl is talking to her dad.

1) The girl's favorite TV show is a _____.

    a. weekly reality show

    b. monthly documentary

    c. weekly quiz show

    d. monthly talk show

2) What is NOT true about the conversation?

    a. The show was about animals.

    b. The show is not on this week.

    c. The show was cancelled.

    d. The show was about lovers.

1

I never miss this _____. The guests are not only famous people but also ordinary people like you and me. But it is never _____. It's the show's host Natalie Jones that makes it so _____. With her, _____ _____ and talk about themselves. Last week Natalie told about herself: her unhappy childhood, her marriage, and her _____. It was very _____.

2

W   This show is _____. I don't know why it is so popular.

M   It is a _____ show. What do you expect from reality?

W   It's so _____ and embarrassing.

M   I like it. _____. It only shows real life. Hey, don't change the _____!

3

M   Mom, where is the _____ show?

W   I guess _____ WBC, Channel 12.

M   It's at 6:30, right?

W   I think so. But why? You don't watch it _____.

M   One of my teachers _____ on the show. _____. I guess he will beat the other two contestants easily.

W   Stop the channel there. _____ Channel 11, not 12.

4

M   Did you see the documentary _____ _____?

W   No, I didn't. Did you?

M   Yes, it was about _____.

W   Too bad! My _____ plays on a _____.

M   Oh, it was so _____ that it's being shown, again.

W   What day is it on?

M   It's on _____ at 10.

W   I'll tell my husband! _____!

5

W   Where is my _____ TV show, tonight?

M   _____? "The Animal Lover?"

W   Yes. Is it not on this week? Have they _____ the program?

M   I think they did.

W   Why? It's a very touching but _____ show about real animals and the people who _____ them.

M   Right. I remember sometimes you cried for the hurt or _____.

I don't think so.

Answers p. 71

GETTING READY

1   Write 'A' for agreement, and 'D' for disagreement.

1. I think so.   _____

2. I agree.   _____

3. I don't think so.   _____

4. Me, too.   _____

5. Me, neither.   _____

6. Sounds like a good idea.   _____

7. I don't think that's a good idea.   _____

8. So do I.   _____

9. Well, I don't know.   _____

10. I don't agree with you.   _____

2   Match the expressions with the responses.

1. I don't like dogs.   •   •   a. I think so, too. It is excellent.

2. I'll miss him.   •   •   b. Me, neither.

3. Let's get together this Friday.   •   •   c. So am I.

4. That movie is good.   •   •   d. Sounds like a good idea.

5. I am nervous.   •   •   e. Me, too. He's a good guy.

6. I think he should marry her.   •   •   f. I don't think so. She is too young.

Listening Task

Is it good news or bad news? Check one.

1 Good news _____ Bad news _____

2 Good news _____ Bad news _____

3 Good news _____ Bad news _____

4 Good news _____ Bad news _____

Listen Again

A. Listen again and choose the correct answer.

1 What's true about the conversation?

a. Both feel the same about their friend.

b. Jerry is very happy now.

c. Caroline is unhappy now.

2 What's true about the conversation?

a. Carl got a job in Texas.

b. It will happen next week.

c. Both of them are sorry about the news.

3 What's NOT true about the conversation?

a. Alex has worked hard after school.

b. Alex needed money to go to university.

c. Both think Friday is a good day to celebrate.

B. Listen again and choose the best summary.

4

a. ☐ Janet has a new puppy.

b. ☐ Janet's mother has a new baby.

Listening 2

Do they agree or disagree? Check one.

1　Agree _____　　Disagree _____

2　Agree _____　　Disagree _____

3　Agree _____　　Disagree _____

4　Agree _____　　Disagree _____

Listen Again

A. Listen again and choose the correct answer.

1　What is true about the conversation?

　　a. Both agree the man is not good any more.

　　b. The man is in his fifties.

　　c. Both agree the man is not young any more.

2　What is true about the conversation?

　　a. Both agree used cars are cheaper.

　　b. Both agree buying a used car will save them money.

　　c. The man will change his mind about buying a used car.

3　What is NOT true about the conversation?

　　a. They agree a man doesn't have to be rich to become a good husband.

　　b. Both hope the female character will marry Bill.

　　c. John is rich but not handsome.

B. Listen again and choose the correct sentence.

4　a. ☐　　　　　b. ☐

Review

Answers p. 73

✳ **Listen and fill in the blanks.**

1

M I think I'll buy a _____ car.

W I don't think that's a good _____.

M But it will save me some money.

W I don't think _____. You will have to spend more money to _____ it.

2

W Did you _____ Max is moving?

M Yes, I'll really _____ him.

W Me, _____.

3

M Pam _____ a cute little puppy.

W She _____ be happy. _____.
   My mom won't let me have a pet.

M _____ will my mom.

4

W Don't worry. He will play better soon.

M I _____ so. But it seems like he is in _____ today.

W I don't _____ with you.

5

W I don't like the _____. He is too small for a cop.

M Well I don't _____.

W Don't you _____ so?

M No, _____ you have to be big to _____ a cop.

128

On Your Own

Answers p. 74

LISTEN AND WRITE

Listen and write your own answers.

- _____

  _____

  _____

- I _____

  _____

Write the questions you hear.

_____

_____

_____

_____

PRONUNCIATION

/ a / vs / ʌ /

Listen and repeat.

cop   doll   dock

lock   shock

Listen and repeat.

cup   dull   duck

luck   shuck

Listen carefully and notice the difference.

cop / cup   doll / dull

dock / duck   lock / luck

shock / shuck

EXERCISE

Listen and check the words you hear.

☐ cop   ☐ cup

☐ doll   ☐ dull

☐ dock   ☐ duck

☐ lock   ☐ luck

☐ shock   ☐ shuck

✳ **Listen and choose the correct answer.**

1　**Susan is talking to her friend.**

　1) Which of the following is NOT a good response?
　　a. So do I.　　　b. He is.
　　c. Me, neither.　　d. I think so, too.

　2) Which is NOT true about the conversation?
　　a. They're talking about their friend.
　　b. Their friend is going to quit school.
　　c. Their friend wants to make money.
　　d. They agree that their friend should quit school.

2　**A mother is talking with her son.**

　1) Choose the best response that can follow.
　　a. That's a good idea.
　　b. So am I.
　　c. I don't think I do.
　　d. I don't agree with you.

3　**Jeff is talking to Maria.**

　1) What is NOT true about the book?
　　a. It's a history book.
　　b. It's a fantasy.
　　c. It's a long book.
　　d. It's a famous book.

2) Which is NOT true about the conversation?

   a. Maria agrees that the book is exciting.

   b. Maria agrees that the book is famous.

   c. Maria doesn't like fantasy.

   d. Jeff never falls asleep while reading the book.

4 **Paul and Jean are best friends.**

1) What is NOT true about the conversation?

   a. They will learn about Korea together.

   b. They have a Korean movie.

   c. Their meeting is on Wednesday.

   d. They will choose another movie to watch.

5 **The following is from Jane's diary.**

1) What is the speaker's mood?

   a. surprised   b. annoyed

   c. horrified   d. disappointed

2) Which of the following is true about Jane?

   a. She and her mom used to disagree.

   b. She disagrees with Tony.

   c. She doesn't love Tony any more.

   d. She will not marry Tony.

1

W Kevin says he's _____ school.

M Is he? _____?

W He said he is going to _____.

M I don't think that's a good idea.

W Me, _____. I tried to change his mind, but I couldn't.

M Why does he need money _____?

W _____. Maybe he is going to start a business.

M I think he is still _____ for that.

2

M Mom, _____ be a millionaire.

W That would be _____.

M I think I can make a million dollars _____.

W Well... I don't know _____.

M But _____ hard.

3

M I read the book and it was just _____. If you haven't read it yet, read it. _____ _____.

W I did, but I couldn't _____ it. I fell asleep in a few minutes.

M _____. How can you go to sleep while reading such an exciting book? It is long but it is an _____ book.

W _____ it's a famous book. But it's _____. I don't like fantasy.

M You're so _____ me!

4

M Let's get together this Wednesday.

W _____ a good idea.

M Hey, look at this.

W Oh, that movie is good.

M I think so, too. It's excellent for _____ _____ Korea.

W Well, I don't know about that. It's just an adventure movie.

M Maybe we should pick _____.

5

My mom and I usually _____ on things, but _____ we didn't. I think I should marry Tony. My mom _____. She thinks I am _____. I don't agree with her, so _____. I finally agreed with my mom that I have to tell him good-bye for now. _____, but I understand.

132

이것이 THIS IS 시리즈다!

THIS IS GRAMMAR 시리즈

▷ 중·고등 내신에 꼭 등장하는 어법 포인트 분석 및 총정리

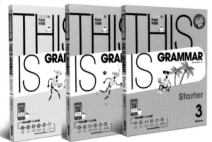

강남인강
강의교재

THIS IS READING 시리즈

▷ 다양한 소재의 지문으로 내신 및 수능 완벽 대비

강남인강
강의교재

THIS IS VOCABULARY 시리즈

▷ 주제별로 분류한 교육부 권장 어휘

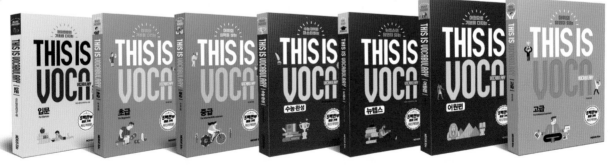

THIS IS 시리즈

무료 MP3 및 부가자료 다운로드
www.nexusbook.com
www.nexusEDU.kr

THIS IS GRAMMAR 시리즈

Starter 1~3	영어교육연구소 지음 | 205×265 | 144쪽 | 각 권 12,000원
초·중·고급 1·2	넥서스영어교육연구소 지음 | 205×265 | 250쪽 내외 | 각 권 12,000원

THIS IS READING 시리즈

Starter 1~3	김태연 지음 | 205×265 | 156쪽 | 각 권 12,000원
1·2·3·4	넥서스영어교육연구소 지음 | 205×265 | 192쪽 내외 | 각 권 10,000원

THIS IS VOCABULARY 시리즈

입문	넥서스영어교육연구소 지음 | 152×225 | 224쪽 | 10,000원
초·중·고급·어원편	권기하 지음 | 152×225 | 180×257 | 344쪽~444쪽 | 10,000원~12,000원
수능 완성	넥서스영어교육연구소 지음 | 152×225 | 280쪽 | 12,000원
뉴텝스	넥서스 TEPS연구소 지음 | 152×225 | 452쪽 | 13,800원

LEVEL CHART

	초1	초2	초3	초4	초5	초6	중1	중2	중3	고1	고2	고3
VOCA	초등필수 영단어 1-2 · 3-4 · 5-6학년용											
			The VOCA + (플러스) 1~7									
			THIS IS VOCABULARY 입문 · 초급 · 중급						고급 · 어원 · 수능 완성 · 뉴텝스			
						WORD FOCUS 중등 종합 5000 · 고등 필수 5000 · 고등 종합 9500						
Grammar	초등필수 영문법 + 쓰기 1~2											
	OK Grammar 1~4											
	This Is Grammar Starter 1~3											
			This Is Grammar 초급~고급 (각 2권: 총 6권)									
				Grammar 공감 1~3								
				Grammar 101 1~3								
				Grammar Bridge 1~3								
				The Grammar Starter, 1~3								
					한 권으로 끝내는 필수 구문 1000제							
					구사일생 (구문독해 Basic) 1~2							
						구문독해 204 1~2						
						그래머 캡처 1~2						
						[특급 단기 특강] 어법어휘 모의고사						

The
best preparation for

LISTENING

Answers

Nexus Contents Development Team · Miran Hong

Integrated Approach to Listening Comprehension

The more language structures are presented,
the better language awareness is improved.

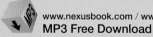
www.nexusbook.com / www.nexusEDU.kr
MP3 Free Download

2
Level

NEXUS Edu

The LISTENING

best preparation for

Answers

Nexus Contents Development Team · Miran Hong

2
Level

NEXUS Edu

UNIT 1
I don't think we've met.

Getting Ready　　　　　　　p. 5

1. S　　F　　F　　S　　F
   S　　S　　S　　F　　F
2. 1. c　　2. a　　3. b　　4. d　　5. e　　6. f

1. 처음 보는 사람에게 쓰는 말이면 'S', 친구를 만났을 때 쓰는 말이면 'F'라고 쓰시오.

처음 뵙겠습니다.	S
요즘 어때?	F
그동안 어떻게 지냈니?	F
어딘가에서 뵌 적이 있는 것 같은데요?	S
요즘 어떻게 지내?	F
만나서 반가워.	S
우리 만난 적 있나?	S
내 이름은 Will Smith야.	S
다시 만나서 반갑다.	F
뭐 하려던 참이야?	F

2. 표현을 응답과 연결시키시오.

1. 우리 전에 본 적 있나요?　　c. 아니, 처음 보는데.
2. 요즘 어때?　　a. 별일 없어.
3. 처음 뵙겠습니다. 저는 Brad에요.
   b. 안녕하세요, 제 이름은 Sue Grant에요.
4. 그동안 어떻게 지냈니?　　d. 아주 잘 지내.
5. 뭐 하려던 참이야?　　e. 병원에 가려고.
6. 여기는 무슨 일이야?　　f. 화학 학위를 따려고 왔어.

Listening Task　　　　　　p. 6~7

Listening 1		Carmen	Hiro	Abdul	Hilga
	나라	Columbia	Japan	Lebanon	the Netherlands
	좋아하는 것	jazz	board games	soccer	reading
	방 번호	305	102	415	307
Listen Again	A	1. b	2. b	3. c	
	B	4. a			
Listening 2		1. X	2. X	3. O	4. O
Listen Again	A	1. a	2. a	3. c	
	B	4. a			

Listening I

아래 단어들을 이용하여 표를 채우시오.

일본	레바논	콜롬비아	네덜란드
축구	재즈	독서	보드게임
307호	102호	415호	305호

스크립트

1. Hi! I am Carmen Gonzales. I'm from Columbia. I am in the second year of high school in my country. I like jazz a lot. My room number is 305. Please drop by my room when you'd like to hear some good jazz.

2. Hello! My name is Hiro Nomura and I'm from Japan. I am a high school freshman in Japan. This is my second visit to America. I like board games. I have plenty of interesting board games and everybody is welcome to challenge me. Oh, my room number is 102.

3. This is Abdul Aziz from Lebanon. He is a high school freshman in Lebanon. He doesn't speak English at all. He likes to play soccer. He hopes there is someone to play soccer with him sometimes. His room number is 415.

4. Hello. My name is Hilga Ingelson. I came from the Netherlands. I am a high school senior in my country. I like to read mystery books, and I'm in a mystery book club here. If you like Sherlock Holmes books, you can join us. By the way, my room number is 307. Remember it's 307.

해석

1. 안녕! 나는 Carmen Gonzales야. Columbia에서 왔어. 우리 나라에서 고등학교 2학년이야. 나는 재즈를 아주 좋아해. 내 방은 305호야. 좋은 재즈 음악을 듣고 싶으면 들러 줘.

2. 안녕! 나는 Hiro Nomura고 일본에서 왔어. 일본에서 고등학교 1학년이야. 미국은 이번이 두 번째고. 난 보드게임을 좋아해. 나에게 재미있는 보드게임이 많이 있으니까, 누구든 도전해도 좋아. 아, 내 방은 102호야.

3. 이 아이는 레바논에서 온 Abdul Aziz야. 레바논에서 고등학교 1학년이지. 영어를 전혀 못 해. 그는 축구 하는 걸 좋아해. 그는 가끔씩 축구를 같이 할 사람이 있었으면 해. 방은 415호야.

4. 안녕. 내 이름은 Hilga Ingelson이야. 네덜란드에서 왔어. 우리나라에서는 고등학교 졸업반이야. 나는 추리 소설 읽는 것

을 좋아하고 여기서 추리 소설 동아리에 들었어. 셜록 홈즈 책을 좋아한다면 가입해도 좋아. 그건 그렇고, 내 방 번호는 307호야. 307호 기억해 줘.

Listen Again

p. 6

A. 다시 듣고 맞는 것을 고르시오.

1. a. Carmen은 재즈를 공부를 하려고 미국에 왔다.
   ★b. 그녀는 자기 자신을 소개하고 있다.
   c. 그녀는 자기 나라에서 대학생이다.

2. a. Hiro는 그의 나라에서 고등학교 졸업반이다.
   ★b. 그는 보드게임을 잘 할 것이다.
   c. 그는 혼자서 보드게임 하는 것을 좋아한다.

3. a. Abdul은 스스로를 소개하고 있다.
   b. Abdul의 발음은 매우 좋다.
   ★c. Abdul은 다른 사람들과 함께 축구를 하고 싶어한다.

B. 다시 듣고 가장 적절하게 요약한 것을 고르시오.

4. a. ★ Hilga는 네덜란드에서 고등학교 졸업반이다.
   b.□ Hilga는 추리 소설 동아리에 가입하려고 미국에 왔다.

Listening 2

p. 7

전에 만난 적이 있다면 'O'를, 아니면 'X'를 쓰시오.

1. ___X___   2. ___X___   3. ___O___   4. ___O___

스크립트

1.

Chris I don't think we've met. I am Chris Jordan.
Juan Hi, I am Juan Perez. Nice to meet you.
Chris Nice to meet you too, Juan. Where are you from?
Juan Mexico.
Chris Oh, I have a friend from Mexico. Do you happen to know Carlos Domingo?
Juan Of course, I do. He is in my math class.

2.

M This is awful. This plane never takes off on time.
W Do you use this flight often?
M Yes. Maybe three times a month.
W That's a lot. I'm on this flight only once or twice a year. I have a sister in Chicago. Why are you going to Chicago?

3.

Susan Excuse me, but don't I know you from somewhere?
Linda No, I don't think so.

Susan Didn't you go to River Hill Elementary School?
Linda I did, but.. Oh, my God. Are you Susan? Susan Brown in Ms. Jones' class!
Susan Yes, Linda.
Linda It is a small world. How have you been?
Susan Great. So what are you up to? Are you sick? Who is your doctor?

4.

Linda Cheryl!
Charles Linda! What's up?
Linda Nothing much. What are all these books for?
Charles I have a paper to write for social studies class.
Linda I heard the teacher gives lots of homework. Right?
Charles Yes, a lot. Oh, it's almost my turn. Where is my library card?

해석

1. Chris 우리 처음 보는 것 같은데. 나는 Chris Jordan이야.
   Juan 안녕, 나는 Juan Perez야. 만나서 반가워.
   Chris 나도 반가워, Juan. 어디에서 왔니?
   Juan 멕시코에서 왔어.
   Chris 오, 멕시코에서 온 친구가 있어. 너 Carlos Domingo 라고 아니?
   Juan 그럼 알지. 나와 같은 수학 수업을 들어.

2. M 정말 끔찍해요. 이 비행편은 제 시간에 이륙하는 법이 없어요.
   W 이 비행편을 자주 이용하세요?
   M 네. 한 달에 세 번 정도요.
   W 자주 이용하시네요. 저는 일 년에 한두 번 밖에 안 타요. 시카고에 여동생이 있어서요. 시카고에는 왜 가시죠?

3. Susan 실례합니다만, 어디선가 당신을 본 적이 있는 것 같은데요.
   Linda 아뇨, 아닌 것 같은데요.
   Susan 리버힐 초등학교에 다니지 않으셨나요?
   Linda 다녔어요, 그런데……. 오, 이럴 수가. Susan이니? Jone 선생님 반의 Susan Brown!
   Susan 맞아, Linda.
   Linda 세상 참 좁다. 그동안 어떻게 지냈니?
   Susan 아주 잘 지냈지. 그런데 여기는 어쩐 일이야? 어디 아프니? 네 의사 선생님은 누구야?

4. Linda Cheryl!
   Charles Linda! 요즘 어때?
   Linda 별일 없어. 이 책들은 다 뭐 하려는 거야?
   Charles 사회 시간에 낼 리포트가 있어.
   Linda 그 선생님은 숙제를 무척 많이 낸다고 들었어. 그래?

3

Charles 응, 많아. 아, 거의 내 차례다. 내 도서관 카드가 어디 있지?

Listen Again
p. 7

A. 다시 듣고 알맞은 답을 고르시오.

1. 대화 내용과 일치하지 않는 것은?
 ★a. Juan은 Columbia에서 왔다.
 b. Juan은 수학 수업을 듣는다.
 c. 두 사람 모두 Carlos를 안다.

2. 대화 내용과 일치하지 않는 것은?
 ★a. 그들은 비행기가 도착하는 것을 기다리고 있다.
 b. 그들은 비행기가 이륙할 것을 기다리고 있다.
 c. 그들은 이 비행편을 전에 타 본 적이 있다.

3. 대화 내용과 일치하지 않는 것은?
 a. Susan과 Linda는 같은 초등학교에 다녔다.
 b. Susan과 Linda는 Jones 선생님 반이었다.
 ★c. Susan과 Linda 초등학교 때부터 가장 친한 친구이다.

B. 다시 듣고 맞는 문장을 고르시오.

4. a.★ Charles는 리포트를 쓰기 위한 책이 필요하다.
 b.□ Charles는 도서관 카드를 찾기 위해 책이 필요하다.

스크립트

a. Charles needs books to write a paper.
b. Charles needs books to look for his library card.

Review
p. 8

1. met, Nice, meet
2. from, freshman, study, play, 102
3. know, somewhere, Didn't
4. morning, This is, was born, speaks, likes
5. new, Have, moved, I'm, Nice to meet you, Nice to meet you, too

✻ 듣고 빈칸을 채우시오.

해석
1. John 우린 만난 적이 없는 것 같아. 내 이름은 John Smith야.
 Jim 안녕! 나는 Jim Brown이야. 만나서 반가워.
 John 나도 반가워.

2. 안녕! 나는 일본에서 온 Kenji Junko야. 일본에서 고등학교 1학년이야. 영어 공부하려고 여기 왔어. 나는 야구하는 걸 좋아해. 아, 내 방 번호는 102호야.

3. W 어딘가에서 뵙지 않았었나요?
 M 글쎄요, 그런 적 없는 것 같은데요.
 W Green Hill 고등학교에 다니지 않으셨나요?
 M 아뇨, 안 다녔는데요.
 W 죄송합니다. 제가 착각을 했어요.

4. 모두 좋은 아침이야. 이쪽은 나의 제일 친한 친구인 Mario야. Mario는 멕시코에서 태어났지만 미국에서 자랐어. 얘는 영어와 스페인 어를 해. 다른 학생들한테 스페인 어 가르치기를 좋아해.

5. Nancy 몇 층에 가세요?
 Cathy 10층이요. 고맙습니다.
 Nancy 처음 뵙는 분이신데요. 막 이사 오셨나요?
 Cathy 네, 일주일 전에, 1003호요.
 Nancy 전 506호에 살아요. 저는 Nancy Brown이에요. 반가워요.
 Cathy 안녕하세요, Cathy Johnson이에요. 저도 만나서 기뻐요.

On Your Own
p. 9

LISTEN & WRITE

듣고 질문을 써 보세요.

스크립트

What do you say when you meet a friend?
What do you say when you meet a stranger?
Introduce your best friend.

해석
친구를 만났을 때 무슨 말을 합니까?
낯선 사람을 만나면 무슨 말을 합니까?
가장 친한 친구를 소개해 보십시오.

PRONUNCIATION

/ʌ/ vs /ə/

☞ 듣고 따라 해 보시오.
 아들, 오다, 돈, 점심, 여름

☞ 듣고 따라 해 보시오.
 아시아, 여분의, 아이디어, 부인, 아빠

단어를 듣고 들은 소리를 표시하시오.

/ʌ/		/ə/
□	~에 대하여	★
★	달리다	□
□	~전에	★
□	해외에	★
□	~이었다	★
★	태양	□
★	점심	□

1. 1) c   2) c   2. 1) c   3. 1) b   2) b
4. 1) a   5. 1) b   2) b

✻ 듣고 알맞은 답을 고르시오.

1. Kate는 길에서 Harry를 만나고 있다.

스크립트

Kate   Excuse me. Harry? Harry Finn?
Harry Yes... And...
Kate   It's me. Kate, Kate Wilson.
Harry I'm sorry but I don't think I remember you.
Kate   Sure you do! I'm the girl who always cried at school.
Harry Oh, the shy girl in Ms. Hill's class. Now I remember you.
Kate   So how are you, Harry?
Harry I'm doing okay. And you? You look pretty good.
Kate   Oh, do I? I'm the class president now. I'm not shy any more.
Harry All right.

해석
Kate   실례합니다. Harry? Harry Finn이야?
Harry 네... 그런데...
Kate   나야. Kate, Kate Wilson.
Harry 죄송하지만 기억이 나질 않는데요.
Kate   왜 안 나! 나 매일 학교에서 울던 그 애야.
Harry 오, Hill 선생님 반의 수줍음 많던 애. 이제 기억난다.
Kate   그래 어떻게 지내니, Harry?
Harry 난 잘 지내. 넌? 아주 좋아 보인다.
Kate   오, 그래? 난 지금 우리 반에서 반장이야. 이젠 수줍어하지 않아.
Harry 그렇구나.

1) 이야기하고 있는 사람들은 어떤 사람들인가?
   a. 사촌   b. 이웃   ★c. 친구   d. 교사
2) 대화 내용과 일치하지 않는 것은?
   a. Kate Wilson은 전보다 좋아 보인다.
   b. 두 사람은 오랫동안 서로를 만나지 못했다.
   ★c. 처음 만난 사람 사이의 대화이다.
   d. Kate Wilson은 더 이상 수줍음을 타지 않는다.

2. 남자와 여자가 이야기하고 있다.

스크립트

M Haven't we met before?
W Well, I don't know.
M Don't you work in the public library?
W No, I don't.
M Oh, I'm sorry. I was mistaken.

해석
M 우리 전에 만난 적이 있지 않나요?
W 글쎄요. 저는 잘 모르겠는데요.
M 공공 도서관에서 일하시지 않으세요?
W 아니오.
M 아, 죄송합니다. 제가 착각을 했어요.

1) 여자가 남자에게 할 말로 적절하지 않은 것은?
   a. 괜찮습니다.   b. 상관없어요.
   ★c. 천만에요.   d. 괜찮아요.

3. Andy와 Patricia는 처음으로 만나고 있다.

스크립트

Andy   Excuse me. Where is Mr. White's room?
Patricia It's 104B. It's right next to the cafeteria.
Andy   Thanks a lot.
Patricia Are you new here?
Andy   Yes, this is my second day in this school.
Patricia Where are you from?
Andy   California.
Patricia Oh, hi, I am Patricia Davis.
Andy   I am Andy Wang. Nice to meet you, Patricia.
Patricia Nice to meet you too, Andy.

해석
Andy   실례지만 White 선생님 사무실이 어딘가요?
Patricia 104B호요. 학교 식당 바로 옆이에요.
Andy   정말 고마워요.
Patricia 전학생인가요?
Andy   네, 이 학교 온 지 이틀째예요.
Patricia 어디서 왔나요?
Andy   캘리포니아요.
Patricia 오, 안녕, 나는 Patricia Davis라고 해.
Andy   나는 Andy Wang이야. 만나서 기뻐, Patricia.
Patricia 나도 만나서 기뻐, Andy.

1) 이야기하는 사람들은 어떤 사람들인가?
   a. 교사 두 사람   ★b. 학생 두 사람
   c. 교사 한 사람과 학생 한 사람   d. 오랜 두 친구

2) 대화 내용과 일치하지 않는 것은?
   a. Andy는 선생님의 방을 찾고 있다.
   ★b. Andy는 학교 식당을 찾고 있다.
   c. Andy는 104B호로 가야 한다.
   d. Andy는 전학생이다.

4. Mike와 Steve가 버스 정류장에서 만났다.

스크립트

Mike	Don't I know you from somewhere?
Steve	No, I don't think so.
Mike	Oh, wait! You came to see Doctor Smith last week.
Steve	That's right. My name is Steve West.
Mike	Hi, I'm Mike Green. I'm Doctor Smith's nurse.
Steve	Oh, I remember you, now.
Mike	So, when are you coming back to see the doctor?
Steve	Next Friday.
Mike	See you then. Bye!
Steve	Bye!

해석

Mike	어딘가에서 우리 만나지 않았나요?
Steve	아뇨, 그런 것 같지 않은데요.
Mike	아, 잠시만요! 지난 주에 Smith 선생님께 진찰받으러 오셨죠?
Steve	맞아요. 제 이름은 Steve West입니다.
Mike	안녕하세요, 전 Mike Green입니다. Smith 선생님의 간호사죠.
Steve	아, 이제 기억나네요.
Mike	그럼, 언제 다시 진찰 받으시러 오실 거죠?
Steve	다음 주 금요일이요.
Mike	그때 뵙죠. 안녕히 가세요.
Steve	안녕히 가세요.

1) 대화 내용과 일치하는 것은 무엇인가?
   ★a. Steve와 Mike는 전에 만난 적이 있다.
   b. Mike는 의사이다.
   c. Steve와 Mike는 Smith 씨의 환자이다.
   d. Mike와 Steve는 오랜 친구이다.

5. John과 Jenny는 이야기를 하고 있다.

스크립트

John	Haven't we met before?
Jenny	No, I don't think so.
John	Are you sure?
Jenny	Yes, because I was at another school last year.
John	Well, I'm John. I'm here to get a degree in chemistry.
Jenny	Hi, I'm Jenny. I'm here to get a degree in English.

해석

John	우리 전에 만난 적이 있나요?
Jenny	아뇨, 그런 것 같지 않은데요.
John	확실한가요?
Jenny	네, 왜냐하면 전 작년에 다른 학교에 있었거든요.
John	아, 전 John이에요. 화학 분야에서 학위를 따려고 이 학교에 왔어요.
Jenny	안녕하세요, 전 Jenny에요. 전 영어 학위를 따려고 이곳에 왔죠.

1) 말하는 사람들은 누구인가?
   a. 교사 ★b. 학생   c. 교사와 학생   d. 회사원

2) 대화에 대해 사실이 아닌 것은?
   a. John는 과학자일 것이다.
   ★b. Jenny와 John은 이전에 만난 적이 있다.
   c. Jenny는 작년에 다른 학교에 다녔다.
   d. Jenny는 영어를 전공하고 있다.

Dictation   p. 12

1. I'm sorry but, Sure, cried at school, remember, look pretty good
2. met before, public library, mistaken
3. next to, Are you new here, from, Nice to meet
4. somewhere, doctor, That's right, coming back, then
5. before, Are you sure, I'm here

UNIT 2
What name and city?

Getting Ready   p. 13

1. 1. operator   2. area code   3. hold
      4. hang   5. press   6. connect

2. 1. b   2. d   3. a   4. c

1. 빈칸을 네모 안에 있는 단어의 기호로 채우시오.

지역 번호	연결하다
교환원	누르다
끊지 않고 기다리다	(전화기를 걸이에) 걸다

1. _____교환원_____ 은 전화를 걸 때 당신을 도와준다.
2. 시카고의 _____지역 번호_____ 는 901이다.
3. _____기다려_____ 주세요. 연결해 드리겠습니다.
4. _____끊지_____ 마세요. 곧 상담원이 도와드릴 것입니다.
5. 예약하고 싶으시면 지금 1을 _____누르세요_____.
6. 408호로 _____연결해_____ 주시겠어요?

2. 질문을 답과 연결시키시오.

1. 성함과 사는 도시를 말씀해 주시겠어요?
   b. 시애틀에 사는 David Brown입니다.
2. 201호로 연결해 주시겠어요?
   d. 기다리세요. 연결해 드리겠습니다.
3. 저에게 전화 온 것 있나요?
   a. 네, Peter가 두세 시간 전에 전화했어요.
4. 메모 남기시겠습니까?
   c. 네, 전화 좀 해 달라고 Jane에게 전해 주세요.

Listening Task   p. 14~15

Listening 1		1. c	2. b	3. a	4. b
Listen Again	A	1. c	2. b	3. b	
	B	4. a			
Listening 2		1. a	2. b	3. b	4. b
Listen Again	A	1. a	2. b	3. a	
	B	4. a			

Listening 1   p. 14

전화 메시지를 듣고, 알맞은 답을 고르시오.

1. 누가 메시지를 남겼는가?
   a. Susan   b. Shirley   ★c. Nancy

2. 누구를 위한 메시지인가?
   a. 치과 의사   ★b. Jeff   c. Gray 의사

3. 어디에서 나오는 메시지인가?
   ★a. 영화관   b. 호텔   c. 항공사

4. 누가 이 메시지를 만들었는가?
   a. 집주인   ★b. 회사   c. 식당

스크립트

1. Hi, Susan! This is Nancy. Jill and Shirley are coming over to my house on Friday for a slumber party. Would you like to come? If you would, please give me a call on my cell phone. I think you have my number, but in case you don't, it's 014-268-3657. Bye!

2. This message is for Jeff. Hi, Jeff. This is Dr. Gray's Dental clinic. We're calling about your appointment this Thursday. We're sorry but Dr. Gray can't make it on Thursday. So, we have to reschedule your appointment. We'll try to reach you again tomorrow morning at 9.

3. You've reached Town Cinema. If you want to make a reservation, please press 1 now. If you want information on the movies playing, please press 2. If you want to cancel or change your reservation, please press 3. If you want directions to the theater, please press 4.

4. Thank you for calling Apple Computer. All our assistants are busy right now. Please hold, and you will be served shortly.

해석

1. 안녕, Susan! 나 Nancy야. Jill하고 Shirley가 금요일 밤에 파자마 파티를 하러 우리 집에 올 거야. 너도 올래? 오려면 내 휴대 전화로 전화해 줘. 내 번호 알겠지만 혹시 모르니, 번호는 014-268-3657이야. 안녕.

2. Jeff에게 보내는 메시지입니다. 여보세요, Jeff 씨. 여기는 Gray 치과입니다. 이번 주 목요일의 예약 때문에 전화 드립니다. 죄송하지만 Gray 선생님께서 목요일에 시간이 안 되셔서요. 그래서 다시 예약하셔야 할 것 같아요. 내일 아침 9시에 다시 전화 드리겠습니다.

3. 타운 극장입니다. 예약을 하시려면 지금 1번을 누르세요. 상영 중인 영화 정보를 원하시면 2번을 누르세요. 예약을 취소하거나 변경하시려면 3번을 누르세요. 영화관의 위치를 알고 싶으시면 4번을 누르세요.

4. 애플 컴퓨터에 전화해 주셔서 감사합니다. 지금은 모든 상담원이 모두 통화 중입니다. 잠시만 기다리시면 곧 상담해 드리겠습니다.

Listen Again

p. 14

A. 다시 듣고 알맞은 답을 고르시오.

1. 메시지의 내용과 일치하는 것은?
   a. Nancy는 다시 전화할 것이다.
   b. Susan은 Nancy의 집 번호로 전화해야 한다.
   ★c. Nancy는 Susan을 초대하고 있다.

2. 메시지 내용과 일치하는 것은?
   a. Jeff는 치과에 전화할 것이다.
   ★b. 치과에서 내일 아침에 Jeff에게 다시 전화할 것이다.
   c. 원래 약속은 금요일이었다.

3. 예약을 변경하려면 _____ 번을 눌러야 한다.
   a. 2   ★b. 3   c. 4

B. 다시 듣고 가장 적절하게 요약한 것을 고르시오.

4. a. ★ 모든 상담원들이 바쁘다.
   b. □ 전화를 거는 사람들은 항상 기다려야 한다.

Listening 2

p. 15

✻ 듣고 빈칸에 알맞은 답을 고르시오.

1. 여자는 _____ 에 전화를 걸고 있다.
   ★a. 전화번호 안내   b. 항공사   c. 병원

2. Amy는 지금 _____
   a. 화가 났다   ★b. 바쁘다   c. 흥분 된다

3. 남자는 _____ 전화하고 있다.
   a. 예약하려고   ★b. 누군가와 이야기하려고
   c. 정보를 물어보려고

4. Simon에게서 온 전화는 _____ 전화이다.
   a. 시내   ★b. 장거리   c. 국제

스크립트

1.
M This is the operator. What city, please?
W San Marino, Florida.
M Yes, go ahead please.
W I'd like the number of Michael McDowell at 124 Forest Road.
M The number is: area code 619-412-0546
W 619-412-0546. Thanks.

2.
Amy Hello.
Jane Hi, Amy! It's me, Jane.
Amy Hi, Jane. What's up?
Jane I have some good news and bad news. The good news is we're going to have no midterms, and the bad news is...
Amy Jane, I'm sorry but I have to go now. My mom is waiting for me in the car. Can I call you back later in the evening?
Jane Sure.

3.
W Plaza Hotel, may I help you?
M Hi, could you connect me to room 1305, please?
W Please hold while I put you through.
M Sure.
W There's no one in the room right now. May I take a message?

4.
M Mom, I'm home. Were there any calls for me?
W There was a long-distance call from Simon.
M Did he leave any messages?
W He wanted you to call him back as soon as possible.
M I see. Thanks, mom.

해석

1. M 교환원입니다. 도시 이름이 무엇입니까?
   W 플로리다 주의 산마리노 시요.
   M 네, 계속하세요.
   W 포레스트 거리 124번지에 사는 Michael McDowell의 번호를 알고 싶습니다.
   M 지역 번호 포함 619-412-0546입니다.
   W 619-412-0546이요. 감사합니다.

2. Amy 여보세요.
   Jane 안녕, Amy! 나 Jane이야.
   Amy 안녕, Jane. 무슨 일이야?
   Jane 좋은 소식과 안 좋은 소식이 있어. 좋은 소식은 중간고사를 안 본다는 거고, 안 좋은 소식은...
   Amy Jane, 미안한데 나 지금 가야 돼. 엄마가 차에서 기다리셔. 이따가 저녁에 전화해도 돼?
   Jane 물론이지.

3. W 플라자 호텔입니다. 무엇을 도와드릴까요?
   M 안녕하세요, 1305호로 연결해 주시겠어요?
   W 연결하는 동안 잠시 기다리십시오.
   M 그러죠.
   W 지금 방에 아무도 안 계십니다. 메모를 남겨 드릴까요?

4. M 엄마, 다녀왔습니다. 저한테 전화 온 것 있었나요?
   W Simon한테서 장거리 전화가 왔다.
   M 메모 남긴 거 있어요?
   W 네가 가능한 한 빨리 전화해 주길 바라던데.
   M 알겠어요. 고마워요, 엄마.

Listen Again
p. 15

A. 다시 듣고 맞는 것을 고르시오.

1 ★a. 여자는 Michael McDowell의 전화번호를 알아야 한다.
  b. 여자는 Michael McDowell의 주소를 알아야 한다.
  c. 여자는 Michael McDowell이 사는 도시의 이름을 알아야 한다.

2. a. Amy는 지금 전화 받으러 올 수 없다.
 ★b. Amy는 전화를 끊어야 한다.
  c. Amy는 메시지를 받을 것이다.

3 ★a. 그가 통화하려는 사람은 외출 중이다.
  b. 그는 번호를 잘못 알았다.
  c. 그는 메시지를 남기고 있다.

B. 다시 듣고 맞는 문장을 고르시오.

4. a. ★ Simon은 전화를 걸었고 전화해 주기를 바란다.
   b. ☐ Simon은 전화를 걸었고 아무 메모도 남기지 않았다.

스크립트

a. Simon called and he wants a return call.
b. Simon called and didn't leave any message.

Review
p. 16

1. city, spell, E, J, area, 2301, 2301
2. reached, busy, hold, be with
3. connect, hold, put, take
4. calling, press, stay
5. calls, hours, leave, later

❋ 듣고 빈칸을 채우시오.

해석
1. W 성함과 주소는요?
   M 볼티모어시에 사는 Kenjo입니다.
   W 이름의 철자를 불러주시겠어요?
   M K-E-N-J-O입니다.
   W 네. 번호는 지역번호 포함 401-725-2301입니다.
   M 401-725-2301이요. 감사합니다.

2. 파크뷰 보험사입니다. 지금 모든 상담원이 통화 중입니다. 기다려 주십시오. 손이 비는 대로 상담원이 잠시 후에 상담해 드리겠습니다.

3. M 여보세요, 701호로 연결해주시겠어요?
   W 물론이죠. 연결하는 동안 끊지 말고 기다려 주십시오.
   M 네.
   W 지금 안에 아무도 없습니다. 메시지를 전해 드릴까요?

4. AT&T에 전화 주셔서 감사합니다. 통화 요금에 대해 궁금하시면 지금 1번을 누르세요. 전화기에 문제가 있으시면, 끊지 말고 기다려 주십시오. 저희 직원이 곧 상담해 드리겠습니다.

5. M 나한테 전화 왔어?
   W 응, Mary가 몇 시간 전에 전화했어.
   M 메시지를 남겼어?
   W 아니, 나중에 전화하겠다고 하더라.

On Your Own
p. 17

LISTEN & WRITE

듣고 질문을 써 보세요.

스크립트

What number did you dial?
Were there any calls for me?
May I take a message?

해석
몇 번에 전화하셨습니까?
나한테 전화 온 것이 있습니까?
메모 남기시겠습니까?

PRONUNCIATION

/θ/ vs /s/
☞ 듣고 따라 해 보시오. 생각하다, 물건, 두꺼운, 작은 길, 수학
☞ 듣고 따라 해 보시오. 가라앉다, 노래하다, 아픈, 지나가다, 큰 덩어리
☞ 주의 깊게 듣고 차이점을 발견해 보시오. 생각하다 / 가라앉다 물건/ 노래하다 두꺼운 / 아픈 작은 길 / 지나가다 수학 / 큰 덩어리

단어를 듣고 들은 단어에 표시하시오.

스크립트 think, sing, sick, path, mass

생각하다	★	가라앉다	☐
물건	☐	노래하다	★
두꺼운	☐	아픈	★
작은 길	★	지나가다	☐
수학	☐	큰 덩어리	★

1. 1) d   2) b   2. 1) b   2) b   3. 1) c
4. 1) c   2) a   5. 1) c   2) a

✖ 듣고 알맞은 답을 고르시오.

1. 한 남자가 전화로 교환원과 이야기하고 있다.

스크립트

Operator	What name and city?
Man	Simpson, Jacob. San Francisco.
Operator	Is that the one on Lakeside Ave.?
Man	Yes.
Operator	Okay. The number is area code 301-672-0253.
Man	Thanks. ......(dialing) Hello, can I speak to Jacob, please?
Woman	What number did you dial?
Man	Isn't this 301-672-0253?
Woman	This is 301-672-2253. I think you dialed the wrong number.
Man	Oh, I'm sorry.
Woman	No problem.

해석

Operator 성함과 사는 도시를 말씀해 주세요.
Man 샌프란시스코의 Jacob Simpson입니다.
Operator 레이크사이드가에 사는 분이신가요?
Man 네.
Operator 네. 번호는 지역 번호 포함 301-672-0253입니다.
Man 고마워요. ......(전화를 건다)
여보세요, Jacob하고 통화할 수 있을까요?
Woman 몇 번으로 거셨어요?
Man 301-672-0253아닙니까?
Woman 여기는 301-672-2253입니다. 잘못 거신 것 같네요.
Man 오, 죄송합니다.
Woman 괜찮습니다.

1) 대화 내용과 일치하지 않는 것은?
　a. 전화 거는 사람은 전화번호 안내를 요청하고 있다.
　b. Jacob은 샌프란시스코에 산다.
　c. Jacob Simpson이 두 명 이상 있을 지도 모른다.
　★d. 교환원이 전화 건 사람에게 번호를 잘못 가르쳐 주었다.

2) 전화 건 사람은 _____ 때문에 Jacob과 전화하지 못했다.
　a. 전화번호를 잘못 알았기
　★b. 전화번호를 잘못 눌렀기
　c. 전화번호를 잊어버렸기

2. Williams씨가 Jeff에게 메시지를 남기고 있다.

스크립트

Hello, Jeff. This is Mr. Williams. I'm calling about the school newspaper this month. How is it going? You must know that the paper should be out by 25th. If you need my help, please drop by my room any time between 2 p.m. and 4 p.m. See you!

해석

여보세요, Jeff. 나 Williams 선생님이야. 이번 달 교내 신문에 대해 이야기하려고 전화했다. 어떻게 되고 있니? 신문이 25일까지 발간돼야 한다는 것은 너도 알아야 해. 내 도움이 필요하면, 오후 2시에서 4시 사이에 아무 때나 내 사무실에 들르거라. 나중에 보자!

1) 전화를 건 사람은 누구인가?
　a. 친구 　★b. 선생님 　c. 아빠 　d. 의사

2) 메시지 내용과 일치하는 것은?
　a. Jeff는 전화 건 사람에게 전화해야 한다.
　★b. Jeff는 교내 신문 제작 일을 하고 있다.
　c. Jeff는 오전에 Williams 선생님을 뵐 수 있다.
　d. 신문은 벌써 나왔다.

3. Susan과 Mary가 이야기하고 있다.

스크립트

Mary	Susan, can you answer my phone while I'm gone? I am waiting for an important call from James.
Susan	No problem. I will take his messages.
Mary	If James calls, could you give him my cell phone number?
Susan	Sure, I will.

해석

Mary Susan, 나 없는 동안에 내 전화 좀 받아 줄 수 있어? James한테서 올 중요한 전화를 기다리고 있어.
Susan 문제 없어. 메시지를 받아 놓을게.
Mary James가 전화하면, 내 휴대 전화 번호를 알려주겠니?
Susan 응, 그렇게.

1) 대화 내용과 일치하지 않는 것은?
　a. Mary는 중요한 전화를 기다리고 있다.
　b. Susan은 Mary를 위해 전화를 받을 것이다.
　★c. Susan은 James에게 Mary의 집 전화번호를 가르쳐 줄 것이다.
　d. Susan은 James의 메시지를 받아 놓을 것이다.

4. Brown 씨가 교환원에게 전화를 건다.

Mr. Brown	Hello, operator?
Operator	This is the operator. How can I help you?
Mr. Brown	I want to place an international call.
Operator	What number, city and country?
Mr. Brown	Could you connect me to 81-902-3678 in Tokyo, Japan?
Operator	One moment, please... Please hold... I'll put you through, now. Go ahead, please.
Mr. Brown	Thank you.

해석

Mr.Brown	여보세요, 교환원인가요?
Operator	교환원입니다. 무엇을 도와드릴까요?
Mr.Brown	국제전화를 걸고 싶습니다만.
Operator	전화번호, 도시와 나라 이름이 어떻게 되나요?
Mr.Brown	일본, 도쿄의 81-902-3678에 연결해 주시겠어요?
Operator	잠시만요. 기다려 주세요. 지금 연결해 드리겠습니다. 말씀하세요.
Mr.Brown	감사합니다.

1) 대화에서 교환원이 필요로 하지 않는 것은 무엇인가?

  a. 전화번호   b. 나라 이름

★c. 우편 번호   d. 도시 이름

2) Brown 씨가 걸려는 번호는?

★a. 81-902-3678   b. 81-902-3687

  c. 81-902-6378   d. 81-920-3678

5. Kim과 Ben은 이야기를 하고 있다.

스크립트

Kim	What is Nina's new cell phone number?
Ben	I don't have it, Kim. Don't you know it?
Kim	No, Ben. I called her home and she's not there. I'll have to call her on her new cell phone.
Ben	Just ask for directory assistance.
Kim	They don't tell you cell phone numbers.
Ben	OK, call and get her work number. Maybe, you can reach her, there.
Kim	You're right.

해석

Kim	Nina의 새 휴대 전화 번호가 뭐지?
Ben	난 본 적 없는데, Kim. 네가 알지 않아?
Kim	아니, Ben. Nina가 집에 없어서. 그녀의 새 휴대 전화에 전화를 걸어야 하겠는데.

Ben	전화번호 상담원에게 물어봐.
Kim	휴대전화 번호는 알려주지 않아.
Ben	그럼, 그럼 전화해서 직장 전화번호를 알아봐. 거기서 넌 그녀와 연락할 수 있을지도 몰라.
Kim	맞아.

1) 여자는 무엇을 찾고 있는가?

  a. Nina의 직장 전화번호   b. 전화번호 상담원

★c. Nina의 새 전화번호   d. Ben의 전화번호

2) Nina의 전화번호에 대해 사실인 것은 무엇인가?

★a. 새 번호는 전화번호 상담원에게서 알아낼 수 없다.

  b. 새 번호는 그녀의 집 전화번호이다.

  c. 새 번호는 그녀의 직장 전화번호이다.

  d. 직장 전화번호는 전화번호 상담원에게서 알아낼 수 없다.

Dictation   p. 20

1. name, Is that the one, number, dial, wrong, No problem
2. calling about, How is it going, between 2 p.m.
3. answer, from, messages, Sure, I will
4. operator, place, country, One moment, Go ahead
5. don't have, not there, directory, reach her

UNIT 3
She is too messy.

Getting Ready   p. 21

1. 1. f   2. a   3. g   4. e   5. c   6. b   7. d
2. 1. c   2. d   3. a   4. b

1. **아래 네모 안에 있는 단어들의 기호를 빈칸에 쓰시오.**

  a. 잘 잊어버리는   b. 지저분한   c. 마음이 넓은
  d. 더러운   e. 밀어 붙이는   f. 으스대는
  g. 심술궂은

1. 그는 뭐든지 자기 식대로 하려고 한다.   f
2. 그는 데이트를 잊어버린다.   a
3. 그는 내 물건을 부숴놓고 사과하지 않는다.   g
4. 그녀는 나에게 더 열심히 일하라고 계속 말한다.   e
5. 그녀는 나의 작은 실수를 용서해 준다.   c
6. 그는 자신의 물건을 바닥에서 치우지 않는다.   b
7. 그는 양치질을 하지 않는다.   d

1. 뭔가 달라진 것 같던가요?
   c. 응, 그런 것 같아요. 그 사람 많이 변했어요.
2. 그 여자 어때요? d. 그 여자는 쾌활하고 친절해요.
3. 이게 더 나을까요? a. 네, 훨씬 나아요.
4. 당신의 남자 친구는 어때요?
   b. 그는 너무 자기 마음대로만 하려고 해요.

Listening Task   p. 22~23

Listening 1	1. b	2. a	3. b	4. b
Listen Again A	1. c	2. a	3. b	B 4. a
Listening 2	1. b	2. a	3. a	4. b
Listen Again A	1. b	2. c	3. a	B 4. a

Listening 1   p. 26

십대들이 라디오 쇼에 나왔다. 알맞은 단어를 골라 빈칸을 채우시오.

1. 그녀의 남자 친구는 너무 _____.
   a. 수줍음이 많다.　★b. 자기 마음대로이다.　c. 조용하다.

2. 그의 어머니는 너무 _____.
   ★a. 밀어 붙인다.　　b. 산만하다.　　c. 심술궂다.

3. 그의 친구는 너무 _____.
   a. 시끄럽다.　★b. 잘 잊어버린다.　c. 자기 마음대로이다.

4. 그녀의 남동생은 너무 _____.
   a. 산만하다.　★b. 심술궂다.　c. 시끄럽다.

스크립트

1. Hi, Angie! I'm calling about my boyfriend. He is a nice guy. He gives me presents all the time. He always takes me home. But he wants to do everything in his own way. He doesn't care what I want. Does he love me?

2. Hello, Angie! It's about my mom. I am not smart and I don't do very well at school. But my mom doesn't think so. She thinks I am not good at school because I don't study hard. She pushes me too hard. I am very unhappy.

3. Hi, Angie! I am a great fan of yours. It's about my friend. She is never on time. She sometimes forgets our appointment. She says sorry, but nothing has changed. We have been friends for years. But I am getting tired of her forgetfulness. What can I do?

4. Hi, Ms. Angie! It's great to talk to you. Well, I am here to talk about my brother. He is too mean. He breaks my things and never says sorry. He even reads my diary. But my mom thinks he is just too young. I can hardly stand him any longer.

해석

1. 안녕하세요, Angie! 제 남자 친구에 대해 얘기하려고 전화했어요. 제 남자 친구는 좋은 사람이에요. 그는 늘 저에게 선물을 줘요. 항상 저를 집에 데려다 줘요. 하지만 그 사람은 무엇이든 자기 식대로 하려고 해요. 제가 원하는 것에는 관심이 없어요. 그 사람이 저를 사랑하긴 하는 걸까요?

2. 안녕하세요, Angie! 저희 엄마에 대한 거예요. 제가 머리가 안 좋아서 학교 성적이 좀 안 좋거든요. 그런데 엄마는 그렇게 생각하지 않으세요. 엄마는 제가 열심히 안 해서 못하는 줄 아세요. 너무 심하게 밀어붙이시죠. 엄마 때문에 아주 불행해요.

3. 안녕하세요, Angie! 저는 당신의 팬이에요. 제 친구 얘기예요. 제 친구는 약속 시간을 제대로 지킨 적이 없어요. 어떨 때는 약속을 잊어버리기도 해요. 미안하다고는 하는데, 바뀌는 건 없거든요. 개하고는 몇 년씩이나 된 친구예요. 근데 저는 걔의 건망증에 점점 지쳐가고 있어요. 어떻게 하면 좋을까요?

4. 안녕하세요, Angie! 이야기하게 돼서 정말 기쁩니다. 음, 제 남동생 얘기 좀 하려고 참여했어요. 걔는 너무 심술궂어요. 제 물건을 부숴놓고 미안하다고도 안 해요. 제 일기까지 읽어요. 그런데 엄마는 그냥 걔가 너무 어려서 그런 거라고 생각하세요. 전 더 이상 그 애를 참을 수가 없어요.

Listen Again   p. 22

A. 다시 듣고 틀린 것을 고르시오.

1. a. 그녀의 남자 친구는 항상 그녀에게 선물을 준다.
   b. 그녀의 남자 친구는 그녀의 기분에 신경 쓰지 않는다.
   ★c. 그녀의 남자 친구는 그녀를 절대 집에 데려다 주지 않는다.

2. ★a. 그의 엄마는 그가 똑똑하지 않다고 생각한다.
   b. 그의 엄마는 그가 열심히 공부하지 않는다고 생각한다.
   c. 그의 엄마는 그의 마음에 상처를 준다.

3. a. 그의 친구는 만나기로 한 약속을 잊어버린다.
   ★b. 그의 친구는 절대 사과하지 않는다.
   c. 그의 친구는 오랫동안 그의 가장 친한 친구이다.

B. 다시 듣고 가장 적절하게 요약한 것을 고르시오.

4. a. ☒ 그녀는 그녀의 남동생이 너무 심술궂어서 더 이상 참을 수가 없다.
   b. ☐ 그녀는 그녀의 남동생이 너무 어려서 더 이상 참을 수가 없다.

Listening 2

p. 23

좋은 쪽으로 변했는가, 나쁜 쪽으로 변했는가? 체크하시오.

1. a. ☐ 좋은 쪽　　b. ★ 나쁜 쪽
2. a. ★ 좋은 쪽　　b. ☐ 나쁜 쪽
3. a. ★ 좋은 쪽　　b. ☐ 나쁜 쪽
4. a. ☐ 좋은 쪽　　b. ★ 나쁜 쪽

스크립트

1.

W Have you seen Karen lately?

M Yes. Why?

W Didn't you notice any difference?

M Yes! She is totally different. She was such a nice girl: always smiled, and never got angry. But now she is bossy and mean. What's happened to her?

W Her boyfriend dumped her.

2.

M What is your new teacher like?

W This one is a lot better. She is warm and generous. She forgives our small mistakes.

M She is not like your last teacher.

W No. She's not so pretty or smart, but she is really good.

M I hope you don't have to change your mind about her.

3.

M How is Peter lately? Does he wash himself now?

W Absolutely. He takes a shower every morning and brushes his teeth after each meal. And his room... (laugh) You've got to see his room. Everything is in its place. He makes his bed and he even hangs his clothes in the closet.

M Maybe he's in love.

4.

W My new roommate gives me a headache. I miss my old one.

M What is she like?

W She snores and plays loud music. She brings her friends over to play games. She doesn't pick up her things off the floor.

M I think you should ask her to leave.

해석

1. W 요즘에 Karen 봤니?

　M 응. 왜?

　W 뭔가 달라진 거 눈치 챘어?

　M 맞아! 걔 완전히 변했어. 꽤 괜찮은 애였는데. 항상 웃고, 절대 화 안 내고. 그런데 이제는 자기 멋대로에 못되게 굴더라. 무슨 일 생겼대?

　W 남자 친구한테 차였대.

2. M 새로 온 선생님 어때?

　W 이번 선생님이 훨씬 나아. 상냥하고 마음도 넓고, 작은 실수는 용서해 줘.

　M 지난번 선생님하고 다르네.

　W 응. 예쁘거나 똑똑한 건 아니지만, 정말 좋아.

　M 새 선생님에 대한 너의 생각이 달라지지 않았으면 좋겠다.

3. M 요즘에 Peter 어때? 이제 자기가 알아서 씻어?

　W 그럼. 매일 아침 샤워하고, 밥 먹고 나서는 이를 닦아. 그리고 그 애 방... (웃는다)... 네가 걔 방을 좀 봐야 돼. 모든 것이 다 제 자리에 있어. 침대 정리도 하고, 옷장에 옷도 걸어.

　M 어쩜 사랑에 빠졌을지도 몰라.

4. W 새로 온 룸메이트 때문에 골치가 아파. 예전 룸메이트가 그리워.

　M 새로 온 애가 어때서?

　W 코 골고, 노래도 시끄러운 걸로 들어. 게임하자고 친구들도 막 부른다니까. 바닥에 자기 물건이 떨어져 있어도 줍질 않아.

　M 나가달라고 부탁 좀 해야겠다, 너.

Listen Again

p. 23

A. 다시 듣고 알맞은 답을 고르시오.

1. Karen은 무엇 때문에 변했는가?
   a. 친구들　　★b. 남자 친구　　c. 가족

2. 새로 온 선생님에 대해 일치하지 <u>않는</u> 것은?
   a. 그녀는 관대하다.
   b. 그녀는 지난번 선생님과 다르다.
   ★c. 그녀는 예쁘고 똑똑하다.

3. Peter에 대해 일치하지 <u>않는</u> 것은?
   ★a. 자기 옷을 빨래한다. b. 옷을 걸어 놓는다.
   c. 침대를 정리한다.

B. 다시 듣고 맞는 문장을 고르시오.

4. a. ★ 그녀의 룸메이트는 시끄럽고 지저분하다.
   b. ☐ 그녀는 옛 룸메이트가 그리워서 머리가 아프다.

스크립트

a. Her roommate is loud and messy.

b. She has a headache because she misses her old roommate.

Review   p. 24

1. seen, notice, different
2. rude, bossy, way
3. like, messy, miss, neat
4. pretty, nice, friendly, a lot better
5. pushy, nice

✱ 듣고 빈칸을 채우시오.

해석

1. W 요즘에 Ken 봤니?

   M 응, 왜?

   W 뭐 달라진 눈치 못 챘니?

   M 응, 있었어. 걔 완전히 변했더라!

2. 나는 Alex가 싫어. 걔는 아주 무례해. 고맙다거나 미안하다는 말을 절대 하지 않아. 그리고 아주 자기 멋대로야. 뭐든지 자기 식대로 하려고 해. 자기가 우리 학교에서 가장 똑똑하다고 생각해. 난 Terry가 학생 회장으로 더 나은 것 같아.

3. M 새 룸메이트는 어때?

   W 정말로 지저분해.

   M 전에 있던 애가 그립겠구나.

   W 응, 착하고 깔끔했지.

4. 나는 새 선생님이 좋다. 별로 예쁘지는 않지만, 착하고 친절하다. 지난번 선생님보다 훨씬 낫다. 우리 선생님의 반에 있어서 정말 행복하다.

5. M 학교 가기 싫어요.

   W 뭐가 문제니?

   M 우리 선생님은 너무 밀어붙이세요. 숙제도 너무 많이 내주세요. 그리고 별로 친절하지도 않아요.

On Your Own   p. 25

LISTEN & WRITE

들은 질문을 써 보세요.

스크립트

> What is your mother like?
> How do you like your best friend?
> What do you think of your English teacher?

해석

어머니는 어떤 분이십니까?
당신의 가장 친한 친구는 어떻습니까?
당신의 영어 선생님을 어떻게 생각하십니까?

/tʃ/ vs /dʒ/

☞ 듣고 따라 해 보시오.

의자, 변화, 고르다, 어울리다, 바라보다

☞ 듣고 따라 해 보시오.

Janet, 주스, 물 주전자, 다리, 마을

단어를 듣고 들은 소리에 표시하시오.

/tʃ/		/dʒ/
☐	물 주전자	★
★	가격이 싼	☐
★	삐약 삐약 울다	☐
☐	지프차	★
★	많이	☐
☐	대학	★
★	Mitch	☐

Practice Test   p. 26~27

1. 1) c	2) a	2. 1) c	2) d	3. 1) c	2) d
4. 1) a	2) d	5. 1) d	2) a		

✱ 듣고 알맞은 답을 고르시오.

1. 두 친구가 그들의 남자 친구에 대해 이야기하고 있다.

스크립트

Mary What is your boyfriend like, Amy?

Amy   He is nice and gentle. He is very generous. He gives me flowers all the time.

Mary He is perfect, isn't he?

Amy   Well, not exactly.

Mary Why not?

Amy   He is very forgetful. He forgets our date and doesn't show up. I am very upset with him sometimes.

Mary But he is better than my boyfriend. Mine is very bossy.

해석

Mary 네 남자 친구 어때, Amy?

Amy   착하고 상냥해. 마음이 아주 넓어. 항상 나한테 꽃을 줘.

Mary 완벽하네, 안 그러니?

Amy   꼭 그렇다고는 할 수 없어.

Mary 왜?

Amy   건망증이 있어. 데이트도 잊어버리고 나타나질 않아. 어떨 땐 엄청 화 나.

Mary 그래도 걔는 내 남자 친구보다는 낫다. 내 남자 친구는 너무 거만해.

1) Amy의 남자 친구가 완벽하지 못한 이유는?
   a. 너무 관대하다.   b. 너무 지저분하다.
 ★c. 너무 건망증이 심하다.   d. 너무 상냥하다.

2) 그는 무엇을 잊어버리는가?
 ★a. 여자 친구와의 데이트를 잊어버린다.
   b. 여자 친구의 생일을 잊어버린다.
   c. 여자 친구의 전화번호를 잊어버린다.
   d. 여자 친구에게 꽃을 주는 것을 잊어버린다.

2. Sam은 학교에서 Chris에 대해 말하고 있다.

스크립트

Chris is a wonderful person. He works hard and helps others a lot. He is hard on himself but generous to others. He is smart and polite. He doesn't talk much but listens. He can do a lot for our class and our school. I think he will make the perfect class president.

해석

Chris는 아주 좋은 사람입니다. 열심히 공부하고 다른 사람을 많이 도와줘요. 자신에게는 엄격하지만 다른 사람에게는 관대해요. 머리가 좋고 예의 바릅니다. 말을 많이 하기보다 남의 말에 귀를 기울이고요. 그는 우리 반과 학교를 위해 많은 일을 할 수 있어요. 나는 그가 완벽한 반장이 될 거라고 생각합니다.

1) Chris는 _____ 선거에 나가고 있다.
   a. 학생 회장   b. 동아리 부장
 ★c. 반장   d. 회사 회장

2) Chris에 대해 일치하지 않는 것은?
   a. 열심히 공부한다.   b. 도움을 준다.
   c. 예의 바르다.   ★d. 남에게 엄격하다.

3. Jeff와 Brown 부인이 이야기하고 있다.

스크립트

M Mom, Tim's mother is very nice.
W Really?
M She is never angry. She doesn't mind doing Tim's homework.
W Really? Tim must like her very much.
M Of course. And she is very generous. She gives Tim a lot of pocket money.
W Oh, that's why Tim is rude, careless and messy.

해석

W 엄마, Tim의 엄마는 정말 좋으신 분이에요.
W 정말?
W 절대 화를 안 내세요. Tim의 숙제를 기꺼이 해 주세요.

W 정말? Tim이 엄마를 정말 좋아하겠네.
W 그럼요. 그리고 아주 마음이 넓으세요. Tim에게 용돈도 많이 주세요.
W 오, 그래서 Tim이 버릇 없고, 조심성 없고, 지저분한 거구나.

1) Tim의 엄마에 대해 Jeff가 말하지 않은 것은?
   a. 아주 친절하다.   b. 마음이 아주 넓다.
 ★c. Tim의 숙제를 해주지 않는다. d. Tim에게 돈을 많이 준다.

2) Brown부인의 생각에 Tim은 어떤가?
   a. 마음이 넓다. b. 착하다. c. 친절하다.★d. 조심성이 없다.

4. John과 Sue가 이야기를 하고 있다.

스크립트

M Hey, Sue! Have you heard from Gail?
W No, why, John?
M She's late, again.
W But she is always on time!
M I know! But, she has really changed.
W How?
M She often forgets to meet me. She plays loud music all the time and doesn't brush her teeth.
W That's too bad. My boyfriend is like that, except he's always on time.

해석

M 이봐, Sue. Gail에게서 무슨 말 들었니?
W 아니, 왜, John?
M Gail이 또 늦네.
W 하지만 Gail은 항상 제시간에 오잖아!
M 알아! 하지만, 걔 정말로 변했어.
W 어떻게?
M 나를 만나는 걸 자주 잊어버려. 항상 큰 음악을 틀어 놓고 이도 닦지 않아.
W 안됐다. 제 시간에 오는 것만 빼면 내 남자 친구도 그래.

1) Gail은 전에 어떠했는가?
 ★a. 언제나 제시간에 왔다.
   b. John을 만나는 걸 항상 잊었다.
   c. 항상 음악을 크게 틀어놓았다.
   d. 더러웠다.

2) Sue의 남자 친구에 대해 사실이 아닌 것은 무엇인가?
   a. 시끄럽다.   b. 더럽다.
   c. 음악을 크게 틀어놓는다.★d. 항상 모든 일에 늦는다.

5. 한 대학생이 그녀의 할머니와 전화 통화를 하고 있다.

스크립트

Hi, Grandmother! I'm fine. My boyfriend? He is doing fine, too. Of course I still like him. Yes, he used to forget our dates, break my things, and not say he was sorry. But, Grandmother! He has changed a lot. What is he like, now? He is nice and friendly and forgives my small mistakes.

해석

안녕하세요, 할머니! 전 잘 지내고 있어요. 남자 친구요? 역시 잘 지내죠. 물론, 그를 여전히 좋아하죠. 네, 남자 친구는 전에는 우리 데이트를 잊어버리고 제 물건을 망가뜨리고, 미안하다고 말도 하지 않곤 했었죠. 하지만, 할머니! 그가 많이 변했어요. 지금은 어떠냐고요? 착하고 자상하며 제 작은 실수까지 다 용서해 줘요.

1) 그녀의 남자 친구는 이전에 어땠는가?
　　a. 가없은　　b. 관대한　　c. 착한　　★d. 건망증이 있는

2) 대화의 분위기는 어떠한가?
　★a. 편안한　　b. 화난　　c. 두려운　　d. 조급한

Dictation　　　　　　　　　　　　　p. 28

1. What is, like, generous, perfect, not exactly, forgetful, very bossy
2. works hard, He is hard, polite, our school
3. Really, doesn't mind, Of course, that's why, careless
4. Have you heard, She's late, changed, all the time, except
5. fine, break my things, What is he like

UNIT 4
Put the coin in first!

Getting Ready　　　　　　　　　　p. 29

1. 1. Press　　2. Turn　　3. Enter　　4. Click
　　5. Raise, point　　6. Add, mix　　7. Pick, insert
2. a　b　e　c　d　f　g

---

1. 아래 네모 안에서 맞는 말을 골라 빈칸을 채우시오.

넣으시오	드시오	누르시오	클릭하시오
켜시오	입력하시오	들어 올리시오	
섞으시오	첨가하시오	가리키시오	

1. 스크린 위의 버튼을 ___누르시오___.
2. 컴퓨터를 ___켜시오___.
3. ID와 비밀번호를 ___입력하시오___.
4. 마우스로 아이콘을 ___클릭하시오___.
5. 팔을 ___올리고___ 곧게 ___가리키시오___.
6. 소금을 약간 ___넣고___ 재료를 모두 잘 ___섞으시오___.
7. 수화기를 ___들고___ 동전을 ___넣으시오___.

2. 다음은 쌀을 요리하는 방법이다. 순서대로 정리하시오.

　a. 어떻게 하는지 가르쳐 줄래?
　b. 응, 이리 와. 내가 어떻게 하는지 보여줄게.
　c. 다음으로, 씻은 쌀을 냄비에 넣어.
　d. 그리고 쌀에다가 물을 세 컵 넣어.
　e. 먼저, 쌀 두 컵을 씻어.
　f. 그리고 강한 불에서 10분간 끓여.
　g. 마지막으로, 불을 줄여서 약한 불에서 5분 더 끓여.

Listening Task　　　　　　　　p. 30~31

Listening 1	1. 2, 3, 1, 4, 5
	2. 5, 3, 2, 1, 4
Listen Again　1	1) arms　　2) out
	3) knees　　4) feet
2	1) two　　2) salt
	3) fifteen　　4) pot
Listening 2	1. c　2. a　3. b　4. c
Listen Again　A	1. b　2. b　3. b
B	4. b

Listening 1　　　　　　　　　　p. 30

두 가지의 지시 사항이 있다. 듣고 순서대로 그림에 번호를 매기시오.

스크립트

1. This is a warm-up exercise. It is very important to get some exercise before you start to play any sports.
　1. Now stand up straight with your feet apart.
　2. Raise your arms.
　3. Point your arms straight out.
　4. Touch your left foot with your right hand. Don't bend your knees.
　5. Touch your right foot with your left hand.

2. The point is you don't need to wash after eating. Isn't that great? You need only two eggs, one strong zipper bag, and a pot of boiling water.
  1. First, break two eggs into a strong zipper bag.
  2. Add some salt and pepper.
  3. Mix the ingredients in the zipper bag. Make sure there are no holes or openings in the bag.
  4. Put the bag into the pot of boiling water.
  5. Let it stay in the boiling water for 15 minutes.
That's it. There are no dishes to wash.

해석

1. 준비운동입니다. 이건 어떤 스포츠이든 시작하기 전에 해야 할 중요한 운동입니다.
  1. 이제 두 발을 벌리고 똑바로 서세요.
  2. 두 팔을 드세요.
  3. 팔을 곧게 뻗어 바깥쪽을 가리키세요.
  4. 오른손을 왼발에 대세요. 무릎을 굽히지 마세요.
  5. 왼손을 오른발에 대세요.

2. 중요한 건 다 먹은 후에 설거지 할 필요가 없다는 거야. 굉장하지 않니? 달걀 2개, 지퍼 백 튼튼한 거 하나, 끓는 물 한 냄비만 있으면 돼.
  1. 먼저, 튼튼한 지퍼 백에 달걀 두 개를 깨뜨려 넣어.
  2. 소금과 후추를 약간 넣어.
  3. 재료들을 지퍼 백 안에서 섞어. 지퍼 백에 구멍이나 틈이 있는지 확인해야 해.
  4. 그 지퍼 백을 끓는 물에 넣어.
  5. 끓는 물에서 15분간 놔 둬. 그게 다야. 설거지 할 게 없지.

Listen Again
p. 30

다시 듣고 알맞은 것을 고르시오. (위의 그림을 보지 마시오.)

1. 1)(다리를 / 팔을) 들어야 한다.
  2)팔을 뻗어 (바깥으로 / 앞으로) 들어야 한다.
  3)(팔을 / 무릎을) 굽히면 안 된다.
  4)손을 (어깨에 / 발에) 대야 한다.

2. 1)달걀이 (2개 / 3개) 필요하다.
  2)(식용유 / 소금)을(를) 조금 첨가한다.
  3)달걀이 든 지퍼 백을 (20분 / 15분) 동안 끓는 물 속에 둔다.
  4)(접시 / 냄비)가 필요하다.

Listening 2
p. 31

무엇에 대한 지시 사항인가? 듣고 알맞은 답을 고르시오.

1. a. 컴퓨터 켜는 방법
  b. 비밀번호 입력하는 방법

 ★c. 인터넷에 접속하는 방법

2.★a. 자동판매기 사용하는 방법
  b. 캔에 담긴 탄산음료를 마시는 방법
  c. 기계에서 지폐를 동전으로 바꾸는 방법

3. a. 인터넷에서 사진 구입하는 방법
 ★b. 온라인 앨범에 사진 올리는 방법
  c. 인터넷 사이트에 자료를 올리는 방법

4. a. 장거리 전화 거는 방법
  b. 교환원에게 도움 받는 방법
 ★c. 공중전화 이용하는 방법

스크립트

1. Please turn on the computer. Soon you'll see some icons on the screen. Click on the icon named 'Internet Explorer.' The page that you have chosen as your home page will then come up.

2. Insert money into the slot. You'll see small lights on under the names of the drink. Press the button for the drink you want. Now take out your drink and push the change button for change.

3. First, click the 'Browse' button. Find your pictures on your hard drive. Click the picture you want to add to your on-line album. Next, hit the "Upload Image" button. Now all you have to do is wait. After a few seconds the picture will be shown on the album. Simple and easy!

4. First, pick up the receiver. There is no tone until you put the right amount of money in coins. For a local call, you have to put 35 cents in. When you hear the tone, dial the number.

해석

1. 컴퓨터를 켜세요. 곧 화면에 아이콘들이 보일 것입니다. '인터넷 익스플로러'라는 아이콘을 클릭하세요. 그러면 당신이 홈페이지로 선택한 페이지가 나타날 것입니다.

2. 구멍에 돈을 넣으세요. 음료수 이름 아래에 있는 작은 불빛이 보일 겁니다. 원하는 음료수의 버튼을 누르세요. 음료수를 꺼낸 다음, 거스름돈을 받기 위해 거스름돈 버튼을 누르세요.

3. 먼저, '브라우저' 버튼을 클릭하세요. 하드 드라이브에 있는 사진들을 찾으세요. 앨범에 추가하기를 원하는 사진을 클릭하세요. 그 다음, '사진 올리기' 버튼을 누르세요. 이제 기다리기만 하면 됩니다. 몇 초 후에 사진이 앨범에 뜰 거예요. 간단하고 쉬워요!

4. 먼저, 수화기를 드세요. 정해진 액수의 동전을 넣을 때까지 발신음은 들리지 않습니다. 시내 전화를 걸려면, 35센트를 넣어야 합니다. 발신음이 들리면, 전화번호를 누르세요.

Listen Again

p. 31

A. 다시 듣고 알맞은 답을 고르시오.

1. 화면에서 가장 먼저 보이는 것은 무엇인가?
   a. 서버 홈페이지 ★b. 아이콘

2. 먼저 해야 할 행동은?
   a. 거스름돈 받기 ★b. 음료수 꺼내기

3. 먼저 해야 할 행동은?
   a. '사진 올리기' 버튼 누르기
   ★b. '브라우저' 버튼 클릭하기

B. 다시 듣고 맞는 문장을 고르시오.

4. a. ☐ 수화기를 들기 전에 35센트를 넣어야 한다.
   b. ★ 발신음을 듣기 위해서는 35센트를 넣어야 한다.

스크립트

a. You have to put 35 cents in before picking up the receiver.
b. You have to put 35 cents in to hear the tone.

Review

p. 32

1. tell, use, pick, Put, tone, dial
2. stand, Raise, Touch
3. Turn, Click, screen, Enter
4. break, Add, Mix, pan
5. upload, click, find and click, Upload Image, picture, on-line

✲ 듣고 빈칸을 채우시오.

해석

1. M 공중전화를 어떻게 사용하는지 가르쳐 주시겠어요?
   W 먼저, 수화기를 드세요. 구멍에 35센트를 넣으세요.
   M 발신음이 들리네요.
   W 이제 전화번호를 누르세요. 그렇게 하시면 돼요.

2. 준비 운동입니다. 여러분, 똑바로 서 주세요. 팔을 들어 올리세요. 오른손을 왼발에 갖다 대세요.

3. W 인터넷에 어떻게 접속하지?
   M 컴퓨터를 켜.
   W 시작 메뉴가 보여.
   M 화면에서 '인터넷 익스플로러' 아이콘을 클릭해.
   W 서버 홈페이지가 보여.
   M ID와 비밀번호를 입력해.

4. 스크램블드 에그를 만드는 방법입니다. 먼저, 사발에 달걀 2개를 깨뜨려 넣으세요. 소금과 후추를 넣으세요. 잘 섞으세요. 프라이팬에 섞은 것을 부으세요. 이제 익혀서 맛있게 드세요.

5. M 이봐, 내가 사진 올리는 법을 가르쳐 줄게. '브라우저' 버튼을 클릭해 봐.
   W 알았어.
   M 이제 원하는 사진을 찾아 클릭하고 '사진 올리기' 버튼을 치고 기다려 봐. 몇 초 후에 사진이 온라인 앨범에 올라와 있을 거야.

On Your Own

p. 33

LISTEN & WRITE

들은 질문을 써 보세요.

스크립트

Can you tell me how to do a warm-up exercise?
How can you access the Internet?
How can you make fried eggs?

해석

준비 운동 하는 법을 말씀해 주시겠습니까?
인터넷에 어떻게 접속합니까?
달걀 프라이는 어떻게 만듭니까?

PRONUNCIATION

/ m / vs / n /

☞ **듣고 따라 해 보시오.**

우편, 달, 나의 것, 총액, 껌

☞ **듣고 따라 해 보시오.**

손톱, 정오, 아홉, 태양, 총

☞ **주의 깊게 듣고 차이점을 발견하시오.**

우편 / 손톱   달 / 정오
나의 것 / 아홉   총액 / 태양
껌 / 총

단어를 듣고 들은 올바른 단어에 표시하시오.

스크립트 mail, noon, nine, sum, gun

우편	★	손톱	☐
달	☐	정오	★
나의 것	☐	아홉	★
총액	★	태양	☐
껌	☐	총	★

1. 1) c 2) a 2. 1) 4 - 1 - 2 - 3 - 5 - 6 2) d
3. 1) b 2) a 4. 1) c 2) c 5. 1) b 2) c

✽ 듣고 알맞은 답을 고르시오.

1. 민수가 처음으로 전화기를 사용하고 있다.

스크립트

M Can you tell me how to use this phone, please?
W Is it a local call?
M No, it's a long-distance call.
W Then pick up the receiver.
M Okay.
W Now dial the number. Be sure to dial 1 first. Now the operator will tell you how much money you need to put in.
M She says it's $1.75.
W Put the money in the slot. That's it.
M Thanks a lot.
W No problem.

해석

M 이 전화 사용하는 법 좀 가르쳐 주시겠어요?
W 시내 전화인가요?
M 아뇨, 장거리 전화에요.
W 그럼 수화기를 드세요.
M 네.
W 이제 전화번호를 누르세요. 처음에는 꼭 1번을 눌러야 해요. 그러면 교환원이 얼마를 넣어야 하는지 말할 거예요.
M 1달러 75센트라는데요.
W 구멍에 돈을 넣으세요. 그러면 돼요.
M 감사합니다.
W 천만에요.

1) 대화 내용과 일치하지 <u>않는</u> 것은?
  a. 공중전화 사용법에 대한 내용이다.
  b. 장거리 전화 거는 법에 대한 내용이다.
  ★c. 시내 전화 거는 법에 대한 내용이다.

2) 어떤 행동이 먼저인가?
  ★a. 수화기를 든다.   b. 동전을 넣는다.
  c. 교환원과 이야기 한다.

2. 다음은 스크램블드 에그를 만드는 방법이다.

스크립트

1. Break two eggs into a bowl.
2. Add some milk and salt.
3. Mix everything together.
4. Pour the mixture onto a pan and heat it.
5. Stir the eggs until they are cooked.
6. Now turn off the heat and enjoy it.

해석

1 사발에 달걀 두 개를 깨뜨려 넣는다.
2 우유와 소금을 첨가한다.
3 모두 한꺼번에 섞는다.
4 섞은 것을 팬에 붓고 가열한다.
5 익을 때까지 달걀을 저어 준다.
6 이제 불을 끄고 맛있게 먹는다.

1) 듣고 순서대로 그림에 번호를 매기시오.

2) 스크램블드 에그를 만들 때 필요 <u>없는</u> 것은?
  a. 우유   b. 팬   c. 사발   ★d. 설탕

3. 남자는 현금인출기를 처음으로 사용한다.

스크립트

M How can I use this machine? I want to take out some money.
W Put your card in the slot.
M Now what? There is a menu on the screen.
W Touch the 'withdraw' button on the screen.
M Now I need to enter my password.
W Yes, that's right. And enter the amount of money you want to take out.
M Oh, here comes my money. Thank you.
W You're welcome.

해석

M 이 기계 어떻게 사용하는 건가요? 돈을 좀 뽑고 싶은데요.
W 카드를 투입구에 넣으세요.
M 이제 어떻게 해요? 화면에 메뉴가 뜨네요.
W 화면에서 '출금' 버튼을 누르세요.
M 이제 비밀번호를 입력해야 하는군요.
W 네, 맞아요. 그리고 출금하고 싶은 액수를 입력하세요.
M 오, 돈이 나오네요. 감사합니다.
W 천만에요.

1) 남자는 무엇을 하려고 하는가?
  a. 송금   ★b. 출금   c. 예금

2) 어느 행동이 먼저인가?
  ★a. 화면의 버튼을 누른다.   b. 비밀번호를 입력한다.
  c. 명세서를 챙긴다.

4. 엄마와 아들이 이야기를 하고 있다.

스크립트

> W Let's make soup.
> M Can you show me how to do it?
> W Sure! What kind of soup do you want?
> M Let's make potato and rice soup. I'll get the potatoes.
> W Okay. Get five potatoes from the sack. Then wash and peel them. I'll wash and prepare the rice. Two cups of rice in three cups of water. Then, heat for 10 minutes on high.
> M I want to mix them, together.
> W Okay.

해석

W 수프를 끓이자.

M 어떻게 끓이는지 보여 주실래요?

W 물론이지. 무슨 수프를 원하니?

M 감자와 쌀 수프를 만들어요. 감자를 가져올게요.

W 알았어. 자루에서 감자 다섯 개를 가져오렴. 그걸 씻어서 껍질도 벗기고. 난 쌀을 씻고 준비해 둘게. 물 세 컵에 쌀 두 컵. 그러고 나서, 강한 불에 십 분 동안 익힌단다.

M 제가 감자와 쌀을 함께 섞을게요.

W 그러려무나.

1) 마지막에 하는 것은 무엇인가?
   a. 쌀을 씻는다.   b. 감자를 씻는다.
   ★c. 쌀과 감자를 섞는다.   d. 감자 껍질을 벗긴다.

2) 수프를 만드는 데 필요하지 않은 것은 무엇인가?
   a. 쌀   b. 감자   ★c. 자루   d. 물

5. 나이 든 부인이 한 그룹에게 말을 하고 있다.

스크립트

> Turn on your computers and enter your ID's and passwords. Click on the icon with the mouse and double click, here. Very good! Point your mouse at the folder and click twice. This is your word processing program. Now, everyone write a thank-you note and e-mail it to your parents for these new school computers.

해석

컴퓨터를 켜고 아이디와 비밀번호를 입력하세요. 마우스로 아이콘을 클릭하시고 이곳을 더블 클릭하세요. 아주 잘했어요! 폴더에 마우스를 가져가서 두 번 클릭하세요. 이것이 워드 프로세싱 프로그램이에요. 이제, 이 새 학교 컴퓨터에 대해 감사 편지를 쓰고 그걸 여러분의 부모님께 보내세요.

1) 말하는 사람은 누구인가?
   a. 학생   ★b. 교사   c. 부모님   d. 교장

2) 여자의 말에 대해 사실이 아닌 것은 무엇인가?
   a. 워드 프로세싱 프로그램을 사용하는 방법에 관한 것이다.
   b. 부모님께 감사 편지를 쓰는 방법에 관한 것이다.
   ★c. 선생님께 감사하는 방법에 관한 것이다.
   d. 새 컴퓨터를 사용하는 방법에 관한 것이다.

Dictation	p. 36

1. how to use, local, receiver, in the slot, problem
2. Break, Add, cooked, turn off
3. take out, password, that's right, You're welcome
4. show me, Let's make, wash, for 10 minutes
5. Turn on, Point, twice, write, your parents

UNIT 5
The steak is too cold!

Getting Ready	p. 37

1. 1. c   2. a   3. b   4. e   5. d
   6. b   7. a   8. e
2. 1. d   2. c   3. a   4. b   5. e

1. 무엇에 대한 표현들인가? 아래 네모 안에 있는 단어의 기호를 쓰시오.

a. 서비스	b. 음식	c. 위치	d. 가격	e. 분위기

1. 그 음식점은 찾기가 어렵다.   c
2. 종업원들은 정말 다정하고 친절하다.   a
3. 신선하고 맛있다.   b
4. 아늑하다. 음악도 아주 좋다.   e
5. 가격이 너무 비싸다.   d
6. 주방장이 요리를 잘 한다.   b
7. 종업원이 손님을 신경 써 주지 않는다.   a
8. 집같이 편안할 것이다.   e

2. 표현을 응답과 연결시키시오.

1. 그 음식점 어땠어?   d. 좋았어요. 음식이 좋았어요.
2. 멕시코 음식 먹어 봤니?   c. 아니, 안 먹어 봤어. 너는?
3. 배불러. 한 입도 더 못 먹겠어. a. 나도. 배가 꽉 찼어.
4. 맛있게 드셨습니까, 손님?   b. 네, 아주 좋았어요.
5. 먹으려면 얼마나 기다려야 해? e. 영영 안 나올 것 같아.

Listening 1	**3, 1, 4, 2**		
Listen Again A	**1. b**	**2. c**	**3. b**
B	**4. a**		
Listening 2	**1. c**	**2. c**	**3. a**	**4. c**
Listen Again A	**1. a**	**2. a**	**3. b**
B	**4. a**		

Listening 1

p. 38

각각의 상황에 가장 알맞은 음식점은 어느 곳인가? 알맞은 번호를
쓰시오.

해물 요리를 먹고 싶을 때	3
매운 음식을 먹고 싶을 때	1
외식하거나 요리할 시간이 없을 때	4
담백하고 특별한 것을 먹고 싶을 때	2

스크립트

1. Do you like spicy food? Are you tired of
   hamburgers and pizza? Try Castello's on
   North Ave. It's the best Mexican restaurant in
   town. The food is nicely spicy and the service
   is even better. Be sure to try the burrito there.
   You would never forget its taste.

2. If you feel like something light and unusual,
   Thai Palace may be your choice. The food
   is mostly rice, vegetables and noodles. You
   can also enjoy Thai culture there. There
   are Thai paintings on the wall and the
   waitresses serve in traditional Thai dresses.

3. Have you tried Ocean's Bay, the seafood
   restaurant on Queens Ave.? If you haven't,
   and you love seafood, you should go this
   month. They are having a special price this
   month. The food is fresh and delicious.
   Once you're there, be sure to taste the
   steamed crab. You wouldn't want to leave!

4. You are busy and your refrigerator is empty,
   but you want something nice and warm? Then
   call Quick Cuisine at 1-800-204-5700. It's
   a food delivery chain. You can get fine hot
   American meals in 30 minutes. You have to
   pay some delivery fee but it's worth it. Their
   best menu item is grilled chicken barbecue.

해석

1. 매운 음식을 좋아하세요? 햄버거와 피자에 질리셨나요?
   North 가에 있는 Castello's에 가 보세요. 시내에서 멕시코

요리를 제일 잘 하는 집이에요. 음식이 맛있게 맵고 서비스는
음식보다 더 훌륭합니다. Castello's에 가시면 꼭 부리토를
드셔 보세요. 절대 잊지 못할 맛이에요.

*burrito: 고기와 소스 섞은 것을 옥수수 빈대떡으로 싸서 먹는 멕시코 음식

2. 담백하고 특별한 음식을 먹고 싶을 때는, Thai Palace를 선
   택하면 아주 좋죠. 주로 쌀, 채소, 그리고 국수로 된 요리를 합
   니다. 그리고 음식뿐만 아니라 타이의 문화도 즐길 수 있습니
   다. 벽에는 타이 전통 그림이 그려져 있고 종업원들은 타이의
   전통 의상을 입고 서빙을 합니다.

3. Queens 가에 있는 해물 전문 음식점, Ocean's Bay에 가 보
   셨나요? 아직 안 가 보셨고 해물을 좋아하신다면 이번 달에
   꼭 가야 합니다. 이번 달에 특별 가격을 제공합니다. 음식은
   신선하고 맛있습니다. 거기에 가시면 꼭 게찜을 맛보세요. 식
   당을 나오기가 싫어질 거예요!

4. 시간은 없고 냉장고는 비었지만, 뭔가 맛있고 따뜻한 걸 드시
   고 싶은가요? 그럴 땐 Quick Cuisine, 1-800-204-5700으
   로 전화해 보세요. 배달 음식 전문 체인점이랍니다. 30분 안
   으로 따뜻한 미국식 식사를 받을 수 있습니다. 배달비를 내야
   하지만 그럴 만한 가치가 있어요. 가장 맛있는 메뉴는 구운
   치킨 바비큐입니다.

Listen Again

p. 38

A. 다시 듣고 맞는 것을 고르시오.

1. a. 아시아 음식점이다.
   ★b. 음식도 맛있지만 서비스는 더 좋다.
   c. 그곳에서 중국 음식을 먹을 수 있다.

2. a. 베트남 음식점이다.
   b. 고기 요리가 많다.
   ★c. 타이의 문화를 즐길 수 있다.

3. a. 이탈리아 음식점이다.
   ★b. 음식이 신선하고 맛있다.
   c. 항상 특별 가격을 제공한다.

B. 다시 듣고 가장 적절하게 요약한 것을 고르시오.

4. a. ★ Quick Cuisine은 따뜻한 미국식 식사를 30분 안에
      제공한다.
   b. ☐ Quick Cuisine은 무료로 배달해 준다.

Listening 2

p. 39

말하는 이들은 각각 음식점의 어떤 점을 좋아하는가? 알맞은 답을
고르시오.

1. a. 위치	b. 서비스	★c. 음식	
2. a. 가격	b. 서비스	★c. 음식	
3 ★a. 서비스	b. 위치	c. 분위기	
4. a. 가격	b. 음식	★c. 분위기	

1.

M I am full. I can't eat one more bite. The food is really good here.

W Yeah. The chef knows how to cook.

M But this place is hard to find. I had to ask several people how to get here.

W Yes, they need a better location if they want to make money.

M I think so.

2.

M I'm hungry. How much longer do we have to wait?

W Seems like it'll take forever. The waiters are just talking among themselves. They don't care about the customers at all.

M The food is excellent, but the service is really poor.

W Right. I can't stand it any longer. Excuse me, miss.

3.

W Did you enjoy your meal, sir?

M Yes. It was great. Especially the service was super. I really like your place.

W Thank you, sir. Here's your check.

M Oh, why is it so expensive?

W Oh, didn't you read the menu? On weekends, there's an additional service charge.

4.

W It's my favorite restaurant, but how did you like it?

M It was a beautiful place with romantic music and a cozy atmosphere.

W So did you propose to her?

M Yes. We had a wonderful time there. But the food was a little disappointing. The steak was cold and dry and the salad was not so fresh.

해석

1. M 나 배불러. 한 입도 더 못 먹겠어. 여기 음식 진짜 맛있다.
   W 맞아. 주방장이 요리를 잘 하나 봐.
   M 그런데 여기는 찾기가 힘들더라. 여기에 오는 방법을 여러 사람에게 물어 봐야 했어.
   W 맞아, 장사 잘 되려면 더 좋은 장소에 있어야 할 것 같아.
   M 그럴 것 같아.

2. M 배고픈데. 얼마나 더 기다려야 되나?
   W 영영 안 나올 것 같아. 종업원들은 자기들끼리 수다만 떨고 있어. 손님들은 전혀 신경 쓰지 않아.

M 음식은 맛있는데, 서비스가 정말 별로다.

W 맞아. 더 이상 못 참겠다. 실례합니다.

3. W 맛있게 드셨습니까, 손님?
   M 네. 잘 먹었어요. 특히 서비스가 훌륭한데요. 여기 정말 마음에 드네요.
   W 감사합니다, 손님. 여기 계산서입니다.
   M 오, 왜 이렇게 비싸죠?
   W 아, 메뉴를 읽지 않으셨습니까? 주말에는 서비스 요금이 추가됩니다.

4. W 거기는 내가 최고로 좋아하는 음식점인데 넌 어땠어?
   M 낭만적인 음악과 포근한 분위기를 가진 아름다운 곳이었어.
   W 그럼 그녀에게 프러포즈는 했어?
   M 응. 우린 거기서 정말 좋은 시간을 보냈어. 그런데 음식은 약간 별로더라. 스테이크는 식은데다 말랐고, 샐러드는 별로 안 싱싱하더라고.

Listen Again   p. 39

A. 다시 듣고 알맞은 답을 고르시오.

1. 이 음식점의 문제점은 무엇인가?
   ★a. 찾아오기가 힘들다.
   b. 가게가 너무 작다.
   c. 주방장이 미숙하다.

2. 이 음식점의 문제점은 무엇인가?
   ★a. 서비스가 너무 느리다.
   b. 여자 종업원들이 너무 떠든다.
   c. 너무 붐빈다.

3. 이 음식점의 문제점은 무엇인가?
   a. 식사가 너무 비싸다.
   ★b. 서비스 요금이 너무 높다.
   c. 식사가 별로 맛이 없다.

B. 다시 듣고 맞는 문장을 고르시오.

4. a. ★ 그곳은 아늑했지만 음식은 그리 좋지 않았다.
   b. □ 그곳은 아름다웠고 음식이 맛있었다.

a. The place was cozy but the food was not so good.
b. The place was beautiful and the food was delicious.

Review   p. 40

1. enjoy, check
2. try, find, enjoy, serve
3. full, bite, service, slow
4. tired, light, rice, 1, 800, in town, meal
5. tried, food, enjoy

✽ 듣고 빈칸을 채우시오.

해석

1. W 식사 즐겁게 하셨습니까?
   M 네, 정말 좋았어요.
   W 감사합니다. 계산서 여기 있습니다.

2. 멕시코의 음식을 좋아하신다면, 새로운 멕시코 음식점에 가
   보세요. 찾아가기 쉬워요. 거기서 멕시코 전통 문화도 즐길 수
   있어요. 종업원들이 멕시코 전통 의상을 입고 서비스를 제공
   합니다.

3. M 나 배불러. 한 입도 더 못 먹겠어.
   W 음식이 아주 좋은데.
   M 그런데 서비스는 안 좋아. 너무 느려.

4. 햄버거와 피자는 질렸고 부담 없고 특별한 것을 드시고 싶다
   고요. 국물 있는 쌀국수는 어떠세요? 1-800-204-2354로 전
   화하세요. 우리는 시내의 새로운 타이 음식점입니다. 30분 내
   로 맛있는 타이 음식을 드실 수 있습니다.

5. W 새로운 중국 음식점 가 봤어?
   M 아니, 거기 좋아?
   W 응, 음식이 맛있어. 그런데 내가 가장 좋아하는 건 생음악
   을 들을 수 있다는 거야.

On Your Own p. 41

LISTEN & WRITE

들은 질문을 써 보세요.

스크립트

> Have you tried Japanese food?
> How did you like the place?
> Did you enjoy your meal?

해석

일본 음식을 먹어 본 적이 있습니까?
그곳이 마음에 들었습니까?
식사는 맛있었습니까?

PRONUNCIATION

-ed는 어떻게 발음하나?
/ id / vs / t /

☞ 듣고 따라 해 보시오.
원했다, 끝났다

☞ 듣고 따라 해 보시오.
좋아했다, 보았다, 희망했다, 웃었다, 씻었다

듣고 올바른 칸에 각각의 단어를 쓰시오.

스크립트 출발했다, 놓쳤다, 일했다, 기다렸다, 필요했다, 구웠다

/ id /	/ t /
started	missed
waited	worked
needed	baked

Practice Test p. 42~43

1. 1) a	2) d	2. 1) b	2) c	3. 1) c	2) d
4. 1) b	2) b	5. 1) d	2) a		

✽ 듣고 알맞은 답을 고르시오.

1. 두 사람이 무엇을 먹을지 이야기하고 있다.

스크립트

M Let's have dinner together tonight.
W Sure. Where would you like to go?
M How about some Asian food? I'd like something light and different. I'm tired of burgers and fries.
W Me, too.
M Let's go to the Korean restaurant then.
W Is it good?
M Oh, yes. The food there is mostly vegetables and grains. My friend Sandy is crazy about bibimbap there. She says it's really tasty and healthy, too.

해석

M 오늘 같이 저녁 먹으러 가자.
W 그래. 어디로 가고 싶어?
M 아시아 음식 어때? 가볍고 색다른 걸 먹고 싶어. 햄버거와 감
   자 튀김은 질렸어.
W 나도.
M 그러면 한국 음식점에 가자.
W 거기 좋아?
M 어, 그럼. 거기 음식은 거의 채소랑 곡물이야. 내 친구 Sandy
   는 거기 비빔밥을 진짜 좋아해. 아주 맛있고 건강에도 좋대.

1) 두 사람이 오늘 저녁에 먹지 않을 음식은?
   ★a. 스테이크   b. 한국 음식
   c. 가벼운 음식   d. 색다른 음식

2) 말하는 이들에 의하면, 한국 음식에 대한 설명으로 옳지 않은
   것은?
   a. 위에 부담 없다.
   b. 건강에 좋다.
   c. 대부분 채소와 곡물로 되어 있다.
   ★d. 건강에는 좋지만 맛이 없다.

2. 한 남자가 어떤 음식점에 대해 말하고 있다.

스크립트

It's my favorite restaurant. First of all, the food is fresh and delicious. Second, the service is excellent. It is never slow. You never have to wait more than twenty minutes to eat. The waiters and waitresses are friendly. And it is not expensive. The only problem is the location. It is hard to find.

해석

그 음식점은 제가 제일 좋아하는 곳입니다. 무엇보다, 음식이 신선하고 맛있습니다. 둘째로, 서비스가 뛰어납니다. 음식이 늦은 적이 없어요. 절대 20분 이상 기다릴 필요가 없습니다. 남녀 종업원들은 친절합니다. 그리고 비싸지도 않아요. 문제는 위치예요. 찾기가 힘들죠.

1) 이 음식점의 문제점은 무엇인가?
   a. 음식   ★b. 위치   c. 서비스   d. 분위기

2) 이 음식점에 대한 설명으로 틀린 것은?
   a. 서비스가 빠르다.
   b. 종업원이 친절하다.
   ★c. 약간 비싸다.
   d. 찾기가 힘들다.

3. 두 사람이 무엇을 먹을지 이야기하고 있다.

스크립트

M Let's eat out this evening.
W I don't want to.
M But there's nothing to eat in the refrigerator. I'd like something nice and hot.
W Why don't we order something at home?
M Like what? Pizza? No way.
W There's a food delivery chain. I have the phone number here. Let's try it. Everybody says the food is nice and hot, even though it's a little expensive.
M Sounds great.

해석

M 오늘 저녁 나가서 먹자.
W 난 그러고 싶지 않아.
M 하지만 냉장고에 먹을 것이 아무 것도 없잖아. 난 맛있고 따뜻한 걸 먹고 싶어.
W 집으로 뭔가 시켜 먹는 게 어때?
M 어떤 거? 피자? 싫어.
W 음식 배달 체인점이 있어. 여기 전화번호도 있고, 먹어 보자. 다들 음식이 맛있고 따뜻하대. 조금 비싸지만 말이야.
M 좋아.

1) 대화 내용과 일치하는 것은?
   a. 그들은 외식을 할 것이다.
   b. 그들은 냉장고에 있는 무언가를 먹을 것이다.
   ★c. 그들은 뭔가를 집으로 배달시켜 먹을 것이다.
   d. 그들은 피자를 먹을 것이다.

2) 음식에 대한 설명으로 틀린 것은?
   a. 인기가 많다.   b. 맛있다.   c. 약간 비싸다.   ★d. 차갑다.

4. Tim이 Kelly에게 이야기하고 있다.

스크립트

M Kelly, have you tried Mexican food before?
W Yes, it was great! Haven't you ever tried it, Tim?
M No, I think it might be too hot and strange for me.
W Oh, this chef knows how to cook it right. The food is fresh and delicious with lots of rice.
M Rice! I would enjoy that meal!

해석

M Kelly, 전에 멕시코 음식 먹어본 적 있어?
W 응, 맛있었어! 넌 먹어 본적 없어, Tim?
M 아니, 너무 맵고 이상할 것 같아.
W 아, 이 주방장은 요리를 어떻게 하는지 안다니까. 음식이 신선하고 맛있어. 밥도 많고.
M 밥이라고! 그 음식 맛있을 것 같네!

1) 대화는 어디에서 일어나고 있는가?
   a. 멕시코   ★b. 멕시코 음식점   c. 시장   d. 온천

2) 대화의 내용 중 사실이 아닌 것은 무엇인가?
   a. Kelly는 이전에 멕시코 요리를 먹어보았다.
   ★b. 주방장은 음식을 맵고 이상하게 요리한다.
   c. Tim은 밥을 좋아한다.
   d. 주방장은 음식을 맛있게 만든다.

5. 한 여자가 이야기하고 있다.

스크립트

My favorite restaurant has some problems. It's hard to find and it's a little expensive to eat there. And in my opinion, they serve too much food. However, I go there almost every weekend because of the great food and service. The food is really delicious and the waitresses are really nice and friendly. They really care about their customers.

해석

내가 가장 좋아하는 식당은 몇 가지 문제점을 가지고 있다. 그 식당은 찾기가 어렵고 식사를 하기엔 조금 비싸다. 또한 내 생각에,

음식을 너무 많이 주는 것 같다. 하지만, 나는 거의 매 주말마다 그곳에 가는데 음식과 서비스가 좋기 때문이다. 음식은 정말 맛있고 종업원들은 정말 상냥하고 친절하다. 손님들에게 정말 신경 써주는 종업원들이다.

1) 여자는 _____에 대해서 이야기하고 있다.
    a. 그녀가 일하는 식당   b. 음식과 서비스
    c. 그녀가 매일 식사하는 식당 ★d. 그녀가 가장 좋아하는 식당

2) 식당의 문제점 중의 하나가 <u>아닌</u> 것은 무엇인가?
    ★a. 손님들   b. 위치   c. 음식의 양   d. 가격

Dictation
p. 44

1. together, How about, I'm tired of, then, crazy about, healthy
2. favorite, First of all, never, friendly, not expensive, find
3. eat out, I'd like, order, Let's try it, Sounds great
4. tried, too hot, how to cook, enjoy
5. problems, in my opinion, delicious, care about

UNIT 6
I want a refund.

Getting Ready
p. 45

1. 1. CU 2. CU 3. CL 4. CU
   5. CU 6. CL 7. CL
2. 1. e 2. d 3. b 4. a 5. c

1. 가게 점원이 하는 말이면 'CL', 손님이 하는 말이면 'CU'를 쓰시오.

1. 이 제품을 환불 받고 싶습니다.	CU
2. 고객 서비스센터가 어디에요?	CU
3. 잘 어울리시네요.	CL
4. 세일 언제 끝나요?	CU
5. 다른 걸로 교환할 수 있나요?	CU
6. 5% 더 깎아드릴 수 있습니다.	CL
7. 영수증 가지고 계십니까?	CL

2. 표현을 응답과 연결시키시오.

1. 현금으로 결제하셨습니까, 카드로 결제하셨습니까?
    e. 현금으로요.
2. 이 제품을 환불 받고 싶습니다.
    d. 무엇이 문제이십니까?
3. 깎아주실 수 있어요?

b. 아니오, 이미 세일한 가격입니다.
4. 한 사이즈 작은 거 있어요?
    a. 아뇨, 그렇지만 하나 주문해 드릴 수 있어요.
5. 저 어때요?
    c. 멋지네요.

Listening Task
p. 46~47

Listening 1	1. a	2. c	3. b	4. b
Listen Again A	1. b	2. b	3. c	
B	4. a			
Listening 2	1. b	2. b	3. b	4. a
Listen Again A	1. a	2. c	3. a	
B	4. b			

Listening 1
p. 46

말하는 이가 이야기하고 있는 옷을 고르시오.

1 ★a. 봄 블라우스   b. 여름 블라우스   c. 봄 드레스
2. a. 모직 코트   b. 정장   ★c. 모피 코트
3. a. 신발   ★b. 재킷   c. 모자
4. a. 정장   ★b. 신발   c. 스웨터

스크립트

1. Hey! The blouse looks good on you. It's a little too long but they can shorten it for you. I like the color and style. Green is a popular color this spring. It's a little expensive but it's worth it, I think.

2. Do you like it? The fur coat looks great on you. I know it's not cheap. But if money is the problem, we can give you an extra 5 percent off. This is only for you, as you're an important customer.

3. I really like this jacket. I like the color, material, style—everything. But it's a little big for me. I wear a size 6, one size smaller than this. Could you order one for me?

4. It's buy-one-get-one-free. If you buy one, you get the second one free. This is an excellent chance to get these fabulous shoes at half the price. It is the last sale of the year. And the sale ends tomorrow. So hurry!

1. 그 블라우스 너한테 어울린다! 좀 긴 것 같긴 한데 가게에서 줄여주기도 하니까. 색깔하고 옷 모양이 마음에 들어. 초록색이 올 봄에 유행이잖아. 좀 비싸긴 하지만 그만한 가치는 있는 것 같아, 내 생각엔.

2. 마음에 드세요? 털 코트가 아주 잘 어울리시네요. 싼 가격이 아닌 걸 알아요. 가격이 문제이시면, 5% 더 깎아드릴게요. 우리 가게의 중요한 고객이시니까 손님께만 해 드리는 거예요.

3. 이 재킷 정말 마음에 들어요. 색, 소재, 모양 다요. 그런데 저에겐 조금 크네요. 저는 이것보다 한 사이즈 작은 6사이즈를 입어요. 하나 주문해 줄 수 있어요?

4. 한 개 사시면 하나 더 드립니다. 한 켤레를 사시면, 두 켤레 째는 공짜로 드립니다. 이 멋진 구두를 반 가격에 살 수 있는 절호의 기회입니다. 이게 올해 마지막 세일입니다. 내일 끝납니다. 서두르세요!

Listen Again   p. 46

A. 다시 듣고 틀린 것을 고르시오.

1. a. 그 물건은 초록색이다.
   ★b. 가격이 싸다.
   c. 그것은 그 손님에게는 길다.

2. a. 그것은 꽤 비싸다.
   ★b. 그 손님은 전에 여기 온 적이 없다.
   c. 그 물건은 이미 세일 중이다.

3. a. 그녀는 그 옷의 옷감을 좋아한다.
   b. 그녀는 그 옷의 스타일을 좋아한다.
   ★c. 그녀는 더 큰 사이즈를 원한다.

B. 다시 듣고 가장 적절하게 요약한 것을 고르시오.

4. a. ★ 가게에 있는 그 물건은 50% 할인 판매 중이다.
   b. □ 그건 올해의 첫 할인 판매이다.

Listening 2   p. 47

사람들이 가게 안에 있다. 듣고 맞는 것을 고르시오.

1. 손님은 _____ 있다.
   a. 상품 가격을 지불하고
   ★b. 환불 받고
   c. 상품을 교환하고

2. 손님은 _____ 있다.
   a. 무언가 살 물건을 찾고
   ★b. 상품을 교환하고
   c. 가게에 대한 것을 물어보고

3. 손님은 _____ 것이다.
   a. 다른 회사의 라디오를 고를
   ★b. 그의 돈을 되돌려 받을
   c. 뭔가 다른 물건을 살

4. 손님은 _____ 있다.
   ★a. 계산서를 정정하고
   b. 불만 사항을 말하고
   c. 환불 받고

1.
W These boots are not very comfortable. I'd like a refund.
M Do you have the receipt with you?
W Yes, here it is.
M Did you pay by cash or credit card?
W By cash.
M It's... $89.50. Here's your money.
W Thanks.

2.
M Where is the customer service?
W It's across the hall down this aisle.
M Can I exchange this sweater for a new one? There is a small hole in it.
W2 Oh! Sorry about that. Sure, take another one.

3.
M I'd like to get a refund on this radio.
W What is the problem with it?
M The antenna is broken.
W Why don't you exchange it for another brand?
M No, thanks. I just want my money back.
W Okay, then. I need to see the receipt, please.

4.
M I think there's a mistake on the bill.
W Really? What is it?
M You put the wrong price for the pan. See? It must be $16.99, not $60.99.
W Oh, I am so sorry.
M Sure.
W Here, I've fixed it. The total is $128.90. Have a nice day.

1. W 이 부츠가 별로 편하지 않네요. 환불 받고 싶은데요.
   M 영수증 가지고 계십니까?
   W 네, 여기 있어요.
   M 현금으로 계산하셨나요, 아니면 신용 카드로 계산하셨나요?
   W 현금으로요.
   M 가격이... 89달러 50센트입니다. 돈 여기 있습니다.
   W 감사합니다.

2. M 고객 서비스 센터가 어디에 있나요?
   W 이 통로를 따라 내려가시면 홀 맞은편에 있습니다.

M 이 스웨터 새것으로 교환할 수 있을까요? 작은 구멍이 하나 났던데요.

W2 오! 죄송합니다. 그럼요, 다른 걸로 가져가십시오.

3. M 이 라디오 좀 환불 받고 싶은데요.

W 무엇이 문제이신지요?

M 안테나가 부러졌더라고요.

W 다른 회사 제품으로 교환하지 않으시겠습니까?

M 아뇨, 됐어요. 그냥 돈으로 받고 싶어요.

W 네, 알겠어요. 그럼 영수증을 보여주십시오.

4. M 계산서가 잘못 된 것 같은데요.

W 아 그렇습니까? 어디가 잘못되었나요?

M 프라이팬 가격을 잘못 쓰셨어요. 보이시죠? 60달러 99센트가 아니고 16달러 99센트예요.

W 아, 정말 죄송합니다.

M 괜찮아요.

W 여기 맞게 고쳤습니다. 합계 128달러 90센트입니다. 좋은 하루 되십시오.

Listen Again p. 47

A. 다시 듣고 맞는 문장을 고르시오.

1★a. 그녀가 환불 받기 위해서 영수증을 가지고 있어야 한다.
b. 그녀는 신용 카드로 지불했다.
c. 그녀는 색깔이 마음에 들지 않아서 물건을 바꾸고 있다.

2. a. 상품이 너무 작았다.
b. 그는 상품을 환불 받고 싶어한다.
★c. 고객 서비스 센터가 이 문제를 해결할 것이다.

3★a. 그는 영수증을 보여 줘야 한다.
b. 그는 서류를 작성해야 한다.
c. 그는 라디오를 스스로 수리해야 한다.

B. 다시 듣고 맞는 문장을 고르시오.

4. a. ☐ 프라이팬은 60달러 99센트였는데 점원이 실수로 16달러 99센트라고 썼다.
b. ★ 프라이팬은 16달러 99센트였는데 점원이 실수로 60달러 99센트라고 썼다.

스크립트

a. The pan was $60.99 and the clerk put $16.99 by mistake.
b. The pan was $16.99 and the clerk put $60.99 by mistake.

Review p. 48

1. refund, receipt, cash
2. on, color, popular, on sale
3. exchange, hole, another
4. on, get, chance, ends, buy
5. size, wear, order

✱ 듣고 빈칸을 채우시오.

해석

1. W 이 모자를 환불 받고 싶어요.
M 영수증 가지고 계세요?
W 네, 여기 있어요.
M 현금으로 지불하셨어요, 카드로 결제 하셨어요?

2. 코트가 잘 어울리시네요. 색깔과 모양이 좋은 것 같아요. 분홍색이 올해 유행이에요. 게다가 별로 비싸지도 않아요. 세일 중이어서 원래 가격에서 40% 할인해 드려요.

3. W 이 셔츠 새것으로 교환할 수 있을까요?
M 무슨 문제가 있으십니까?
W 작은 구멍이 하나 났던데요.
M 아, 죄송합니다. 그럼요. 다른 것으로 가져가세요.

4. 이 바지 나에게 잘 어울리는 것 같아. 그리고 이건 하나 사면 하나 더 주는 세일 중이었어. 이 좋은 바지를 반 가격에 살 수 있는 좋은 기회였지. 세일은 오늘 끝나는데, 올해의 마지막 세일이야. 하나 더 사야 할 것 같아.

5. W 한 사이즈 작은 거 있으세요? 이건 저한테 조금 커요. 저는 6 1/2 사이즈를 입거든요.
M 죄송해요, 그 사이즈는 지금 당장은 없어요. 하지만 주문해 드릴 수는 있어요.
W 얼마나 걸려요?
M 3일 내로 옵니다.

On Your Own p. 49

LISTEN & WRITE

듣고 질문을 써 보세요.

스크립트

What is the clothing item you bought lately?
Do you like it?
How does it look on you?
Was it on sale?

해석

당신이 최근에 산 의류 품목은 무엇입니까?
그것이 마음에 듭니까?
당신에게 그것이 어울립니까?
그것은 세일 중이었습니까?

억양

↗ **vs** ↘

☞ 듣고 질문들을 따라 해 보시오.

Amy는 집에 있습니까?

앞으로 쭉 가나요?

오른쪽에 있습니까?

☞ 듣고 질문들을 따라 해 보시오.

사과 파이는 어떻게 만듭니까?

제 가방은 어디에 두면 됩니까?

저는 언제 집에 갈 수 있습니까?

질문을 듣고 위(↗) 또는 아래(↘)를 표시하시오.

	↗	↘
왼쪽으로 돌까요?	★	□
금요일에 무엇을 하실 겁니까?	□	★
나중에 제가 전화 드려도 될까요?	★	□
어떻게 지내세요?	□	★

* Yes/No로 대답하는 질문들은 보통 올라가는 억양입니다.
* Wh-와 how가 있는 질문들은 보통 내려가는 억양입니다.

Practice Test
p. 50~51

1. 1) c	2) b	2. 1) d	2) d	3. 1) b	2) d
4. 1) d	2) b	5. 1) a	2) d		

✻ 듣고 알맞은 답을 고르시오.

1. 한 남자가 점원과 이야기하고 있다.

스크립트

M I'd like to get a refund on this TV.

W Is there a problem?

M Yes, the screen is cracked.

W You need to take it to customer service. They will take care of it.

M Where is customer service?

W It's across the hall next to the other door.

M Thanks a lot.

W Sure.

해석

M 이 TV를 환불 받고 싶습니다.

W 무슨 문제라도 있습니까?

M 네, 화면에 금이 갔어요.

W 고객 서비스 센터로 가져가셔야겠네요. 거기서 해결해 드릴 겁니다.

M 고객 서비스 센터가 어디에요?

W 홀 건너편에 또 다른 문 옆입니다.

M 감사합니다.

W 천만에요.

1) 남자는 _____ 하려고 한다.

　a. 상품을 교환　　　b. 상품을 수리

★c. 상품을 환불　　　d. 계산서를 정정

2) 대화 내용과 일치하는 것은?

　a. 화면에 구멍이 났다.

★b. 그는 상품을 고객 서비스 센터로 가져가야 한다.

　c. 고객 서비스 센터는 입구에서 멀다.

　d. 상품은 VCR이다.

2. 한 여자가 이야기하고 있다.

스크립트

This dress is beautiful. I like the color. Pink is my favorite color. I like the style, too. It's not too long and not too short. It's cute. I also like the soft silky material. The problem is the price. It's too expensive. It's on sale, but it still costs too much money. Can you give me a discount?

해석

이 드레스 예쁘네요. 색깔이 마음에 들어요. 분홍색은 제가 제일 좋아하는 색이에요. 모양도 마음에 들고요. 너무 길지도 짧지도 않네요. 귀엽고요. 부드러운 실크 같은 소재도 좋아요. 문제는 가격이에요. 너무 비싸네요. 세일하는 건데도 너무 많이 들겠어요. 좀 더 깎아 줄 수 있나요?

1) 여자는 드레스의 _____(이)가 마음에 들지 않는다.

　a. 색깔　　b. 모양　　c. 소재　　★d. 가격

2) 내용과 일치하는 것은?

　a. 그녀는 드레스를 환불 받고 싶어 한다.

　b. 그녀는 더 싼 것을 원한다.

　c. 그녀는 드레스를 교환하고 싶어 한다.

★d. 그녀는 할인 받기를 원한다.

3. Jeff와 친구가 이야기하고 있다.

스크립트

M What's wrong with the computer? It doesn't work.

W Yes. The problem started yesterday. When it happens, I have to start it all over again.

M When did you buy it?

W In June.

M You'd better take it to the store right now. You can get a refund within three months after you buy it.

W I think I should.

M 컴퓨터 뭐가 잘못 된 거야? 작동되질 않아.

W 응. 어제부터 이래. 이렇게 되면, 처음부터 전부 다시 시작해야 해.

M 언제 샀어?

W 6월에.

M 당장 가게로 가져가는 게 좋을 것 같아. 구입한 지 3달 내에는 환불 받을 수 있어.

W 그래야 할 것 같아.

1) 컴퓨터의 무엇이 문제인가?
   a. 부서졌다.   ★b. 작동되지 않는다.
   c. 아예 켜지질 않는다.   d. 소음이 난다.

2) 대화와 일치하는 것은?
   a. 그녀는 컴퓨터를 환불 받을 수 없다.
   b. 거의 석 달 전에 샀다.
   c. 그녀는 컴퓨터를 수리 받고 싶어 한다.
  ★d. 그녀는 환불 받으러 컴퓨터를 가게에 가져갈 것이다.

4. 한 소녀가 쇼핑을 하고 있다.

M You'll look great in this hat!

W No, I'll try on a different one. How about this one?

M Yes, that looks good on you. You should get that one.

W Do you have this one size smaller in blue?

M Don't worry! We have it.

W I won't have any money until Saturday. When does the sale end?

M On Sunday.

M 이 모자를 쓰면 잘 어울릴 거예요!

W 아뇨, 다른 걸 써 볼게요. 이건 어때요?

M 네, 손님이 쓰니 예뻐 보이네요. 그걸 사셔야겠어요.

W 이 모자 파란색으로 한 치수 작은 게 있나요?

M 염려 마세요! 있어요.

W 토요일이나 되어야 돈이 생기는데. 할인이 언제 끝나죠?

M 일요일에요.

1) 말하는 사람은 누구인가?
   a. 손님 두 명   b. 점원 두 명
   c. 아빠와 딸   ★d. 점원과 소녀

2) 소녀가 다음에 무엇을 할까?
   a. 모자를 산다.   ★b. 가게를 떠난다.
   c. 모자를 쓴다.   d. 다른 모자를 산다.

5. 한 여자가 상점에 있다.

W Can I exchange this skirt for a different one?

M What's the problem?

W It's too big for me.

M Do you have the receipt with you?

W Yes, but do you have it one size smaller?

M No, yours is the only one.

W Then, I'd like to get a refund.

M Don't you want to exchange it for another item?

W No, thanks. I just want my money back.

W 이걸 다른 것과 교환할 수 있을까요?

M 무슨 문제가 있나요?

W 저한텐 너무 크네요.

M 영수증 가지고 계신지요?

W 네. 그런데 그 치마 한 치수 작은 것으로 있나요?

M 아뇨, 손님이 사신 치마는 하나밖에 없는 거예요.

W 그렇다면 환불을 받았으면 하는데요.

M 다른 물건과 교환하기를 원하시지는 않으신가요?

W 아뇨, 됐습니다. 그냥 돈을 돌려받고 싶어요.

1) 대화에 대해 사실인 것은 무엇인가?
  ★a. 그녀의 치마는 너무 컸다.
   b. 영수증의 액수는 너무 적다.
   c. 그녀는 가게에서 마지막 남은 치마를 샀다.
   d. 그녀는 다른 치마를 샀다.

2) 그녀는 _____ 것이다.
   a. 한 치수 작은 것을 살   b. 교환을 할
   c. 할인을 받을   ★d. 환불을 받을

Dictation   p. 52

1. get a refund, need, customer service, across, Sure
2. style, not too short, price, expensive, discount
3. started, over again, You'd better, I should
4. smaller, We have it, money
5. big for me, do you have it, exchange, money back

UNIT 7
I'd like to make a reservation.

1. 1. CU   2. CU   3. CL   4. CU   5. CL
     6. CU   7. CL   8. CU   9. CU

2. 1. d   2. a   3. e   4. b   5. c   6. f

1. 상점의 점원이 하는 말이면 'CL', 손님이 하는 말이면 'CU'를 쓰시오.

1. 2인 테이블을 예약하고 싶습니다.	CU
2. 이틀 묵을 건데 방 하나 주세요.	CU
3. 예약하셨습니까?	CL
4. 예약을 취소하고 싶습니다.	CU
5. 뒷좌석 괜찮으시겠어요?	CL
6. 예약 확인하고 싶어서 전화했어요.	CU
7. 죄송합니다만 30분 기다리셔야 합니다.	CL
8. John Smith라는 이름으로 예약했습니다.	CU
9. 티켓이 남아있나요?	CU

2. 표현을 응답과 연결하시오.

1. 자리 남았습니까?   d. 지금은 없습니다.
2. 어느 쪽으로 앉으시겠습니까?   a. 창가로 해 주세요.
3. 흡연석과 금연석 중 어느 걸로 하시겠습니까?
   e. 금연석으로 해 주세요.
4. 몇 시에 도착하게 될까요?   b. 오후 8시요.
5. 예약을 취소해야겠습니다.   c. 네. 성함이 어떻게 되십니까?
6. 얼마 동안 머무르시겠습니까?   f. 3일이요.

Listening 1	1. a	2. b	3. b	4. a
Listen Again A	1. b	2. c	3. a	
B	4. a			
Listening 2	1. c	2. b	3. c	4. a
Listen Again A	1. c	2. b	3. b	
B	4. a			

Listening 1   p. 54

사람들이 전화로 메시지를 남기고 있다. 알맞은 답을 고르시오.

1. _____를(을) 예약하기 위한 메시지이다.
   ★a. 식당 자리   b. 호텔 방   c. 콘서트 좌석

2. _____에게 온 메시지이다.
   a. 교사   ★b. 의사   c. 치과 의사

3. 이 사람은 _____에 전화했다.
   a. 식당   ★b. 호텔   c. 극장

4. 이 사람은 _____에 전화했다.
   ★a. 항공사   b. 식당   c. 병원

스크립트

1. Hello. I'd like to reserve a table for two, for 7 p.m. Friday the 15th. I'd like the non-smoking section. If it's possible please make it by the window so we can overlook the lake while eating. My name is Barbara Johnson, and my phone number is 402-562-2673.

2. Hi! This is from Mrs. Jordan. I'd like to see Dr. Cell for my daughter. She has a bad headache all this week. Please let me know what time is possible. I'd like the appointment as soon as possible. My phone number is 715-812-6428.

3. Hello. I'd like to make a reservation for a double room for three nights from the 11th to the 13th. Please give me a call and let me know if it is possible. You can reach me at 203-256-2400.

4. Hi! My name is Kevin Clark. I'd like to make a reservation for the flight to New York this Saturday around 3 p.m. I will be alone and I prefer a window seat. I need you to return my call within today. My phone number is 512-902-562.

해석

1. 여보세요. 15일 금요일 오후 7시에 두 사람 좌석을 예약하고 싶은데요. 금연석으로요. 가능하면 먹으면서 밖의 호수도 내려다볼 수 있게 창가 쪽으로 하고 싶어요. 제 이름은 Barbara Johnson이고, 전화번호는 402-562-2673이에요.

2. 안녕하세요! 저는 Jordan 부인입니다. Cell 선생님한테 우리 딸 진찰 좀 받고 싶은데요. 우리 딸이 이번 주 내내 머리가 너무 아파서요. 언제쯤 가능할지 연락 좀 주세요. 되도록 빨리 약속을 잡고 싶어요. 전화번호는 715-812-6428이에요.

3. 여보세요. 11일에서 13일까지 3일간 2인실 예약하고 싶습니다. 가능한지 전화 좀 해 주세요. 203-256-2400으로 거시면 됩니다.

4. 안녕하세요! 저는 Kevin Clark입니다. 이번 주 토요일 오후 3시쯤으로 뉴욕 행 비행기를 예약하고 싶어요. 저 한 명이고, 창가 쪽으로 앉고 싶어요. 오늘 안으로 전화 주셨으면 좋겠어요. 제 전화번호는 512-902-562입니다.

Listen Again

p. 54

A. 다시 듣고 맞는 것을 고르시오.

1. a. 여자는 흡연석을 원한다.
   ★b. 식당 옆에 호수가 있다.
   c. 여자는 많은 사람들과 함께 올 것이다.

2. a. 여자는 예약을 변경하고 싶어 한다.
   b. 그녀의 딸은 치통에 시달리고 있다.
   ★c. 여자는 가능한 한 빨리 예약하고 싶어 한다.

3. ★a. 그는 2인실을 원한다.
   b. 그는 호텔에 이틀간 머물 것이다.
   c. 그는 나중에 전화할 것이다.

B. 다시 듣고 가장 적절하게 요약한 것을 고르시오.

4. a. ★ 그는 오늘 회신 전화를 받기를 원한다.
   b. ☐ 그는 친구와 함께 뉴욕에 갈 것이다.

Listening 2

p. 55

대화하는 장소는 어디인가? 알맞은 답을 고르시오.

1. a. 식당   b. 호텔   ★c. 여행사

2. a. 영화관   ★b. 공연장   c. 항공사

3. a. 호텔   b. 영화관   ★c. 식당

4. ★a. 항공사   b. 호텔   c. 식당

스크립트

1.

W Dream Tour, Casey speaking. May I help you?
M Hi! I'm calling to confirm my reservation.
W Can I have your name, please?
M Jack Kennedy.
W It's the package trip to India on the 17th. Right?
M Yes, that's right.
W Your reservation has been confirmed. Thank you, sir.

2.

W Excuse me, but I think there is a mistake on my ticket.
M What do you mean, ma'am?
W I asked for a front row seat and this ticket is for a back row seat.
M Oh, I'm sorry about that. But front seats are sold out.
W Then I'd like a refund. I don't want to watch the concert from the back.
M Sure.

3.

W Have you made a reservation, sir?
M No, we haven't. How long is the wait for four people?
W I'm afraid you have to wait around 30 minutes.
M We'll wait.

4.

W Is this the American Airlines ticket counter?
M Yes, it is. How may I help you?
W I'd like to cancel my reservation for flight #709 to L.A.
M No problem. Please tell me your name and the time of reservation.
W My name is Linda Gray, and the time is Monday the 3rd, 6:30.
M Okay. Your reservation has been canceled.
W Thanks, bye.

해석

1. W 드림 투어의 Casey입니다. 무엇을 도와드릴까요?
   M 안녕하세요! 예약 확인을 하려고 전화했어요.
   W 성함이 어떻게 되세요?
   M Jack Kennedy요.
   W 17일 날 떠나는 인도 패키지 여행. 맞으시죠?
   M 네, 맞아요.
   W 예약 확인되었습니다. 감사합니다, 고객님.

2. W 죄송한데요, 제 표가 잘못된 것 같은데요.
   M 어떻게 잘못 되었나요, 손님?
   W 저는 앞줄로 달라고 했는데 이 표는 뒷자리 표예요.
   M 오, 죄송합니다. 그런데 지금은 앞자리가 매진이네요.
   W 그럼 환불해 주세요. 공연을 뒤에서 보고 싶지는 않아요.
   M 네.

3. W 예약하셨습니까. 손님?
   M 아뇨, 우린 안 했어요. 네 사람 자리는 얼마나 더 기다려야 해요?
   W 죄송하지만 30분쯤 기다리셔야 할 것 같습니다.
   M 기다릴게요.

4. W American Airlines 항공권 판매대인가요?
   M 네 그렇습니다. 무엇을 도와드릴까요?
   W L.A. 행 709 비행편 예약을 취소하고 싶습니다.
   M 알겠습니다. 성함과 예약 시간을 말씀해 주십시오.
   W 이름은 Linda Gray고요, 예약 시간은 3일 월요일 6시 30분이에요.
   M 네. 예약 취소되었습니다.
   W 고마워요, 안녕히 계세요.

Listen Again
p. 55

A. 다시 듣고 알맞은 답을 고르시오.

1. 대화와 일치하지 <u>않는</u> 것은?
   a. 남자는 인도 여행을 가려고 한다.
   b. 여행은 이번 달로 계획되어 있다.
   ★c. 그는 아직 예약하지 않았다.

2. 대화와 일치하는 것은?
   a. 여자는 뒷좌석에서 공연을 볼 것이다.
   ★b. 여자는 공연을 보지 않을 것이다.
   c. 여자는 앞 좌석에서 공연을 볼 것이다.

3. 대화와 일치하는 것은?
   a. 그는 혼자 있다.
   ★b. 그는 얼마 동안 기다릴 것이다.
   c. 그는 다른 곳으로 먹으러 갈 것이다.

B. 다시 듣고 맞는 문장을 고르시오.

4. a. ★ 여자는 예약을 취소하고 있다.
   b. ☐ 여자는 예약을 위해 이름을 불러주고 있다.

스크립트

a. The woman is cancelling her reservation.
b. The woman is giving her name for the reservation.

Review
p. 56

1. reserve, prefer
2. reservation, alone, window
3. confirm, confirmed
4. cancel, Tuesday, call, phone, 2445
5. mistake, double, available

✽ 듣고 빈칸을 채우시오.

해석

1. W 4인석 테이블 예약하고 싶습니다.
   M 네. 언제로 하시겠습니까?
   W 금요일 오후 6시 30분이요.
   M 금연석을 원하십니까, 아니면 흡연석을 원하십니까?
   W 금연석으로, 창가로 주세요.

2. 이번 금요일 오후에 L.A.행 비행편을 예약하고 싶은데요. 저 한 사람이고요. 창가 자리로 해주시면 좋겠어요.

3. M 예약 확인하려고 전화했어요.
   W 성함을 말씀해 주시겠습니까?
   M Brian Nelson이요.
   W L.A.행 605 비행편 예약이 확인되었습니다.

4. 여보세요. 죄송하지만 시카고행 342편 예약을 취소해야 할 것 같습니다. 제 이름은 Jane Pond고, 예약한 시간은 12일 화요일 7시예요. 전화 주셔서 가능한지 알려주세요. 제 전화 번호는 715-254-2445입니다.

5. M 예약이 잘못 된 것 같아요.
   W 무슨 말씀이신지요, 고객님?
   M 1인실이 아니라 2인실을 예약했는데요.
   W 기록을 확인해 보겠습니다. 말씀하신 게 맞네요. 정말 죄 송합니다. 그런데 지금 비어 있는 2인실이 있습니다. 방을 하나 잡으시겠어요?

On Your Own
p. 57

LISTEN & WRITE

듣고 질문을 써 보세요.

스크립트

Have you ever made a reservation for a restaurant?
Where do you prefer to seat?
Do you usually make an appointment to see a doctor?

해석
식당 예약을 해 본 적이 있습니까?
어디에 앉는 것을 더 선호합니까?
진찰을 받기 위해 보통 예약을 하십니까?

PRONUNCIATION

강세

시작 **vs** 끝

☞ 듣고 따라 해 보시오.
파일럿, 치과 의사, 진료소, 사무실, 운전사

☞ 듣고 따라 해 보시오.
기타, ~이전에, 일본, 타이완, 일상

✽ 듣고 강세가 앞에 있으면 "b"를 쓰고 끝에 있으면 "e"를 쓰시오.

항공사	b	정직한	b
너 자신	e	CD	e
월요일	b	~아래에	e

Practice Test
p. 58~59

1. 1) c 2) b   2. 1) b 2) d   3. 1) c 2) c
4. 1) c 2) d   5. 1) c 2) a

✽ 듣고 알맞은 답을 고르시오.

1. 남자가 전화로 이야기하고 있다.

스크립트

M Hello, I'd like to reserve a room for this coming Saturday.

w Certainly. How long will you be staying?
M Just one night.
w Would you like a single or a double room?
M A double room, please.
w I'm sorry but we don't have any double rooms available.
M Then make it two single rooms, please.
w All right, sir. Two single rooms for Saturday the 5th.

해석
M 이번 주 토요일에 방을 하나 예약하고 싶습니다.
W 네. 얼마 정도 머무르시겠어요?
M 하룻밤이요.
W 1인실로 하시겠어요, 2인실로 하시겠어요?
M 2인실 하나 주세요.
W 죄송합니다만 비어 있는 2인실이 없네요.
M 그러면 1인실 두 개로 해 주세요.
W 알겠습니다, 고객님. 5일 토요일 1인실 두 개입니다.

1) 무엇을 위한 전화 통화인가?
   a. 음식점 자리 예약   b. 공연 좌석 예약
   ★c. 호텔 방 예약   d. 비행기 좌석 예약

2) 대화 내용과 일치하지 <u>않는</u> 것은?
   a. 그는 하룻밤 머물 것이다.
   ★b. 2인실 하나를 예약했다.
   c. 그는 이번 주에 호텔에 머문다.
   d. 비어 있는 2인실이 없다.

2. 남자가 전화로 이야기하고 있다.
스크립트

M Hello, can I reserve a train ticket over the phone?
w Certainly.
M I'd like to reserve a one-way ticket from Boston to Chicago.
w When will you be travelling?
M May 28th.
w Which class would you like?
M First class, please.
w Okay. Can I have the name for the reservation?
M Please make it for Nick Wilson.

해석
M 여보세요, 전화로 기차표 예약할 수 있나요?
W 물론입니다.
M 보스턴에서 시카고로 가는 편도표를 사고 싶어요.
W 며칠에 가실 건가요?

M 5월 28일이요.
W 어떤 좌석으로 드릴까요?
M 일등석으로 해 주세요.
W 네. 예약하실 성함을 말씀해 주시겠습니까?
M Nick Wilson으로 예약해 주세요.

1) 남자는 무엇을 예약하고 있는가?
   a. 버스표   ★b. 기차표   c. 항공권   d. 공연 표

2) 예약 내용과 일치하지 <u>않는</u> 것은?
   a. 편도 표이다.   b. 일등석이다.
   c. 5월 출발이다.   ★d. 보스턴행이다.

3. 여자가 전화로 이야기하고 있다.
스크립트

w I'm calling to change my reservation.
M Sure. Can I have your name and the time of reservation, please?
w It's under my name Karen Johnson, Tuesday at 8:00 p.m.
M How would you like to change it?
w Please make it a table for six, not two.
M Okay. Anything else?
w No, everything else is the same.

해석
W 예약을 변경하려고 전화했어요.
M 네. 성함과 예약 시간을 말씀해 주시겠습니까?
W 제 이름인 Karen Johnson으로 했고요, 화요일 오후 8시입니다.
M 어떻게 변경하시겠어요?
W 2인용이 아니라 6인용 테이블로 해 주세요.
M 네. 다른 게 더 있으신가요?
W 아뇨, 다른 건 모두 같아요.

1) 여자는 무엇을 하고 있는가?
   a. 예약을 하고 있다.   b. 예약을 취소하고 있다.
   ★c. 예약을 변경하고 있다.   d. 예약을 확인하고 있다.

2) 대화 내용과 일치하지 <u>않는</u> 것은?
   a. 여자의 이름은 Karen Johnson이다.
   b. 여자는 음식점에 전화하고 있다.
   ★c. 여자는 다른 두 사람과 함께 갈 것이다.
   d. 아직 화요일이 아니다.

4. 다음은 전화 통화이다.
스크립트

w Park Lake Inn! How can I help you?
M I'd like to make a reservation for a room, please.
w Certainly! How long are you going to stay?

M For two nights.

W Do you prefer smoking or non-smoking?

M Non-smoking, please. Quiet with a view of the lake, if possible!

W Sure! What's your name, please?

해석

W 파크 레이크 호텔입니다! 무엇을 도와드릴까요?

M 방을 하나 예약하고 싶은데요.

W 네! 얼마나 오래 머무르실 건가요?

M 이틀 밤이요.

W 흡연실 아니면 금연실 중에서 어느 방을 선호하시나요?

M 금연실요. 가능하다면 호수가 보이는 조용한 방으로 부탁 드려요.

W 물론이죠! 성함이 어떻게 되세요?

1) 남자가 전화를 한 곳은 어디인가?

   a. 기차역　　　　　b. 여행사

★c. 호텔　　　　　d. 아파트 임대 사무소

2) 남자가 원하지 <u>않는</u> 것은 무엇인가?

   a. 조용한 방　　　　b. 호수가 보이는 곳

   c. 이틀 밤을 지낼 방　★d. 흡연실

5. 다음은 전화 통화이다.

스크립트

W I'm calling to confirm my flight on Saturday.

M Certainly.

W I made the reservations under the name of Jenny Smith.

M Yes, what time are you arriving?

W At 11 a.m. Are there any seats left by the window?

M Not right now. But would back row seats be okay with you?

W Sure.

M All three of you are confirmed.

해석

W 토요일의 제 비행편을 확인하려고 전화했는데요.

M 네.

W Jenny Smith라는 이름으로 예약했습니다.

M 네, 몇 시에 도착하는 비행편입니까?

W 오전 11시요. 창문 옆에 남은 좌석이 있나요?

M 지금 당장은 없습니다. 뒷줄에 있는 좌석도 괜찮으신지요?

W 네.

M 손님과 일행 세 분 예약이 확인되었습니다.

1) 여자의 예약에 대해 사실이 <u>아닌</u> 것은 무엇인가?

a. 그녀는 비행기를 탈 것이다.

b. 그녀와 다른 두 명의 예약이 확인되었다.

★c. 그녀는 밤 11시에 도착한다.

d. 그녀는 토요일에 떠난다.

2) 여자는 _____ 앉지 않을 것이다.

★a. 창문가에　　b. 뒷줄 좌석에　　c. 다른 두 명과

Dictation　　　　　　　　　　　　　　p. 60

1. reserve, Just one night, a double room, I'm sorry but, All right

2. over the phone, one-way ticket, traveling, reservation, make it for

3. I'm calling to, How would you like, table, everything else

4. How long, For two nights, non-smoking, possible

5. confirm, what time, any seats, okay with you

UNIT 8
What's going on?

Getting Ready　　　　　　　　　　　　p. 61

1. 1. neighborhood　　2. stains
   3. rent　　　　　　　4. upstairs
   5. floor　　　　　　　6. view
   7. story

2. 1. c　　2. a　　3. b　　4. d

1. 아래 네모 안의 단어로 빈칸을 채우시오.

위층에　얼룩　동네　층(floor)　층(story)　임대료　전망

1. 우리 ____동네____ 에는 가게가 너무 많다.

2. 벽이 ____얼룩____ 로(으로) 뒤덮였다. 너무 더럽다.

3. 집이 낡고 더러워서, ____임대료____ 가(이) 아주 낮다.

4. 내 방은 ____위층에____ 있는데, 다락방 바로 아래에 있다.

5. 내 아파트는 그 건물의 10____층____ 에 있다.

6. ____전망____ 이 아주 좋다.

7. 우리 집은 2____층____ 집이다.

2. 표현을 응답과 연결하시오.

1. 싱크대에서 물이 새.　　　　　　c. 배관공을 불러야겠다.

2. 여기서 얼마 동안 살았어?　　　a. 4살 때부터.

3. 방은 무슨 색으로 할 거니?　　　b. 초록색으로 칠할 거야.

4. 다른 지역으로 이사 가세요?　　d. 아니오, 같은 동네로요.

Listening Task
p. 62~63

Listening 1		1. a	2. b	3. b	4. a
Listen Again	A	1. a	2. c	3. a	
	B	4. a			
Listening 2		4, 2, 1, 3			
Listen Again	A	1. a	2. a	3. b	
	B	4. a			

Listening 1
p. 62

자신들의 집에 대해 이야기하고 있다. 맞는 그림에 표시하시오.

스크립트

1.

Pat Hello, Jeff! It's me, Pat.

Jeff Hi, Pat! What's up?

Pat I have new roller-blades. Why don't you go out with me?

Jeff Sorry, I can't. I'm waiting for a plumber. There is a leak in the sink, and we have to get it fixed. My mom told me to stay home for that.

Pat Okay. Maybe tomorrow then.

2.

Amy What a mess! What is going on here, Jeff?

Jeff Be careful. We're painting the whole house.

Amy What color will your room be?

Jeff It will be deep blue. I want it to be like an ocean.

Amy That would be cool!

3.

Jeff Look at you, Amy. You are covered with dust.

Amy I am helping my mom clean the garage. There are so many things piled up. Maybe we will have a garage sale.

Jeff Then my family may join you.

Amy Sounds great. That will make a better sale.

Jeff Come on. Let's talk about it with my mom.

4.

M How long have you been living here?

W Since I was four, so it has been twelve years.

M That is a long time.

W Yes. There are a lot of good and bad memories around this house: playing in the tree house, falling from the roof...

M Oh, do you have a tree house? Can I see that?

W Sure.

해석

1. Pat 안녕, Jeff! 나야, Pat.

   Jeff 안녕, Pat! 무슨 일이야?

   Pat 새 롤러 블레이드가 생겼어. 나랑 같이 나가지 않을래?

   Jeff 미안하지만 안 돼. 배관공을 기다리고 있거든. 싱크대에서 물이 새서 고쳐야 돼. 그것 때문에 엄마가 집에 있으라고 하셨어.

   Pat 그래. 그럼 내일 만나든가 하자.

2. Amy 웬 난장판이야! 여기 뭐 하는 거야, Jeff?

   Jeff 조심해. 집에 모두 페인트를 칠하고 있어.

   Amy 방은 무슨 색으로 할 거야?

   Jeff 짙은 파랑으로 할 거야. 바다같이 만들고 싶어.

   Amy 그거 멋지겠다!

3. Jeff 너 좀 봐, Amy. 너 먼지를 뒤집어썼구나.

   Amy 차고 청소하는 엄마를 돕고 있어. 쌓인 물건이 너무 많아. 아마 차고 세일을 할 것 같아.

   Jeff 그러면 우리 가족이 같이 할 수도 있겠다.

   Amy 좋은 생각이야. 그러면 더 잘 될 거야.

   Jeff 이리 와. 우리 엄마와 이야기해 보자.

4. M 여기서 산 지 얼마나 됐어?

   W 네 살부터니까, 12년 됐어.

   M 정말 오래되었구나.

   W 응. 이 집에 대한 좋은 기억과 안 좋은 기억이 많아. 나무 위 오두막집에서 논 일, 지붕에서 떨어진 일….

   M 오, 나무 위에 오두막집이 있어? 봐도 돼?

   W 그럼.

Listen Again
p. 62

A. 다시 듣고 일치하지 않는 것을 고르시오.

1★a. Jeff는 새 롤러 블레이드가 생겼다.

   b. Jeff는 지금 집에 혼자 있다.

   c. 배관공은 오늘 싱크대를 고칠 것이다.

2. a. 집은 지금 아주 지저분하다.

   b. Jeff의 방은 파란색으로 칠할 것이다.

   ★c. 집 전체를 파란색으로 칠할 것이다.

3★a. 차고 세일 중이다.

   b. 차고에는 먼지가 아주 많다.

   c. Amy는 차고를 청소하고 있다.

B. 다시 듣고 가장 적절하게 요약한 것을 고르시오.

4. a. ★ 그녀는 그 집에서 12년째 살고 있다.

   b.□ 그녀는 놀다가 나무 위의 오두막집에서 떨어졌다.

Listening 2

p. 63

자신의 집에 대해 말하고 있다. 그림에 번호를 매기시오.

스크립트

1. I live in an apartment. It is on the tenth floor of a high-rise building. It has a great view. We can see a park and a river from the window in the living room. There is a swimming pool and a tennis court in the apartment complex. The best thing about our complex is I can swim and play tennis every day.

2. My home is a two-story house. My room is upstairs right under the attic. My mom likes it because it is not far from the mall or public transportation. My dad likes it because

it's safe and quiet. I like it because I can play basketball in the yard.

3. I live in an old apartment. The walls are covered with stains, and the doors and windows shake when wind blows. It is almost falling apart. Only my mom likes it. Why? The rent is good. But who would want to live in this kind of dirty old place?

4. There are big and small shops in my neighborhood. My home is right next to a large supermarket. It is never quiet. There are lots of cars coming in and out. There are so many people around. It is even more annoying at night. I can't study with the window open. I wish we could move out of this place.

해석

1. 나는 아파트에서 살아. 고층 건물의 10층에 있어. 전망이 아주 좋아. 거실에서 창문으로 공원과 강을 볼 수 있어. 아파트 단지 안에 수영장과 테니스장이 있어. 우리 단지의 제일 좋은 점은 매일 수영을 할 수 있고 테니스를 칠 수 있다는 거야.

2. 우리 집은 2층집이야. 내 방은 위층에 있는데, 다락방 바로 아래야. 대중교통과 쇼핑몰에서 멀지 않아서 엄마가 좋아하셔. 아빠는 안전하고 조용해서 좋아하시고. 나는 마당에서 농구를 할 수 있어서 좋아해.

3. 나는 오래 된 아파트에서 살아. 벽은 얼룩으로 덮였고, 바람이 불면 문과 창문이 흔들려. 거의 무너져 가고 있어. 우리 엄마만 좋아하셔. 왜냐고? 집세가 싸거든. 하지만 누가 이렇게 더럽고 오래 된 곳에서 살고 싶어 하겠어?

4. 우리 동네에는 크고 작은 가게들이 있어. 우리 집은 큰 슈퍼마켓 바로 옆이야. 조용할 때가 없어. 들어오고 나가는 차들이 많아. 주변에 사람도 아주 많고, 밤에는 훨씬 더 짜증 나. 창문을 열어놓고 공부할 수가 없어. 나는 여기서 이사 갔으면 좋겠어.

Listen Again

p. 63

A. 다시 듣고 알맞은 답을 고르시오.

1. 아파트에 대한 내용과 일치하는 것은?
   ★a. 전망이 좋다. b. 운동 시설이 없다. c. 옆에 호수가 있다.

2. 집에 대한 내용과 일치하지 않는 것은?
   ★a. 조용하지 않다.
   b. 대중교통과 가까이 있다.
   c. 가족 모두가 집을 좋아한다.

3. 아파트에 대한 내용과 일치하지 않는 것은?
   a. 집세가 싸다.
   ★b. 바람이 불면 벽이 흔들린다.
   c. 그녀의 엄마가 이 아파트를 좋아한다.

B. 다시 듣고 맞는 문장을 고르시오.

4. a. ☒ 그는 너무 시끄러워서 자신의 집을 싫어한다.
   b. ☐ 그는 자신의 집이 너무 커서 싫어한다.

스크립트

a. He doesn't like his house because it's too noisy.
b. He doesn't like his house because it's too large.

Review
p. 64

1. going, whole, color
2. story, far, quiet, since
3. floor, view, rent
4. apartment, noisy, neighborhood
5. cleaning, garage sale

✴ 듣고 빈칸을 채우시오.

해석

1. W 여기서 뭐 하고 있는 거야?
   M 집 전체를 칠하고 있어.
   W 거실은 무슨 색으로 할 거야?
   M 옅은 녹색으로 할 거야.

2. 우리 집은 2층집이다. 대중교통과 멀리 떨어져 있긴 하지만, 안전하고 조용하다. 나는 태어났을 때부터 이곳에 살았다. 이 집과 관련된 추억이 많이 있다.

3. M 새 집 마음에 드세요?
   W 네. 고층 아파트 건물 15층에 있어요. 전망이 아주 좋아요. 제 방에서 지역 전체가 보여요.
   M 집세는 얼마인가요?
   W 싸요. 월세 1500달러밖에 안 해요.

4. 우리 가족은 막 이사했다. 나의 오래된 아파트는 너무 소음이 심해서 좋아하지 않았다. 이제 나는 안정이 된다. 동네가 좋아서, 멋지고 조용하다.

5. M 위에서 뭐 해?
   W 다락방 청소하는 중이야. 쌓인 물건이 너무 많아.
   M 그 물건들로 다 뭐 할 거야?
   W 차고 세일을 하려고 해.

On Your Own   p. 65

LISTEN & WRITE

들은 질문을 쓰시오.

스크립트

Do you live in a house or an apartment?
Can you describe your house?
Are there many stores around your
neighborhood?

해석

주택에 삽니까 아파트에 삽니까?
살고 있는 곳이 어떤 집인지 설명할 수 있겠습니까?
동네에 가게가 많이 있습니까?

PRONUNCIATION

/ e / vs / æ /
☞ 듣고 따라 해 보시오.   내기하다, 머리, 즐거운, 말했다, 한 벌(짝)
☞ 듣고 따라 해 보시오.   방망이, 가졌다, 결혼하다, 슬픈, 앉았다

☞ 주의 깊게 듣고 차이점을 발견하시오.
  내기하다 / 방망이   머리 / 가졌다
  즐거운 / 결혼하다   말했다 / 슬픈
  한 벌(짝) / 앉았다

단어를 듣고 들은 단어에 표시하시오.

스크립트 bat, had, merry, said, sat

내기하다	☐	방망이	★
머리	☐	가졌다	★
즐거운	★	결혼하다	☐
말했다	★	슬픈	☐
한 벌(짝)	☐	앉았다	★

Practice Test   p. 66~69

1. 1) a	2) b	2. 1) c		3. 1) c 2) d
4. 1) d	2) b	5. 1) d	2) b	

✽ 듣고 알맞은 답을 고르시오.

1. Amy와 Jane이 이야기하고 있다.

스크립트

Jane	We're moving next month.
Amy	Are you moving out of town?
Jane	No, in the same neighborhood.
Amy	So you can still go to school with me.
Jane	Sure.
Amy	Why are you moving?
Jane	My mom thinks this house is too small and old. In the new house my room is upstairs and it has a great view. It is bigger too. I'll hang my favorite pictures on the wall. I can't wait to show it to you.

해석

Jane	우리 다음 달에 이사해.
Amy	다른 동네로 가?
Jane	아니, 같은 동네야.
Amy	그러면 여전히 나랑 같이 학교 갈 수 있겠네.
Jane	물론이지.
Amy	왜 이사 가는 거야?
Jane	엄마는 이 집이 너무 작고 오래 됐다고 생각해서. 새집에서 내 방은 위층에 있고 전망이 아주 좋아. 더 크기도 하고. 내가 제일 좋아하는 그림을 벽에 걸 거야. 빨리 너에게 보여주고 싶어.

1) 대화와 일치하지 않는 것은?
   ★a. Jane은 다른 동네로 이사를 간다.
   b. Jane는 이사 간다는 것으로 흥분해 있다.
   c. 새집은 더 크고 새것이다.
   d. 새집은 1층 이상이다.

2) Jane의 새 방은 _____.
   a. 아래층이다.   ★b. 전망이 좋다.
   c. 별로 크지 않다.   d. 벽에 포스터가 붙을 것이다.

2. 한 소녀가 자신의 집에 대해 말하고 있다.

스크립트

Look, Mom. I can't study with the window open. It is too noisy outside. I can hear all the cars and people from the street and the market. And this house is too old. The doors and windows shake when wind blows. There are stains all over the walls. I can't bring my friends home. Let's move out of here. Please, Mom.

해석

보세요, 엄마. 창문을 열어놓고는 공부할 수가 없어요. 밖이 너무 시끄러워요. 길하고 시장에서 들리는 자동차랑 사람들 소리가 다 들려요. 그리고 이 집은 너무 오래됐어요. 바람이 불면 문과 창문이 흔들려요. 벽은 얼룩으로 뒤덮였고요. 친구들을 집에 데려올 수도 없어요. 이사 가요. 제발, 엄마.

1) 소녀에 의하면 집의 문제점이 <u>아닌</u> 것은 무엇인가?
   a. 너무 시끄럽다.   b. 너무 지저분하다.
  ★c. 학교에서 너무 멀다.   d. 너무 낡았다.

3. Brown 부인과 Jeff는 집에 대하여 이야기하고 있다.

스크립트

w The sink is leaking. The floors are squeaking. The paint is fading. I don't know what to start with.

M Why don't we sell this house and move?

w I don't want to. I like this neighborhood. It's safe and quiet. Besides it is in walking distance from the town center.

M I'll help you, Mom. Maybe I can paint my room.

해석

w 싱크대에서 물이 새네. 바닥은 삐걱거려. 페인트는 다 벗겨졌고. 뭐부터 시작해야 할지를 모르겠어.

M 이 집을 팔고 이사 가는 것은 어때요?

w 나는 그러고 싶지 않아. 이 동네가 좋아. 안전하고 조용해. 게다가 시내 중심으로 걸어갈 수 있는 거리잖아.

M 제가 도울게요, 엄마. 아마 제 방은 제가 칠할 수 있을 거예요.

1) 이 집의 문제점은 무엇인가?
   a. 너무 작다.
   b. 너무 시끄럽다.
  ★c. 너무 낡았다.
   d. 안전하지 않다.

2) 대화 내용과 일치하는 것은?
   a. Brown 부인은 이사 가고 싶어 한다.
   b. Jeff는 자신이 문제를 모두 해결할 수 있다고 생각한다.

   c. 시내 중심에서 멀다.
 ★d. 집에 수리해야 할 것이 많다.

4. Jim과 Pete가 이야기를 하고 있다.

스크립트

Jim Hey, up there! What's going on, Pete?

Pete We're painting the whole two-story house, Jim.

Jim Oh, what color will the house be?

Pete Well, this outside color will be blue.

Jim Even your room will be blue?

Pete No, you know me! It will be orange and brown. My two favorite colors.

해석

Jim 어이, 거기 위에! 무슨 일이야, Pete?

Pete 이 층집 전체를 페인트 칠 하고 있어, Jim.

Jim 오, 집이 무슨 색이 되는데?

Pete 이 바깥쪽 색은 파란색이 될 거야.

Jim 네 방도 파란 색으로 칠할 거니?

Pete 아니, 알잖아! 내 방은 주황색과 갈색이 될 거야. 내가 가장 좋아하는 색 두 가지.

1) 대화에 대해 사실인 것은 무엇인가?
   a. 주황색과 갈색은 Jim이 가장 좋아하는 색이다.
   b. Jim은 페인트공이다.
   c. Pete와 Jim은 집을 함께 페인트칠하고 있다.
 ★d. Pete는 그의 이층집을 페인트칠할 것이다.

2) 말하는 사람들은 어디에 있는가?
   a. 집 안 ★b. 집 밖   c. 페인트 가게 안   d. 그림 가게 안

5. 한 여자가 그녀의 동네에 대해 이야기하고 있다.

스크립트

I have lived in my neighborhood since I was four. The houses used to be nice. Now, they are old and dirty, so the rent is low. They are far from public transportation, and many shops have closed. I am moving out of here, soon. I can't wait to live in my new apartment. It has a great view!

해석

나는 네 살 이후로 이 동네에 살고 있다. 이 동네 집들은 한때는 좋았었다. 지금은 오래되고 지저분해져서 집세가 싸다. 대중교통과 멀리 떨어져 있고, 많은 가게들이 문을 닫았다. 나는 곧 여기서 이사 갈 것이다. 빨리 새 아파트에서 살고 싶다. 거기는 전망이 좋다!

1) 여자의 동네는 _____.
   a. 좋다.   b. 막혀 있다.
   c. 새 아파트가 있다. ★d. 대중교통과 멀리 떨어져 있다.

2) 여자는 어떤 기분인가?
   a. 낯선   ★b. 흥분한
   c. 참는   d. 지루한

Dictation   p. 68

1. We're moving, out of town, too small, hang, show it
2. window, noisy, shake, over the walls, move out
3. what to start, sell, neighborhood, quiet, Maybe
4. painting, will be, Even, orange
5. since I was four, far from, soon, live in, view

UNIT 9
Where to, sir?

Getting Ready   p. 69

1. 1. B   2. T   3. S   4. A   5. A
   6. B   7. T   8. S
2. 1. d   2. a   3. b   4. c   5. f   6. e

1. 이 표현들을 어디에서 들을 수 있는가? 버스는 B, 택시는 T, 지하철은 S, 비행기는 A를 쓰시오.

   1. 요금 내세요!   B
   2. 어디로 갈까요, 손님?   T
   3. 미술관역에 가려면 1호선을 타세요.   S
   4. 유나이티드 항공사로 시카고에 가려면 여기서 탑승 수속을
      하나요?   A
   5. 여권을 보여 주시겠습니까?   A
   6. 정확한 요금을 넣으세요.   B
   7. 시청으로 가 주세요.   T
   8. 유니언 역에서 파란 선으로 갈아타세요.   S

2. 질문을 답과 연결시키시오.

1. 여기서 상점가는 어떻게 가요?   d. 저기서 버스를 타세요.
2. 여권을 보여 주시겠습니까?   a. 네, 여기요.
3. 시청역까지 요금이 얼마예요?   b. 3달러 50센트예요.
4. 왕복 얼마예요?   c. 70달러입니다.
5. 거기까지 얼마나 걸려요?   f. 40분쯤요.
6. 거기까지 가장 빨리 갈 수 있는 방법이 뭐예요?
                               e. 지하철을 이용하세요.

Listening Task   p. 70~71

Listening 1	2 - 4 - 1 - 3			
Listen Again A	1. c	2. b	3. a	
B	4. b			
Listening 2	1. b	2. a	3. c	4. b
Listen Again A	1. b	2. b	3. b	
B	4. a			

Listening 1   p. 70

사람들이 대중교통을 이용하려 한다. 그들은 지금 어디에 있는가? 그림에 번호를 붙이시오.

스크립트

1. The airport gives limousine service. The bus stops at the major hotels in town. It runs every thirty minutes. You have to wait twenty more minutes for the next bus. If you are in a hurry and don't mind paying more money, you can call a taxi here.

2. $45.67 for one-way, and just $80 for the round-trip. You save more than ten dollars if you get the round-trip ticket. It takes a little longer than the bus, but the scenery is beautiful. The train passes through mountains and fields. Of course, it is more relaxing, too.

3. Put 55 cents in the fare box, please. No, no, you can't put more than that. Exact change only. See the sign over there? I don't carry change.

4. Please take me to the bus terminal. I'm in a hurry. How long will it take? I have to be there in thirty minutes. Do you think you can make it? If you do, I'll give you a ten-dollar tip.

해석

1. 공항에서 리무진 서비스를 제공합니다. 리무진 버스는 시내 주요 호텔에 정차합니다. 버스는 30분마다 출발합니다. 다음 버스까지는 20분 이상을 기다리셔야 해요. 시간은 급하고 돈이 좀 들어도 상관없다면 여기서 택시를 타셔도 돼요.

2. 편도는 45달러 67센트, 왕복은 80달러밖에 안 합니다. 왕복 표를 사시면 10달러 넘게 아끼실 수 있어요. 시간은 버스보다 약간 더 걸리지만, 경치가 아름답죠. 기차가 산과 들을 통과하니까요. 물론 더 편안하기도 합니다.

3. 요금 통에 55센트 넣으세요. 아니, 아니, 더 넣지 마세요. 딱 맞게 넣으세요. 저기 안내 간판이 보이세요? 저희는 거스름돈

은 가지고 다니지 않습니다.

4. 버스 터미널로 가 주세요. 정말 급해요. 얼마나 걸릴까요? 30분 후에는 도착해야 되거든요. 갈 수 있으세요? 가능하시면 팁으로 10달러를 드릴게요.

Listen Again

p. 70

A. 다시 듣고 알맞은 답을 고르시오.

1. 리무진 버스는 _____ 운행한다.
   a. 1시간마다   b. 20분마다   ★c. 30분마다

2. 왕복표를 사면 _____ 달러를 절약할 수 있다.
   a. 약 40   ★b. 약 10   c. 약 18

3. 요금 통에 _____ 을(를) 넣어야 한다.
   ★a. 55센트   b. 토큰   c. 1달러 지폐

B. 다시 듣고 가장 적절하게 요약한 것을 고르시오.

4. a. ☐ 그녀는 10분 내로 버스 터미널에 도착하기를 원한다.
   b. ★ 그녀는 30분 내로 버스 터미널에 도착해야 한다.

Listening 2

p. 71

사람들이 서로 다른 대중교통을 이용하려 한다. 어떤 교통수단들인가?

1. a. 지하철   ★b. 버스   c. 택시
2. ★a. 택시   b. 버스   c. 지하철
3. a. 버스   b. 택시   ★c. 지하철
4. a. 버스   ★b. 비행기   c. 기차

스크립트

1.
w How can I get to the mall from here?
m There's a bus to the mall every twenty minutes. But make sure it is orange. The other buses don't go to the mall.
w Where is the bus stop?
m It's over there in front of the bank.

2.
m Where to?
w The Garden Cinema.
m That's the one next to City Hall, isn't it?
w No, that is Town Cinema. This one is the one across from the Tower Hotel.
m Oh, I see. All right. I'll have you there in no time.

3.
w Excuse me. How can I get to the National Museum?
m Take the red line to Market Place, and change for the yellow line. It's the third stop, Museum Station.
w Thank you very much.

4.
w Do I check in here for American Airlines to New York?
m Yes. Do you have your ticket?
w Yes, here it is.
m Thank you. May I see your passport?
w There you go.
m Can you put your luggage up here, please?

해석

1. w 여기서 상점가에 가려면 어떻게 해야 돼요?
   m 20분마다 상점가로 가는 버스가 있어요. 그런데 반드시 주황색 버스인지 확인하셔야 돼요. 다른 색 버스는 상점가로 안 가요.
   w 정류장이 어디에요?
   m 저기 은행 앞이요.

2. m 어디로 갈까요?
   w 가든 극장으로 가 주세요.
   m 시청 옆에 있는 극장 말이죠?
   w 아니오, 그것은 타운 극장이에요. 가든 극장은 타워 호텔 맞은편에 있어요.
   m 아, 그렇군요. 좋습니다. 금방 모셔다 드리지요.

3. w 실례합니다. 국립 박물관에 어떻게 가나요?
   m 시장역에 가는 붉은 선을 타고, 노란 선으로 갈아타세요. 박물관역은 세 번째 역이에요.
   w 정말 감사합니다.

4. w 뉴욕행 아메리칸 항공사의 탑승 수속을 여기서 하면 되나요?
   m 네, 표 있으십니까?
   w 네, 여기 있어요.
   m 감사합니다. 여권을 보여 주시겠습니까?
   w 여기 있습니다.
   m 여기에 짐을 올려 주시겠습니까?

Listen Again

p. 71

A. 다시 듣고 알맞은 답을 고르시오.

1. 대화 내용과 일치하는 것은?
   a. 버스는 10분마다 운행한다.
   ★b. 다른 색 버스는 가는 길이 다르다.
   c. 버스정류장은 바로 근처에 있다.

2. 목적지는 어디에 있는가?
   a. 시청 옆에 있다.   ★b. 타워 호텔 맞은편에 있다.
   c. 기사는 목적지가 어디에 있는지 모른다.

3. 이 사람은 _____ 으로 가려 한다.
   a. 음악 공연장 ★b. 박물관   c. 국립 미술전시관

B. 다시 듣고 맞는 문장을 고르시오.

4. a. ★ 이 사람은 뉴욕행 비행기의 탑승 수속을 하고 있다.
   b. ☐ 이 사람은 뉴욕을 떠나고 있다.

<u>스크립트</u>

  a. The person is checking in for a flight to New York.
  b. The person is leaving New York.

Review   p. 72

1. get, subway, stop
2. fare, change, sign, carry
3. ticket, round, Here
4. take us, How long, take, hurry
5. check in, passport, Here, luggage

✻ **듣고 빈칸을 채우시오.**

해석
1. W 여기서 기차역은 어떻게 가나요?
   M 버스를 타거나 지하철 타시면 돼요.
   W 버스정류장이 어디에 있어요?
   M 저기 다음 블록 끝에요.

2. 요금 통에 55센트를 넣어 주세요. 정확한 요금만 넣어 주세요. 저기 안내 간판 보이세요? 저는 거스름돈이 없습니다.

3. W Baltimore까지 표 값이 얼마예요?
   M 편도 42달러 50센트, 왕복 80달러입니다.
   W 편도표 한 장 주세요.
   M 여기 있습니다.

4. 종합 병원에 데려다 주세요. 제 아내가 아파요. 얼마나 걸릴 것 같아요? 될 수 있는 한 빨리 도착해야 해요. 돈은 달라고 하시는 대로 드릴게요. 서둘러 주세요!

5. W 여기서 시카고 행 유나이티드 항공사의 탑승 수속을 하나요?
   M 네. 여권을 보여 주시겠습니까?
   W 여기 있습니다.
   M 짐을 여기에 올려 주시겠습니까?

On Your Own   p. 73

LISTEN & WRITE

들리는 질문을 써 보세요.

스크립트

How can I get to the bus stop from here?
What is the best way to get to City Hall from here?
What is the fare to City Hall from here?

해석
여기서 버스 정류장에 어떻게 갑니까?
여기서 시청에 가는 가장 좋은 방편은 무엇입니까?
여기서 시청까지 요금은 얼마입니까?

PRONUNCIATION

/ ʌ /   **vs**   / ʌr /
☞ 듣고 따라 해 보시오.
상반신, 갈매기, 오두막, 닫다, 톤
☞ 듣고 따라 해 보시오.
터지다, 소녀, 다치게 하다, 셔츠, 돌다
☞ 주의 깊게 듣고 차이점을 발견해 보시오.
상반신 / 터지다   갈매기 / 소녀
오두막 / 다치게 하다   톤 / 돌다
닫다 / 셔츠

들리는 단어에 표시하시오.

스크립트 burst, gull, hut, shirt, ton

상반신	☐	터지다	★
갈매기	★	소녀	☐
오두막	★	다치게 하다	☐
닫다	☐	셔츠	★
톤	★	돌다	☐

Practice Test   p. 74~75

1. 1) d   2) c   2. 1) c   2) c
3. 1) 1, 3   2) Central Station, City Hall Station
   3) fifth   4) 5
4. 1) b   2) a   5. 1) a

※ 듣고 알맞은 답을 고르시오.

1. Susan은 택시를 부르고 있다.

스크립트

M City Cab. Where are you going?
W Lakeside Hospital.
M Where are you now?
W 256 Lincoln Ave.
M What's your phone number?
W It's 301-245-7890.
M A taxi will be there in five to ten minutes.

해석

M 시티 택시입니다. 어디로 가실 건가요?
W Lakeside 병원이요.
M 지금 위치가 어디세요?
W Lincoln 가 256번지요.
M 전화번호가 어떻게 되나요?
W 301-245-7890이요.
M 5분에서 10분 후에 택시가 갈 겁니다.

1) 택시 회사는 _____를 물어보지 않았다.
   a. Susan의 주소
   b. Susan의 전화번호
   c. Susan이 갈 곳
   ★d. Susan의 이름

2) 대화 내용과 일치하지 않는 것은?
   a. Susan은 5분에서 10분 후에 택시에 탈 것이다.
   b. Susan은 병원에 가려고 한다.
   ★c. Susan의 목적지는 링컨 가이다.
   d. 택시 회사의 이름은 시티 택시이다.

2. Brown 씨는 표를 사고 있다.

스크립트

M Hi. What time is your next flight to New York?
W 3:45 p.m. There are some seats available.
M What's the one-way fare?
W It's $249.80 with tax.
M Okay. Here you go. Put it on my card, please.
W All right. Just a second.

해석

M 안녕하세요. 뉴욕으로 가는 다음 비행기는 몇 시에 있어요?
W 오후 3시 45분에 있습니다. 자리가 좀 남아있네요.
M 편도는 얼마예요?
W 세금 포함 249달러 80센트입니다.
M 좋아요. 여기 있습니다. 카드로 해 주세요.
W 알겠습니다. 잠시만 기다려 주세요.

1. Brown 씨는 _____에 있다.
   a. 기차역   b. 버스 터미널
   ★c. 항공권 판매소   d 전철역

2. 대화 내용과 일치하는 것은?
   a. 그는 현금으로 지불하고 있다.
   b. 그는 왕복표를 사고 있다.
   ★c. 그는 뉴욕으로 가려 한다.
   d. 비행기표에는 세금이 붙지 않는다.

3. 두 사람이 길을 묻고 답하고 있다.

스크립트

M What is the best way to get to your house?
W Use the subway. Line number 3. Where are you coming from?
M I take Line one, at Central Station.
W Then you can change for Line three at City Hall Station. Get off at Market Street. It's the fifth stop from there. I'll be waiting for you at Exit 5.

해석

M 너희 집에 가는 가장 빠른 방법이 뭐야?
W 지하철을 타. 3호선이야. 어디서 오고 있는데?
M 1호선 센트럴역이야.
W 그러면 시청역에서 3호선으로 갈아 탈 수 있겠다. 마켓 스트리트에서 내려. 거기서 다섯 번째 역이야. 5번 출구에서 기다릴게.

1. (1 / 3)호선을 먼저 타고 (3 / 1)호선으로 갈아타야 한다.

2. (센트럴역 / 시청역)에서 지하철을 타고 (시청역 / 마켓 스트리트)에서 갈아탄다.

3. 갈아 탄 후 (네 번째 / 다섯 번째) 역에서 내려야 한다.

4. 친구는 (3 / 5)번 출구에서 기다릴 것이다.

4. 한 여자가 서울에서 런던으로 갈 예정이다.

스크립트

M I'll take your bags. Now, where to, Ma'am?
W The airport, please. I'm flying back to London.
M Which one?
W Do you have more than one airport?
M Yes. May I see your ticket?
W Sure. Here it is.
M Oh, you want Incheon Airport. I'll help you with your bags and take you right to the airline check-in desk.
W Wonderful!

M 제가 가방을 들어 드리겠습니다. 자, 어디로 모실까요, 부인?

W 공항으로 가 주세요. 런던으로 다시 돌아갈 거거든요.

M 어느 공항을 말씀하시는 건지요?

W 공항이 두 개 이상인가요?

M 네. 표를 좀 볼 수 있을까요?

W 네. 여기 있어요.

M 아, 인천 공항으로 가셔야겠네요. 가방 옮기는 걸 도와드리고 곧장 공항 체크인 데스크로 모셔다 드리겠습니다.

W 감사합니다!

1. 대화는 어디에서 일어나고 있는가?
   a. 기차역에서   ★b. 택시 안에서
   c. 버스 안에서   d. 전철 안에서

2. 대화 내용과 일치하지 <u>않는</u> 것은 무엇인가?
   ★a. 그녀는 하나 이상의 공항을 향해 비행할 것이다.
   b. 서울 근방에는 두 개의 공항이 있다.
   c. 그녀는 공항에서 체크인을 해야 한다.
   d. 남자는 그녀가 가방을 옮기는 것을 도울 것이다.

5. 한 여자가 L.A.에서의 그녀의 경험에 대해 이야기를 하고 있다.

스크립트

I went to L.A. last year. Once, I took the bus because I wanted to use all forms of public transportation over there. However, I didn't see a sign that said to pay the driver with exact change only. The driver made a gesture toward the sign. I had to get off the bus and use the subway.

해석

작년에 L.A.에 갔어. 한번은 거기에 있는 모든 형태의 대중교통을 이용해 보고 싶어서 버스를 탔어. 그런데 난 정확한 금액의 요금을 운전사에게 내라고 쓰여 있는 표지를 보지 못했지. 운전사는 그 표지 쪽으로 손짓을 했어. 난 버스에서 내려 전철을 타야 했어.

1. 이야기와 일치하지 <u>않는</u> 것은 무엇인가?
   ★a. 그녀는 버스를 이용했다.
   b. 그녀는 전철을 이용했다.
   c. 그녀는 정확한 금액의 요금을 가지고 있지 않았다.
   d. 그녀는 버스에서 전철로 바꿔 탔다.

Dictation   p. 76

1. going, Hospital, phone number, be there, minutes
2. flight, seats available, one-way, tax, Here you go, second
3. the best way, Use, take, Get off, fifth, waiting
4. bags, where to, back, more than, take, airline
5. took the bus, use, sign, change, get off, subway

UNIT 10
I'd like to open an account.

Getting Ready   p. 77

1. 1. d   2. f   3. a   4. b   5. c   6. e
2. 1. b   2. d   3. a   4. c

1. 장소 이름 옆에 그곳에서 들을 수 있는 말 묶음의 기호를 쓰시오.

   a. 소포, 우편 번호, 항공 우편, 선박 우편, 우표
   b. 룸서비스, 체크인, 체크아웃, 2인실, 헬스클럽, 인터넷 연결
   c. 전지, 엔진, 무연의, 엔진오일 점검(윤활유 점검)
   d. 탑승, 비행, 승객, 티켓
   e. 드라이클리닝, 다림질, 바느질, 얼룩
   f. 수표, 현금(현금으로 바꾸다), 저축 예금 계좌, 당좌 예금 구좌

1. 공항   d   2. 은행   f
3. 우체국   a   4. 호텔   b
5. 주유소   c   6. 세탁소   e

2. 표현과 응답을 연결시키시오.

1. 이 소포를 보내고 싶습니다.
   b. 알았습니다. 항공 우편인가요, 선박 우편인가요?
2. 계좌를 만들고 싶습니다.
   d. 네. 어떤 종류의 계좌로 하시겠어요?
3. 콜로라도 주 푸에블로 시의 우편 번호가 뭐예요?
   a. 81009입니다.
4. 제 세탁물을 가지러 왔습니다.
   c. 여기 있습니다.

Listening 1	1. b	2. b	3. a	4. b
Listen Again A	1. a	2. a	3. b	
B	4. a			
Listening 2	1. b	2. c	3. a	4. a
Listen Again A	1. b	2. c	3. c	
B	4. a			

Listening 1   p. 78

어디에서 들을 수 있는 말인가? 알맞은 그림을 고르시오.

스크립트

1. Attention passengers: This is the last boarding call for Flight 168 to Chicago. The flight will be departing shortly. Passengers with young children can now board the flight.

2. I need these shirts and pants dry-cleaned and ironed. One shirt has a button missing. Can you sew the button back on? One more thing—there is a small ink spot on the pants. Can you get that out? My father needs them back before Friday. Can I pick them up on Thursday?

3. This package is not labeled right. The address is in the wrong place. The sender's address has to go up here, not on the back. And you forgot the zip code. Now do you want to send this by air mail or surface mail?

4. This is not the room I made the reservation for. I wanted a double room, not single. And this room doesn't have an Internet connection. It is also not quiet enough; it is too close to the entrance. I want to change rooms.

해석

1. 승객 여러분께 알립니다. 시카고 행 168 비행편의 마지막 탑승 안내입니다. 비행기가 곧 출발합니다. 어린이를 동반한 승객들께서는 이제 탑승이 가능합니다.

2. 이 셔츠하고 바지를 드라이클리닝하고 다림질해 주세요. 셔츠 하나는 단추가 하나 떨어졌어요. 다시 달아 주실래요? 한 가지 더요. 바지에 작은 잉크 얼룩이 있어요. 그것 좀 빼 주실래요? 저희 아버지께서 금요일 전까지는 필요하다고 하세요. 목요일에 찾아갈 수 있을까요?

3. 이 소포는 표기가 제대로 안 되어 있네요. 주소를 제 자리에 안 썼어요. 보내는 사람 주소는 뒤쪽이 아니라 이 위에다 써야 돼요. 그리고 우편 번호도 잊으셨군요. 그럼 항공 우편으로 하실래요, 선박 우편으로 하실래요?

4. 이건 제가 예약한 방이 아닙니다. 저는 1인실이 아니라, 2인실을 원했어요. 그리고 이 방은 인터넷 연결도 안 되네요. 전혀 조용하지도 않고, 입구랑 너무 가까워요. 방을 바꿔 주세요.

Listen Again   p. 78

A. 다시 듣고 맞는 것을 고르시오.

1★a. 비행기는 시카고 행이다.
  b. 모든 승객이 지금 탑승한다.
  c. 탑승 전에 안내 방송을 또 할 것이다.

2★a. 바지에 작은 잉크 얼룩이 있다.
  b. 바지는 단추가 하나 떨어졌다.
  c. 금요일에 옷을 찾고 싶어 한다.

3. a. 주소가 틀렸다.
 ★b. 우편 번호가 없다.
  c. 보내는 사람 이름이 없다.

B. 다시 듣고 가장 적절하게 요약한 것을 고르시오.

4. a.★ 그녀는 소음 때문에 그 방을 바꾸고 싶어 한다.
  b.□ 인터넷이 연결되어 있기 때문에 그녀는 그 방을 원한다.

Listening 2   p. 79

사람들이 각각 다른 장소에 있다. 어디에 있는가? 알맞은 답을 고르시오.

1. a. 세차장에   ★b. 주유소에   c. 슈퍼마켓에
2. a. 할인매장에   b. 약국에   ★c. 은행에
3★a. 음반 가게에   b. 라디오 방송국에   c. 서점에
4★a. 정비소에   b. 주유소에   c. 약국에

스크립트

1.
M Yes, ma'am. What can I do for you?
W Hi! Fill it up, please.
M Regular unleaded or super?
W Regular unleaded.
M Check the oil?
W Yes, please.

2.

W Next! Good morning.

M Good morning. I'd like to cash this check, please.

W Okay, $150. Oh, you haven't signed it.

M Really? Oh, I'm sorry. There you go.

W How would you like your money?

M Five twenties and five tens, please.

3.

M Excuse me. Do you have the new Carl Estefan album?

W Yes, we do. It's number five this week. Do you want a CD or a cassette?

M A CD, please.

W It's right here.

4.

Mr. Brown Hi, Lee. My car won't start.

Lee Hi, Mr. Brown. Did you check the battery?

Mr. Brown Sure, I did.

Lee It seems like there is some problem with the engine. Leave it here so I can have a look at it. I'll call you when I've finished checking.

해석

1. M 네, 손님. 어떻게 해 드릴까요?

   W 네! 가득 채워 주세요.

   M 무연 일반이요, 고급이요?

   W 무연 일반이요.

   M 오일을 점검해 드릴까요?

   W 네, 해 주세요.

2. W 다음 손님! 안녕하세요.

   M 안녕하세요. 이 수표를 현금으로 바꾸고 싶은데요.

   W 네, 150달러네요. 아, 수표에 서명을 아직 안 하셨네요.

   M 정말요? 아, 죄송합니다. 지금 할게요.

   W 어떻게 바꾸시겠습니까?

   M 20달러짜리 5장하고 10달러짜리 5장이요.

3. M 실례합니다. Carl Estefan의 새 앨범 있어요?

   W 네, 있어요. 이번 주 5위에요. CD로 드릴까요, 카세트테이프로 드릴까요?

   M CD요.

   W 여기 있습니다.

4. Mr.Brown 안녕하세요, Lee 씨. 제 차가 시동이 안 걸려요.

   Lee 안녕하세요, Brown 씨. 배터리는 체크하셨어요?

   Mr.Brown 물론 했죠.

   Lee 엔진에 문제가 있는 것 같은데요. 제가 한번 보게 여기 맡겨 주세요. 점검이 끝나면 전화 드릴게요.

A. 다시 듣고 맞는 것을 고르시오.

1. a. 여자는 고급 무연 가솔린을 원한다.
   ★b. 여자는 오일을 점검 받고 싶어 한다.
   c. 여자는 차에서 내려야 한다.

2. a. 수표는 100달러짜리이다.
   b. 남자는 돈은 모두 10달러짜리 지폐로 바꾸고 싶어 한다.
   ★c. 남자는 돈을 받기 전에 서명을 해야 한다.

3. a. 이 음반은 카세트테이프로는 나오지 않는다.
   b. 점원은 이 음반에 대해 알지 못한다.
   ★c. 이 음반은 인기가 많다.

B. 다시 듣고 맞는 문장을 고르시오.

4. a. ★ Brown 씨의 차는 엔진에 이상이 있는 듯하다.
   b. □ Brown 씨는 Lee씨에게 배터리를 점검해 달라고 정비소에 갔다.

스크립트

a. Mr. Brown's car seems to have some problem with the engine.

b. Mr. Brown went to see Mr. Lee to check the battery.

Review p. 80

1. cash, How, tens
2. ironed, sew, spot
3. Fill, check
4. boarding, departing, minutes
5. address, up, back, air mail

✽ 듣고 빈칸을 채우시오.

해석

1. M 이 수표를 현금으로 바꾸고 싶습니다.

   W 네. 60달러군요. 돈을 어떻게 받으시겠습니까?

   M 20달러짜리 한 장과 10달러짜리 4장이요.

2. 이 셔츠 드라이클리닝하고 다림질해 주세요. 단추 하나가 떨어졌어요. 다시 달아 주실래요? 그리고 등에 잉크 얼룩 좀 빼 주세요. 화요일 전까지 해 주세요.

3. W 가득 채워 주세요!

   M 무연 일반이요, 고급이요?

   W 무연 일반이요. 그리고 오일을 점검해 주세요.

4. 승객 여러분께 알립니다. Miami행 324 비행편의 마지막 탑승 안내입니다. 비행기가 5분 후에 출발합니다.

5. W 아, 주소를 잘못된 위치에 쓰셨네요.

   M 진짜요? 원래 어디에다 쓰는 거죠?

   W 보내는 사람 주소는 뒤쪽이 아니라, 여기 위에다 써야 해요. 그리고 항공 우편인가요, 선박 우편인가요?

LISTEN & WRITE

들리는 질문을 써 보세요.

스크립트

> What can I do for you?
> How would you like your money?
> What is your zip code?
> Do you want to send this by air mail?

해석
무엇을 도와드릴까요?
돈은 어떻게 해 드릴까요?
우편 번호가 어떻게 되십니까?
항공우편으로 보내드릴까요?

PRONUNCIATION

> ### / s / vs / ʃ /
>
> ☞ **듣고 따라 해 보시오.**
> 같은, 구하다, 찔끔찔끔 마시다, 보인(see의 과거분사), 팔다, 계급
>
> ☞ **듣고 따라 해 보시오.**
> 부끄러움, 면도하다, 배, 광택, 껍질, 충돌
>
> ☞ **주의 깊게 듣고 차이점을 발견하시오.**
>
> | | |
> |---|---|
> | 같은 / 부끄러움 | 구하다 / 면도하다 |
> | 찔끔찔끔 마시다 / 배 | 보인 / 광택 |
> | 팔다 / 껍질 | 학급 / 충돌 |

들리는 단어에 표시하시오.

스크립트 same, save, ship, seen, shell, class

같은	★	부끄러움	☐
구하다	★	면도하다	☐
찔끔찔끔 마시다	☐	배	★
보인	★	광택	☐
팔다	☐	껍질	★
학급	★	충돌	☐

> 1. 1) package 2) air mail
> 2. 1) b 2) d 3. 1) c 2) a
> 4. 1) b 2) a 5. 1) c 2) c

✱ 듣고 알맞은 답을 고르시오.

1. Jeff는 우체국에 있다.

스크립트

> M Hi! I'd like to send this package to Los Angeles.
> W Sure. What's in it?
> M Some books.
> W Let's see. It's 8 pounds. You can send it by air mail or by surface mail. Which way would you like?
> M How much is it by air?
> W Let me check... $16.80.
> M I'll send it by air.

해석
M 안녕하세요! Los Angeles로 이 소포를 부치고 싶은데요.
W 네. 내용물이 뭐죠?
M 책 몇 권요.
W 어디 봅시다. 8파운드네요. 항공 우편하고 선박 우편이 있어요. 어떤 걸로 하시겠습니까?
M 항공으로 하면 얼마죠?
W 확인해 볼게요. 16달러 80센트입니다.
M 항공으로 해 주세요.

1) Jeff는 (편지 / 소포)를 부치려 한다.

2) (항공 우편 / 선박 우편)으로 보내려 한다.

2. Brown 부인은 은행에 있다.

스크립트

> W I want to take out $300 from my savings account.
> M Sure. Could you fill out this form?
> W Okay. Here you go.
> M How would you like your money?
> W Two hundreds and five twenties, please.

해석
W 제 예금 계좌에서 300달러 인출하고 싶습니다.
M 네. 이 서류 좀 써 주시겠습니까?
W 네. 여기 있어요.
M 돈은 어떻게 받으시겠습니까?
W 100달러짜리 2장하고 20달러 5장 부탁합니다.

1) Brown 부인은 무엇을 하고 있는가?
   a. 수표의 현금 교환   ★b. 예금 인출
   c. 예금   d. 송금

2) 대화 내용과 일치하는 것은?
   a. 은행 직원이 Brown 부인을 위해 서류를 작성했다.
   b. Brown 부인은 현금인출기를 사용하고 있다.

c. Brown 부인은 돈을 모두 100달러 지폐로 받을 것이다.

★d. Brown 부인은 그녀의 예금 계좌에서 돈을 인출하고 있다.

3. Brown 씨는 세탁소에 있다.

스크립트

> M I'd like to pick up my laundry. Here's my claim ticket.
> W Here it is. That comes to eighteen dollars.
> M Oh, my jacket is not clean yet. Look! The stains are still there.
> W Sorry, but we couldn't get them out. That's the best we could do.
> M I see. Thanks anyway. Here's the money.

해석

M 제 세탁물을 찾아 가고 싶어요. 접수표 여기 있어요.

W 여기 있습니다. 18달러입니다.

M 오, 재킷이 안 깨끗하네요. 보세요! 얼룩이 아직도 있어요.

W 죄송합니다만, 지울 수가 없었어요. 그게 최선을 다한 거예요.

M 알겠어요. 어쨌든 고마워요. 돈 여기 있어요.

1) Brown 씨는 무엇을 하고 있는가?
   a. 세탁물을 맡기고 있다.
   b. 불만을 말하고 있다.
   ★c. 세탁물을 찾고 있다.
   d. 세탁소에 대해 물어보고 있다.

2) 대화 내용과 일치하는 것은?
   ★a. 세탁소 직원은 얼룩을 빼지 못했다.
   b. Brown 씨는 세탁 결과에 만족했다.
   c. Brown 씨는 20달러 넘게 지불했다.
   d. 세탁소 직원은 얼룩이 있는지 몰랐다.

4. 한 여자가 미용실에 있다.

스크립트

> M How would you like your haircut, today?
> W I'd like to have a simple style that's easy to take care of.
> M Would you like it the same length?
> W No, a little shorter.
> M Sure. What kind of color?
> W I'd like to see some samples, please.
> M Okay. Mine are beautiful!
> W How much is color?
> M Only $25 extra.
> W Oh!

해석

M 오늘은 머리를 어떻게 하고 싶으세요?

W 관리하기 쉬운 단순한 스타일로 하고 싶어요.

M 같은 길이로 해드릴까요?

W 아뇨, 조금 더 짧게요.

M 네. 색상은요?

W 견본을 좀 보고 싶군요.

M 좋습니다. 제 머리 색도 예뻐요!

W 염색은 얼마죠?

M 25달러만 추가하시면 돼요.

W 오!

1) 여자가 결정한 것은 무엇인가?
   a. 그녀의 머리 색상
   ★b. 그녀의 머리 길이
   c. 오늘 얼마나 돈을 쓸지
   d. 어느 미용실에 갈지

2) 여자의 자른 머리는 _____ 지지 않을 것이다.
   ★a. 이전보다 길어   b. 이전보다 간편해
   c. 관리하기 더 쉬워   d. 더 화려해

5. 두 사람이 이야기를 하고 있다.

스크립트

> M I'd like to open an account.
> W Sure. Savings or checking?
> M A checking account, please.
> W I need you to fill out this form, and I need to get a photo ID.
> M OK. Here is my driver's license.
> W Sign at the bottom of the form, please.
> M Here?
> W Right. Well, we are all set.

해석

M 계좌를 개설하고 싶습니다.

W 네. 예금 계좌와 당좌 계좌 중 어느 것을 원하십니까?

M 당좌 계좌로 하겠습니다.

W 이 양식을 작성하시고 사진이 있는 신분증을 주세요.

M 네. 여기 운전면허증이요.

W 그 양식 아래에 서명해 주세요.

M 여기요?

W 네. 자, 모두 다 준비됐네요.

1) 대화는 어디에서 일어나고 있는가?
   a. 주유소   b. 시장
   ★c. 은행   d. 우체국

2) 대화에 대해 사실이 아닌 것은 무엇인가?
   a. 남자는 은행 계좌를 개설하고 있다.
   b. 여자는 은행에서 일한다.
   ★c. 남자는 돈을 예금하고 있다.
   d. 여자는 남자의 사진이 있는 신분증을 요구하고 있다.

UNIT 11
Which house appliance?

Getting Ready   p. 85

1. 1. c 2. b 3. d 4. e 5. a 6. f
2. 1. c 2. b 3. a 4. d

1. 아래 네모 안에 있는 가전제품의 기호로 빈칸을 채우시오.

| a. TV 세트 | b. 냉장고 | c. 카세트 재생기 |
| d. 세탁기 | e. 재봉틀 | f. 오븐 |

1. 테이프가 안에서 엉켜서 나오지 않는다.   c
2. 식품을 더 이상 신선하게 보관하지 못하며, 물이 샌다.   b
3. 얼룩이 심하게 진 빨랫감이 많다.   d
4. 나만의 옷을 만들고 싶다.   e
5. 뉴스와 날씨 볼 때만 본다.   a
6. 빵을 굽고, 생선을 굽고, 고기를 굽는다.   f

2. 질문을 답과 연결하시오.

1. 이거 잘 빨아져요?
   c. 그럼요, 어떤 얼룩이든 잘 빠집니다.
2. 언제 받을 수 있어요?   b. 배송 기간은 3일입니다.
3. 카세트 재생기가 왜 이래요?   a. 테이프가 안에서 엉켰어요.
4. 이거 얼마나 빨라요?   d. 1분당 25페이지를 출력해요.

Listening Task   p. 86~87

Listening 1		1. b	2. a	3. c	4. b
Listen Again	A	1. b	2. b	3. c	
	B	4. a			
Listening 2		1. b	2. c	3. b	4. a
Listen Again	A	1. c	2. a	3. c	
	B	4. a			

Listening I   p. 86

어떤 물건에 대한 내용인가? 알맞은 그림을 고르시오.

스크립트

1. I don't know what's happened to it. The tape is stuck and won't come out. This is not the first time it has happened. It has ruined several of my tapes already. Do you think you can fix it?

2. Uh oh! The paper is jammed again. This machine always gives me trouble when I'm busy. Yesterday, the ink ran out while I was printing out an important paper. And now the paper jam, it's never any help.

3. It makes a buzzing sound. Sometimes the lines get crossed and I hear other people talking. Other times it just doesn't work and there is no sound at all. It all started last week–when I dropped it on the floor.

4. It leaks. I don't know where the water is leaking from. And it makes noise. At night the noise is really irritating. But I don't want to throw it away because it works okay. It still keeps food fresh and cold. I need to get it fixed.

해석

1. 이게 왜 이러는지 모르겠어요. 테이프가 걸려서 안 나와요. 처음 이러는 게 아니에요. 벌써 테이프 여러 개 망쳤다고요. 고치실 수 있을 것 같나요?

2. 아 이런! 종이가 또 걸렸네요. 이 기계는 항상 내가 바쁠 때 고장이 나요. 어제는 중요한 서류를 출력하고 있는데 잉크가 떨어졌어요. 그리고 이번엔 종이가 걸리다니, 도움이 안 돼요.

3. 이 기계에서 지직거리는 소리가 나요. 어쩔 땐 혼선이 돼서 다른 사람이 말하는 게 들려요. 다른 땐 그냥 작동이 안 되고 아무 소리도 안 나고요. 이건 다 지난주부터 시작됐어요. 제가 전화기를 바닥에 떨어뜨렸거든요.

4. 물이 새요. 어디서 나오는 건지 모르겠어요. 게다가 소음도 나요. 밤에는 진짜 거슬려요. 하지만 작동은 잘 되니까 버릴 생각은 없어요. 아직까지 음식을 신선하고 차갑게 유지시켜 주거든요. 수리하고 싶어요.

Listen Again

p. 86

A. 다시 듣고 맞는 것을 고르시오.

1. a. 이 문제는 이번이 처음이다.
   ★b. 여러 번 일어난 일이다.
   c. 이 사람이 고칠 수 있다.

2. a. 이 사람은 이 기계를 좋아한다.
   ★b. 이 사람은 바쁘다.
   c. 지금 잉크가 다 떨어졌다.

3. a. 이 사람은 이것을 물속에 빠뜨렸다.
   b. 이것은 전혀 작동하지 않는다.
   ★c. 소음이 난다.

B. 다시 듣고 가장 적절하게 요약한 것을 고르시오.

4. a. ★ 그것은 물이 새고 소음이 나지만 여전히 음식을 신선하게 유지시켜 준다.
   b. □ 그것은 소음만 나는데 그 소리 때문에 밤에 정말 거슬린다.

Listening 2

p. 87

이들은 무엇을 사려고 하는가? 알맞은 답을 고르시오.

1. a. 전축   ★b. TV세트   c. 비디오카메라
2. a. 밥솥   b. 토스터   ★c. 오븐
3. a. 건조기   ★b. 세탁기   c. 식기세척기
4. ★a. 재봉틀   b. VCR   c. 다리미

스크립트

1.
M It's too big. We don't watch it very often, only for news and weather.
W Sorry, it is the only model on sale right now.
M How about the 20-inch model over there?
W That's not on sale. But it is smaller and it is twenty dollars cheaper.

2.
M This is new. You can do many things with this. You can bake, grill, roast and everything.
W How about cleaning? It is hard to clean an oven.
M For cleaning there is nothing to worry about, because it is a self-cleaning oven. Just push the button. It only takes five minutes to clean itself.
Girl Mom, let's buy it. I want to bake cookies.

3.
W Does it wash well? I have a lot of laundry with heavy stains.
M Absolutely. This is a very popular brand. And it comes with a ten-year warranty. They will repair any problems for free for the next ten years.
W Wow! And it is the same model as on the TV commercial. Right?
M Right.
W Hmm... When can I get it?
M It'll take about three days to deliver.

4.
Amy What do you need it for, Mom?
Mom I want to make you some dresses. I'm tired of the ones in the stores. They all look the same to me.
Amy Do you know how to use it?
Mom Of course, I do. Your grandmother always made dresses for me. I learned from her.

해석

1. M 너무 크네요. 우리는 이걸 그렇게 자주 안 봐요. 뉴스하고 날씨만 보거든요.
   W 죄송하지만, 지금 세일하고 있는 건 그 모델밖에 없어요.
   M 저기 20인치짜리는요?
   W 세일 중은 아니에요. 하지만 크기는 더 작고 20달러 더 싸요.

2. M 이것은 신상품입니다. 여러 가지 하실 수 있어요. 빵도 굽고, 생선을 구워도 되고, 고기를 구울 수도 있고, 다 됩니다.
   W 청소는요? 오븐 청소하기 힘들잖아요.
   M 자동으로 청소가 되니까, 청소라면 걱정할 게 없어요. 버튼만 누르세요. 자동 청소하는데 5분 밖에 안 걸려요.
   Girl 엄마, 이거 사요. 나 과자 굽고 싶어요.

3. W 이 세탁기 빨래 잘 돼요? 얼룩이 심하게 진 빨랫감이 많거든요.
   M 물론 잘 됩니다. 이 상품이 제일 인기 있는 거예요. 그리고 10년 무상 수리가 됩니다. 10년간은 어떤 고장도 다 공짜로 수리해 드려요.
   W 와! 그리고 이거 TV 광고에서 나온 거랑 같은 모델이죠?
   M 맞습니다.
   W 음... 언제 받을 수 있죠?
   M 배달하는 데 약 3일 정도 걸립니다.

4. Amy 이거 어디다 쓰실 거예요, 엄마?
   Mom 네 옷을 만들려고 해. 가게에서 파는 옷들은 질렸어. 다 똑같아 보여.
   Amy 어떻게 사용하는지 아세요?
   Mom 물론 알지. 네 외할머니께서 항상 내 옷을 만들어 주셨거든. 할머니께 배웠어.

Listen Again

p. 87

A. 다시 듣고 맞는 것을 고르시오.

1. a. 그들은 세일 중인 제품을 마음에 들어 한다.
   b. 세일하는 모델은 20인치 짜리밖에는 없다.
   ★c. 그들은 큰 제품을 좋아하지 않는다.

2. ★a. 새 모델이다.   b. 청소하는 데 50분이 걸린다.
   c. 여자는 요리를 할 줄 몰라서 걱정이다.

3. a. 제품을 오늘 집에 가져갈 수 있다.
   b. 10개월 동안 무상으로 수리해 준다.
   ★c. 같은 제품이 TV 광고에 나왔다.

B. 다시 듣고 맞는 문장을 고르시오.

4. a. ★ 그녀는 가게에서 산 드레스를 좋아하지 않기 때문에
      드레스를 만들고 싶어 한다.
   b. □ 그녀는 그 기계를 사용하고 싶어서 옷을 만들기를 원한다.

스크립트

> a. She wants to make dresses because she doesn't like
>   the dresses from the store.
> b. She wants to make clothes because she wants to use
>   the machine.

Review

p. 88

1. smaller, sale, brand   2. happened, stuck, fix
3. leaks, keep, throw   4. sound, crossed, work
5. wash, popular, deliver

✻ 듣고 빈칸을 채우시오.

해석

1. W 이건 너무 커요. 더 작은 걸 원해요.
   M 죄송하지만, 세일하는 모델은 이것밖에 없어요.
   W 20인치 모델은요? 좋은 상표인가요?
   M 그럼요. 10년 무상 보증 수리입니다. 아주 좋은 상표입니다. 그런데 세일은 안 하고 있습니다.

2. 왜 이러는지 모르겠어요. 테이프가 안에서 걸려서 꺼낼 수가 없어요. 수리할 수 있으세요?

3. M 무엇이 문제이십니까?
   W 물이 새요. 계속 물이 흘러나와요.
   M 보관은 신선하게 되나요?
   W 아뇨, 안 돼요.
   M 아마도 그럼 폐기하셔야 하겠군요.

4. 계속 지직거리는 소리가 나요. 어떨 때는 혼선이 돼서 다른 사람이 말하는 게 들려요. 다른 때는 아예 작동을 하지 않고 아무 소리가 안 나요.

5. W 세탁이 잘 되나요?
   M 물론입니다. 아주 인기 있는 제품이에요.

W 언제 받을 수 있어요?
M 배송하는 데 일주일이 걸릴 거예요.

On Your Own

p. 89

LISTEN & WRITE

들리는 질문을 써 보세요.

스크립트

> What happened to your computer?
> How fast is your printer?
> How big is your TV?

해석
당신의 컴퓨터에 무슨 문제가 생겼습니까?
당신의 프린터는 얼마나 빠릅니까?
당신의 TV는 얼마나 큽니까?

PRONUNCIATION

/ n / vs / ŋ /
☞ 듣고 따라 해 보시오. 금지하다, 햇볕에 그을음, 죄, 얇은, 톤, 태양
☞ 듣고 따라 해 보시오. 탕 치다, 짜릿한 맛, 노래하다, 것, 혀, 노래한
☞ 주의 깊게 듣고 차이점을 발견해 보시오. 금지하다 / 탕 치다　　　　햇볕에 타다 / 짜릿한 맛 죄 / 노래하다　　　　　　얇은 / 것 톤 / 혀　　　　　　　　　태양 / 노래한

들리는 단어에 표시하시오.

스크립트 bang, tan, sin, thing, ton, sung

금지하다	□	탕 치다	★
햇볕에 타다	★	짜릿한 맛	□
죄	★	노래하다	□
얇은	□	것	★
톤	★	혀	□
태양	□	노래한	★

Practice Test

p. 90~91

1. 1) isn't   2) big   3) age   4) one
2. 1) c   2) c   3. 1) d   2) d
4. 1) b   5. 1) b   2) d

50

※ 듣고 알맞은 답을 고르시오.

1. 남자가 쇼핑을 하고 있다.

스크립트

> W May I help you?
> M Yes, I'm looking for a refrigerator.
> W Do you have a certain brand in mind?
> M No, not really.
> W How about this one?
> M It's too big.
> W It's big but it's on sale. It is cheaper than this smaller one.
> M Why is it so cheap?
> W It's an old model. But it's not so old, only one year old.

해석

W 도와드릴까요?

M 네. 냉장고 좀 보려고요.

W 특별히 생각하고 계신 상표가 있으세요?

M 아뇨. 그렇진 않아요.

W 이 모델은 어떠십니까?

M 너무 크네요.

W 크긴 하지만 세일 중이에요. 더 작은 이 제품보다 가격이 더 저렴해요.

M 왜 이렇게 싸죠?

W 구식 모델이거든요. 그래도 그렇게 오래 되진 않았고, 일 년 됐어요.

1) 남자는 특정한 상표를 (찾고 있다 / 찾고 있지 않다).
2) 남자는 그 상품이 (무겁다 / 크다)고 생각한다.
3) 그 상품은 출시된 (시기 / 상표) 때문에 크기가 더 작은 상품보다 싸다.
4) 그것은 출시된 지 (일 / 이)년 되었다.

2. 손님이 가게에서 쇼핑하고 있다.

스크립트

> M This one is new. It works really well.
> W How fast is it?
> M It prints 25 pages a minute.
> W That is fast.
> M And the image is very clear and alive. Look! What do you think?
> W That is impressive! I'll take it.

해석

M 이건 신상품입니다. 작동이 정말 잘 됩니다.

W 얼마나 빠른데요?

M 1분에 25페이지를 출력해요.

W 빠르군요.

M 그리고 해상도가 아주 선명하고 생생하죠. 보세요! 어떠세요?

W 정말 잘 되네요! 이걸 사겠어요.

1) 어떤 가전 제품에 대해 이야기하고 있는가?
   a. 세탁기   b. 냉장고   ★c. 프린터   d. 비디오카메라

2) 내용과 일치하지 <u>않는</u> 것은?
   a. 작업 속도가 빠르다.
   b. 손님과 점원의 대화이다.
   ★c. 손님은 이 제품을 별로 마음에 들어 하지 않는다.
   d. 새 제품이다.

3. 다음은 어떤 전자 제품에 관한 것이다.

스크립트

> TV, radio, computer, and telephone are all in one. You can watch TV while chatting with your friend in a foreign country. You can check your e-mail on the subway while listening to some good music. You have the world right in your hand. It is small and light. You can even carry it even in your pocket. It is still very expensive but it's worth it.

해석

TV, 라디오, 컴퓨터, 전화기가 모두 하나에 들어 있습니다. 다른 나라에 있는 친구와 통화하면서 TV를 볼 수 있습니다. 지하철 안에서 좋은 음악을 들으면서 이메일을 확인할 수도 있지요. 당신의 손 안에 세계를 가지는 것입니다. 작고 가볍습니다. 심지어 주머니에 넣고 다닐 수도 있죠. 아직 상당히 비싸지만 그만한 가치가 있습니다.

1) 이 제품으로 사용할 수 없는 기능은 무엇인가?
   a. 전화기   b. 컴퓨터   c. TV   ★d. 주머니

2) 이 제품에 대한 내용과 일치하지 <u>않는</u> 것은?
   a. 이 제품으로 여러 가지를 할 수 있다.
   b. 이 제품으로 이메일을 확인할 수 있다.
   c. 이 제품으로 지하철에서 TV를 볼 수 있다.
   ★d. 이 제품은 작지만 무겁다.

4. Johnny가 엄마에게 이야기하고 있다.

스크립트

> M Mom! I need help.
> W Oh, really? What's wrong?
> M Yes, something happened to my cassette player.
> W Again? Oh, my! The tape is stuck inside, and it won't come out. This will take some work to remove.
> M Can you fix it?
> W _____Sure, it will just take some time._____

M 엄마! 도움이 필요해요.

W 아, 정말? 뭐가 문제니?

M 네, 제 카세트 플레이어가 뭔가 잘못됐어요.

W 또? 아, 이런! 테이프가 안에 끼여서 빠지질 않네. 이걸 제거하려면 손 좀 봐야겠는걸.

M 고치실 수 있겠어요?

W _____ 그럼, 시간이 좀 걸릴 뿐이야. _____

1) 다음에 이어질 수 있는 가장 적절한 대답은 무엇인가?

   a. 고맙지만 됐어.   ★b. 그럼, 시간이 좀 걸릴 뿐이야.

   c. 그래, 알지.   d. 그래, 그가 해 볼 거야.

5. Paul은 그의 새 오븐에 대해 말하고 있다.

스크립트

M I have a new wonderful oven that cooks everything!

W Really?

M Yes, it bakes, grills, and roasts!

W Sounds like it's really a good oven.

M I think with this new oven I'm going to become a chef soon.

W I like to cook, too. Where can I buy one?

M Here is the number. It'll take several days to deliver after you call.

해석

M 나는 뭐든지 요리할 수 있는 멋진 새 오븐이 있어!

W 그래?

M 응, 빵도 굽고, 생선도 굽고, 고기도 구울 수 있어!

W 정말 좋은 오븐인가 보네.

M 이 새 오븐으로 난 곧 요리사가 될 거야.

W 나도 요리하는 것을 좋아해. 어디서 살 수 있지?

M 여기 번호가 있어. 전화를 하고 배달되는 데 며칠 걸릴 거야.

1) 이 가전 제품에 대해 사실이 <u>아닌</u> 것은 무엇인가?

   a. 주문해야 한다.

  ★b. 하루 만에 도착한다.

   c. 주문하려면 전화번호가 필요하다.

   d. 아주 멋지다.

2) 오븐이 하지 못하는 것은?

   a. 빵 굽기   b. 생선 굽기

   c. 고기 굽기   ★d. 음식을 신선하게 보관하기

Dictation p. 92

1. looking, brand, big, on sale, cheaper, old model
2. new, fast, clear, alive, I'll take it
3. radio, watch, listening, small, light, expensive
4. wrong, happened, stuck, come out, remove, fix
5. cooks, bakes, roasts, buy, after you call

UNIT 12
Did you see the news last night?

Getting Ready p. 93

1. 1. a   2. c   3. f   4. d   5. e   6. b
2. 1. b   2. d   3. c   4. a

1. 다음은 신문 기사에 나온 문장들이다. 빈칸에 면의 기호를 쓰시오.

   a. 스포츠 면   b. 경제 면   c. 날씨 면

   d. 사건사고 면   e. 기술과학 면   f. 오락 면

1. Lakers가 Bulls에 79대 78로 졌다.   a

2. 기온은 30도 초반에서 40도 후반일 것이다.   c

3. 톱스타 Tim Brown과 Nicole White가 결혼을 발표했다.   f

4. 비행기가 L.A. 근처의 숲에 추락했다.   d

5. 마이크로소프트 사가 새로운 소프트웨어를 개발했다.   e

6. Bill Gates가 작년에 미국에서 가장 많은 돈을 벌었다.   b

2. 표현을 응답과 연결시키시오.

1. 흥미로운 소식 있어?   b. 인도에 폭우가 내렸대.

2. 내일 날씨는 어떨까?   d. 덥고 햇볕이 강할 거야.

3. 아, 이럴 수가. 저 팀 또 졌네.   c. 이번엔 누구한테?

4. 어젯밤에 뉴스 봤어?   a. 응, 봤어.

Listening Task p. 94~95

Listening 1   3, 4, 1, 2

Listen Again A 1. c   2. a   3. b

         B 4. a

Listening 2   1. a   2. b   3. a   4. a

Listen Again A 1. b   2. b   3. c

         B 4. b

Listening 1

뉴스를 듣고 기사 제목에 번호를 매기시오.

Tom Crane과 Cindy Hoffer 결혼	3
개가 주인을 살리다	4
비행기 추락으로 수백 명 사망	1
폭우 중국 강타	2

스크립트

1. Good evening, this is Ann Slinger with the Nine o'clock Report from WLTV. Our top story tonight: French Air Flight 709 traveling from Paris to New York has crashed in the woods near Los Angeles. All the passengers and the crew members aboard the plane are dead. The police are looking for the plane's black box.

2. Heavy rains hit China hard again. It has been raining for a week. Several towns have been destroyed. About thirty people are dead and hundreds are still missing. Thousands have lost their homes.

3. Top stars Tom Crane and Cindy Hoffer announced they're going to get married. The couple has been dating since 2002 when they starred in the same movie. The wedding is scheduled for May 25. They say they will be going to a Caribbean island for their honeymoon.

4. A brave dog saved his owner from a fire. The owner was in a deep sleep when the house caught fire. The dog didn't leave him and kept shaking him. He finally woke up and escaped from the fire with his dog. The house fell to the ground only a few minutes after they escaped.

해석

1. 안녕하십니까, WLTV 9시 보도의 Ann Slinger입니다. 오늘 밤 주요 소식입니다. 파리발 뉴욕행의 프렌치 에어 플라이트 709편이 로스앤젤레스 근처 숲에서 추락했습니다. 탑승했던 승객과 승무원 전원이 사망했습니다. 경찰은 숲 속에서 블랙박스를 찾고 있습니다.

2. 폭우가 중국을 다시 강타했습니다. 비는 일주일간 계속 내리고 있습니다. 여러 도시가 파괴됐습니다. 약 30명이 사망했고 수백 명이 아직 실종된 상태입니다. 수천 명이 집을 잃었습니다.

3. 인기스타 Tom Crane과 Cindy Hoffer가 결혼을 발표했습니다. 두 사람은 2002년에 같은 영화에 주연으로 출연했을

때부터 만남을 유지했다고 합니다. 결혼식은 5월 25일로 예정되어 있습니다. 두 사람은 신혼여행으로 캐리비언의 섬에 갈 것이라고 했습니다.

4. 용감한 개가 자신의 주인을 불에서 구했습니다. 주인은 집에 불이 났을 때 깊은 잠에 빠져 있었습니다. 개는 떠나지 않고 계속해서 주인을 흔들고 있었습니다. 그는 결국 깨어나서 개와 함께 불에서 탈출했습니다. 그들이 탈출한 지 몇 분 후에 그 집은 무너졌습니다.

Listen Again

다시 듣고 틀린 것을 고르시오.

1. a. 비행기는 뉴욕으로 향하고 있었다.
   b. 비행기를 타고 있던 사람은 아무도 살아남지 못했다.
   ★c. 블랙박스는 발견되었다.

2. ★a. 폭우로 이미 수천 명의 사람들이 사망했다.
   b. 비는 일주일 동안 계속되었다.
   c. 중국에서 일어난 일이다.

3. a. 두 사람은 모두 영화배우이다.
   ★b. 그들은 지금 신혼여행 중이다.
   c. 결혼은 5월로 계획되어 있다.

B. 다시 듣고 가장 적절하게 요약한 것을 고르시오.

4. a. ★ 집에 불이 났을 때 용감한 개가 그의 주인을 구출했다.
   b. ☐ 한 집에 화재가 발생했고 개와 주인이 죽었다.

Listening 2

사람들이 무엇에 대해 이야기하고 있는가? 알맞은 답을 고르시오.

1. ★a. 새로운 소프트웨어 프로그램
   b. 새로운 컴퓨터 회사
   c. 장애인

2. a. 그림
   ★b. 절도 사건
   c. 도둑

3. ★a. 날씨
   b. 미식축구경기
   c. 소풍

4. ★a. TV의 스포츠 방송
   b. 농구 선수
   c. 농구화

1.

Jane   Any interesting news, Dad?

Mr. Brown   Yes, Microsoft has developed a new software program.

Jane   What kind of program is it?

Mr. Brown   It's for handicapped people who can't move their hands. With the program, they can use computers by moving their eyes.

2.

W   Did you watch the news last night?

M   About what?

W   The national museum in Washington D.C. was robbed. Several famous paintings were stolen.

M   That's a shame. Have the robbers been caught yet?

W   No, but they were videotaped and the police are looking for them.

3.

M   What will the weather be like tomorrow?

W   It will be a little cold and cloudy.

M   What about the temperature?

W   It'll be in the low 25s to the high 30s, it says.

M   But nothing about rain?

W   No. You can play football.

4.

W   Oh, no! They were beaten again.

M   Who?

W   The Chicago Bulls. They got shut down by the Lakers. This is the third time this year.

M   I know. What was the score?

W   78 to 79. It was a close game.

해석

1. Jane   아빠, 재미있는 소식 있어요?

Mr.Brown   응, 마이크로소프트사가 새로운 소프트웨어 프로그램을 개발했대.

Jane   어떤 프로그램인데요?

Mr.Brown   손을 못 움직이는 장애인들을 위한 거래. 이 프로그램이 있으면 눈의 움직임으로 컴퓨터를 사용할 수 있대.

2. W   어젯밤에 뉴스 봤어?

M   무슨 뉴스?

W   워싱턴 D.C. 국립박물관이 도난을 당했대. 유명한 그림을 여러 점 도둑맞았대.

M   저런. 도둑은 잡혔대?

W   아니, 그런데 감시 카메라에 찍혀서 경찰이 찾고 있대.

3. M   내일 날씨 어떨대?

W   좀 춥고 구름 낄 거래.

M   기온은요?

W   최저 25도에서 최고 30도라고 했어.

M   비는 안 오고요?

W   안 온대. 너 축구 할 수 있겠네.

4. W   아, 이런! 저 팀 또 졌어.

M   어떤 팀?

W   Chicago Bulls. Lakers에 완전 패했어. 올해로 세 번째야.

M   맞아. 점수는?

W   78 대 79. 팽팽한 경기였어.

Listen Again   p. 95

A. 다시 듣고 틀린 것을 고르시오.

1. a. 손이 없는 사람들이 이 프로그램을 사용할 수 있다.
★b. 눈이 안 보이는 사람들이 이 프로그램을 사용할 수 있다.
c. 장애인을 위해 만들어졌다.

2. a. 그림을 도둑맞았다.
★b. 도둑들은 잡혔다.
c. 도둑들은 감시 카메라에 찍혔다.

3. a. 그는 내일 축구를 할 수 있다.
b. 춥고 흐릴 것이다.
★c. 햇볕은 강하나 바람이 불 것이다.

B. 다시 듣고 맞는 문장을 고르시오.

4. a. ☐ Lakers가 Bulls보다 훨씬 많은 득점을 했다.
b. ★ Chicago Bulls는 올해 좋은 성적을 거두지 못하고 있다.

스크립트

a. The Lakers scored far more than the Bulls.
b. The Chicago Bulls are not good this year.

Review   p. 96

1. interesting, killed, weather
2. crashed, died, looking for, crashes
3. Did you hear, album, I didn't know that, newspaper
4. Report, top story, residential, London, looking
5. caught, That's good news, escaped

✱ 듣고 빈칸을 채우시오.

해석

1. M   흥미로운 소식 있니?

W   응. 태풍이 일본을 강타해서 수백 명이 죽었대.

M 아, 또야. 요즘엔 날씨가 점점 문제를 많이 일으켜.

2. 프랑스 비행기가 시카고 근처의 숲에 추락했습니다.
   승객과 승무원 전원이 사망했습니다.
   사람들은 숲에서 블랙박스를 찾고 있습니다.
   올해에만 비행기 추락 사고가 3번 일어났습니다.

3. W Bill Jones가 새 음반을 발표했다는 소식 들었어?
   M 그래? 몰랐어.
   W 그리고 올해 그래미상을 받을 거래.
   M 어디서 들었어?
   W 오늘 신문에 났더라.

4. 안녕하십니까, BBS 8시 뉴스의 John Watson입니다. 오늘 아침 주요 소식입니다. 영국 항공 405편이 런던 근처의 거주 지역에 추락했습니다. 탑승자 전원이 사망한 것으로 보입니다. 경찰은 아직 생존자를 찾고 있습니다.

5. M 은행 강도가 어제 아침에 잡혔대.
   W 좋은 소식이네.
   M 그런데 어젯밤에 도망쳤대.
   W 그거 안 좋네.

On Your Own   p. 97

LISTEN & WRITE

들리는 질문을 써 보세요.

스크립트

Did you watch the news last night?
Any interesting news?
Did you watch the weather forecast today?

해석
어젯밤에 뉴스를 봤습니까?
흥미로운 기사가 있습니까?
오늘 일기예보를 봤습니까?

PRONUNCIATION

/ t / vs / θ /
☞ 듣고 따라 해 보시오.
탱크, 깡통, 팀, 방망이, 매트
☞ 듣고 따라 해 보시오.
감사하다, 얇은, 주제, 목욕, 수학
☞ 주의 깊게 듣고 차이점을 발견해 보시오.
탱크 / 감사하다   깡통 / 얇은   팀 / 주제
방망이 / 목욕   매트 / 수학

들리는 단어에 표시하시오.

스크립트 thank, tin, theme, bath, mat

탱크	☐	감사하다	★

깡통	★	얇은	☐
팀	☐	주제	★
방망이	☐	목욕	★
매트	★	수학	☐

Practice Test   p. 98~99

1. 1) a	2) c	2. 1) c	3. 1) b	2) c
4. 1) d	2) d	5. 1) d	2) b	

※ 듣고 알맞은 답을 고르시오.

1. 다음은 9시 뉴스이다.

스크립트

M Our top story tonight. A National Bank in downtown Chicago was robbed yesterday. There was a security system but it was not working. This is Chicago's third bank robbery this year.

W Next story. A twelve-year-old boy has entered one of the best universities in the U.S. He scored the second highest on this year's SAT. He is a Chinese-American and his father runs a small restaurant in L.A.'s China Town.

해석
M 오늘 밤 주요 소식입니다. 시카고 중심가에 있는 국립 은행이 어제 도난을 당했습니다. 보안 시스템은 있었지만 작동하지 않았습니다. 이것은 올해 들어 시카고에서 발생한 세 번째 은행 도난 사건입니다.

W 다음 소식입니다. 12살 소년이 미국 최고의 대학 중 한 곳에 입학했습니다. 그는 올해 SAT에서 두 번째로 높은 점수를 받았다고 합니다. 이 소년은 중국계 미국인이며 소년의 아버지는 L.A.의 차이나 타운에서 작은 중국 음식점을 운영하고 있다고 합니다.

1) 듣고 맞는 것을 고르시오.
   ★a. 은행 도난 사건은 시카고에서 일어났다.
   b. 올해 시카고에서는 은행 도난 사건이 없었다.
   c. 보안 시스템은 작동했지만 도둑을 막지 못했다.
   d. 도둑들은 잡혔다.

2) 듣고 맞는 것을 고르시오.
   a. 소년은 부잣집 출신이다.
   b. 소년은 올해 SAT에서 가장 높은 점수를 받았다.
   ★c. 소년은 13살보다 어리다.
   d. 소년은 한국계 미국인이다.

2. 두 사람이 뉴스에 관해 이야기하고 있다.

스크립트

M What's new?
W Bill Gates earned the most money in the U.S. last year.
M That's not new. How much did he earn this time?
W About $13 million.
M $30 million?
W No. 13.

해석

M 새로운 거 있어?
W Bill Gates가 작년에 미국에서 돈을 가장 많이 벌었대.
M 새로운 소식도 아니네. 이번에는 얼마 벌었대?
W 천삼백만 달러 정도.
M 삼천만 달러?
W 아니. 천삼백만 달러.

1) 대화 내용과 일치하는 것은 무엇인가?
   a. Bill Gates는 세계에서 돈을 가장 많이 벌었다.
   b. 그는 작년에 삼천만 달러를 벌었다.
   ★c. 남자는 이 소식에 별로 놀라지 않았다.
   d. 그가 미국에서 돈을 가장 많이 번 것은 이번이 처음이다.

3. 두 사람이 뉴스에 대해 이야기하고 있다.

스크립트

W Samsung sold the most cell phones last year!
M Yes, it's amazing. It seems that the company develops a new model almost every month.
W I heard it is one of the world's top 100 companies.
M It is. Samsung is now an international brand. I am proud of them.

해석

W 삼성이 작년에 휴대 전화를 가장 많이 팔았대!
M 응, 놀라워. 그 회사는 거의 매달 신제품을 개발하는 것 같아.
W 거기가 세계 100대 회사 중 하나라고 들었어.
M 맞아. 삼성은 이제 국제적인 회사야. 그 회사가 자랑스러워.

1) 무엇에 대한 대화인가?
   a. 휴대 전화   ★b. 삼성
   c. 세계에서 가장 큰 회사   d. 새로운 소프트웨어 프로그램

2) 대화 내용과 일치하는 것은?
   a. 삼성은 작년에 TV를 가장 많이 팔았다.
   b. 삼성은 세계 10대 회사 중 하나이다.
   ★c. 말하는 이들은 뉴스에 놀라워하고 있다.
   d. 삼성은 새로운 컴퓨터를 개발했다.

4. 동료 직원 두 명이 이야기를 하고 있다.

스크립트

M Did you read the newspaper this morning?
W No. Did you find anything interesting?
M I'll say! There was a tornado in Oklahoma City last night.
W Really? Did many people die?
M Some people are dead and many houses have been damaged.
W That's too bad. I think they had another tornado some years ago, didn't they?
M You're right. They had a bad tornado six years ago.

해석

M 오늘 아침 신문 읽어봤어요?
W 아뇨. 흥미로운 기사가 있었나요?
M 말해 줄게요! 지난 밤에 오클라호마 시에서 토네이도가 있었대요.
W 정말요? 사람들이 많이 죽었나요?
M 몇 명은 죽고 많은 집들이 피해를 입었다네요.
W 정말 안됐네요. 거긴 몇 년 전에도 토네이도가 있었던 것 같은데요, 그렇죠?
M 맞아요. 6년 전에도 토네이도가 있었대요.

1) 대화에 대해 사실이 아닌 것은 무엇인가?
   a. 토네이도는 지난밤에 오클라호마 시에 피해를 입혔다.
   b. 토네이도로 몇 명이 죽었다.
   c. 남자는 토네이도에 대해 읽었다.
   ★d. 오클라호마 시에는 지난 주에 또 다른 토네이도가 있었다.

2) 말하는 사람들의 기분은 어떠한가?
   a. 기쁜   b. 불쾌한   c. 행복한   ★d. 초조한

5. 다음은 뉴스이다.

스크립트

The 58th International Cannes film festival opened at Le Palais de Festival on Wednesday. 21 films are competing this year. Festival jury members including German director Fatih Akin, Mexican actress Salma Hayek and Spanish actor Javier Bardem will pick the winner of the Palme d'Or as well as six other awards. The festival continues until May 22.

해석

제 58회 칸 국제 영화제가 Le Palais de Festival에서 수요일에 개막한다. 올해에는 21개의 영화가 경쟁을 벌일 것이다. 독일의 영화감독 Fatih Akin, 멕시코 여배우 Salma Hayek, 그리고 스페인 배우 Javier Bardem을 포함한 축제 심사 위원들은 다른 6

개의 상과 함께 황금종려상의 수상자를 뽑을 것이다. 축제는 5월 22일까지 계속될 것이다.

1) 뉴스는 무엇에 관한 것인가?
   a. 의학 뉴스　　　　b. 과학과 기술
   c. 날씨　　　　★d. 연예

2) 뉴스에 대해 일치하는 것은 무엇인가?
   a. 최고의 배우 상을 두고 21명의 배우들이 경쟁할 것이다.
   ★b. 멕시코 여배우 Salam Hayek은 축제의 심사 위원이다.
   c. 칸 영화제는 다음 주 수요일까지 지속될 것이다.
   b. 축제의 심사 위원은 6개의 상에 대한 수상자를 뽑을 것이다.

Dictation　　　　　　　　　p. 100

1. top story, robbed, working, third, twelve-year-old, second, runs
2. What's new, earned, this time, 13
3. sold, amazing, companies, am proud of
4. newspaper, interesting, a tornado, die, damaged, That's too bad, six years ago
5. opened, this year, members, actress, winner, until

UNIT 13
I work part time.

Getting Ready　　　　　　　p. 101

1. 1. a　2. b　3. f　4. e　5. c
   6. d　7. g　8. h
2. 1. a　2. d　3. b　4. c

1. 네모에서 알맞은 직업을 골라 빈칸에 기호를 쓰시오.

a. 목수	b. 은행원	c. 공장 근로자
d. 배우	e. 점원	f. 여행사 직원
g. 호텔 접수원	h. 프로 야구 선수	

1. 나는 평생 동안 탁자와 의자를 만들었습니다. ___a___
2. 당좌 예금 구좌를 만드시겠습니까? ___b___
3. 이 말레이시아 패키지는 근사합니다. ___f___
4. 어떤 걸 찾고 계신가요? ___e___
5. 나는 하루 종일 공장에서 일합니다. ___c___
6. 나는 지금까지 12편의 영화에 출연했습니다. ___d___
7. 손님들이 저희 호텔에서 즐겁게 지내기를 바랍니다. ___g___
8. 나는 홈런을 200번 쳤습니다. ___h___

2. 표현을 응답과 연결시키시오.

1. 성함을 말씀해 주실래요?　　a. Joseph Kennedy입니다.
2. 거기까지 얼마나 걸립니까?　　d. 2시간 30분 걸립니다.
3. 어떻게 이렇게 됐어요?　　b. 그는 자전거를 타다 넘어졌어요.
4. 얼마 정도 쓰실 수 있나요?　　c. 100달러 정도요.

Listening Task　　　　　　p. 102~103

Listening 1	1. b	2. b	3. c	4. b
Listen Again　A	1. c	2. b	3. a	
B	4. b			
Listening 2	1. a	2. c	3. b	4. a
Listen Again　A	1. c	2. b	3. b	
B	4. a			

Listening 1　　　　　　　　p. 102

남자의 직업은 무엇일까? 알맞은 답을 고르시오.

1. a. 호텔 지배인　★b. 기차 차장　c. 비행기 승무원
2. a. 계산원　★b. 은행원　c. 호텔 접수원
3. a. 전화 교환원　b. 점원　★c. 여행사 직원
4. a. 약사　★b. 의사　c. 인명 구조원

스크립트

1.
M May I see your ticket, please? I need to punch it, ma'am.
W Oh, I seem to have misplaced it.
M Take your time. I'll come back in a few minutes.
W Oh, here it is. It was under my seat.
M You are going to Petersburg. Have a nice trip.
W Thanks.

2.
W I'd like to open a checking account.
M Sure. You need to fill out a form first. Could I have your name, please?
W Lisa Thompson.
M Your address?
W 254 Maple Drive, Cincinnati, Ohio.
M Please sign here. And can I see your ID, please?

3.

M Good morning. How can I help you?

W I'm interested in your 'Enjoy the Orient Vacation' package.

M Oh, yes! Turkey. It's a wonderful place, where the East meets the West!

W How long does it take to get there?

M Around ten hours. It's a direct flight to Ankara, so it's fast.

W How much is it?

M Oh, it's not expensive. It's only $1,300 for a whole week.

4.

M Oh! How did this happen?

W He was running around outside and tripped and fell.

M Oh, he is bleeding a lot. I have to stop the blood first. OK, now. Just a few stitches and he'll be all right.

W Whew... Thank you very much.

해석

1. M 표를 보여 주시겠습니까? 표를 찍어야 해요, 손님.

   W 오, 어디에 뒀는지 모르겠어요.

   M 천천히 하세요. 몇 분 후에 다시 오겠습니다.

   W 오, 여기 있네요. 제 좌석 밑에 있었어요.

   M Petersburg까지 가시는군요. 즐거운 여행 되세요.

   W 감사합니다.

2. W 당좌 예금 구좌를 만들고 싶습니다.

   M 네, 먼저 서류를 작성하셔야 해요. 성함이 어떻게 되십니까?

   W Lisa Thomson이요.

   M 주소는요?

   W 오하이오 주 신시네티의 메이플 가 254번지요.

   M 여기에 서명해 주세요. 그리고 신분증을 보여 주시겠습니까?

3. M 안녕하십니까. 무엇을 도와드릴까요?

   W '동양에서의 휴가를 즐겨라' 패키지에 관심이 있어서요.

   M 아, 네! 터키요. 동양이 서양과 만나는 굉장한 곳이죠!

   W 가는 데 얼마나 걸리나요?

   M 10시간 정도요. 앙카라 직행이라 빨라요.

   W 얼마죠?

   M 오, 별로 안 비싸요. 일주일 간 1,300달러밖에 안 해요.

4. M 오! 어쩌다 이렇게 됐어요?

   W 밖에서 뛰어다니다가 발을 헛디뎌서 넘어졌어요.

   M 아, 피가 너무 많이 나네요. 피부터 멈춰야겠네요. 네, 됐어요. 이제 몇 바늘 꿰매면 괜찮아질 거예요.

   W 휴... 정말 감사합니다.

Listen Again
p. 102

A. 다시 듣고 알맞은 답을 고르시오.

1. 무슨 일이 일어나고 있는가?

   a. 승객이 표를 잃어버렸다.

   b. 그녀는 표를 사지 않았다.

   ★c. 그녀는 표를 둔 곳을 잊었다.

2. 그는 무엇을 알아야 하는가?

   a. 여자의 전화번호   ★b. 여자의 주소   c. 여자의 치수

3. 대화 내용과 일치하는 것은?

   ★a. 앙카라행 비행기이다.

   b. 가는 데 13시간이 걸린다.

   c. 비행기는 여러 곳을 들를 것이다.

B. 다시 듣고 가장 적절하게 요약한 것을 고르시오.

4. a. ☐ 소년은 자전거를 타다가 다쳤다.

   b. ☒ 소년은 피를 매우 많이 흘리고 있다.

Listening 2
p. 103

※ 듣고 빈칸에 들어갈 알맞은 말을 고르시오.

1. 그의 할아버지의 첫 번째 직업은 _____이었다.

   ★a. 직업 수영 선수   b. 인명 구조원   c. 수영 강사

2. 그녀의 어머니의 첫 번째 직업은 _____이었다.

   a. 여행가   b. 작가   ★c. 관광 안내원

3. 그의 삼촌의 첫 번째 직업은 _____이었다.

   a. 배우   ★b. 의사   c. 가수

4. 그녀의 할아버지의 첫 번째 직업은 _____이었다.

   ★a. 광부   b. 목수   c. 공사장 인부

스크립트

1. My grandfather was a swimming champion in his school days. He won many medals in national and international competitions. He loved swimming. After graduation from college, he became a lifeguard. All his life he worked on the beach, saving hundreds of lives.

2. My mother loves traveling to foreign countries. In her twenties and thirties, she worked as a tour guide. She guided tourists to every corner of the world. In her later years, she became a writer. She put her experience into books. Now she is old, and her books are guiding more people to the wonderful world of traveling.

3. My uncle was a doctor. He was rich and famous. But one day in his forties, he quit his job and became an actor. He said he had always wanted to become an actor. Now he is not rich but he is happier. You can see him in a Broadway theater.

4. My grandfather was a miner all his life. His face was always black, I remember. But he was an excellent woodworker. After work, he made all kinds of things with wood. He was happiest in his work room in the basement. He made tables, chairs and toys for his neighbors. In his old age, he built his own house, where he is living now.

해석

1. 우리 할아버지는 학창 시절 때 수영 챔피언이었어. 국내, 국제 대회에서 많은 메달을 따셨지. 그는 수영을 사랑하셨어. 대학을 졸업한 후, 할아버지는 인명 구조원이 되셨어. 평생을 해변에서 수백 명의 생명을 구하며 사셨어.

2. 우리 엄마는 외국 여행을 좋아하셔서 20대랑 30대 때는 여행 안내원으로 일하셨어. 여행자들에게 세계 구석 구석을 안내하셨지. 나중에는 작가가 되셨어. 경험을 책으로 기록하셨어. 이제 엄마는 늙으셨고, 엄마의 책은 더 많은 사람들에게 여행의 경이로운 세계를 안내하고 있어.

3. 우리 삼촌은 의사셨어. 부유하고 유명하셨지. 그런데 40대의 어느 날 일을 관두고 배우가 되셨어. 항상 배우가 되고 싶었다고 말씀하셨지. 지금 돈은 많지 않지만 더 행복하셔. 브로드웨이 극장에서 우리 삼촌을 볼 수 있을 거야.

4. 우리 할아버지는 평생 동안 광부셨어. 내 기억으로는 할아버지 얼굴은 항상 검은색이었어. 하지만 할아버지는 뛰어난 목수셨어. 일이 끝난 후에는 나무로 여러 가지 물건을 만드셨어. 할아버지는 지하 작업실에서 가장 행복하셨지. 이웃들에게 줄 탁자, 의자, 장난감들을 만드셨어. 나이를 많이 드신 후에는 지금 살고 계신 집을 직접 지으셨어.

Listen Again   p. 103

A. 다시 듣고 맞는 것을 고르시오.

1. a. 그는 결혼 인명 후 구조원이 되었다.
   b. 그는 여전히 해변에서 사람들을 구조하고 있다.
   ★c. 그는 학창 시절 때 수영 챔피언이었다.

2. a. 그녀는 국내 여러 곳을 여행했다.
   ★b. 그녀는 책을 한 권 이상 썼다.
   c. 그녀는 아직도 여행 안내원으로 일하고 있다.

3. a. 그는 30대에 직업을 바꿨다.
   ★b. 그의 꿈은 실현되었다.
   c. 지금 그는 의사로 일하고 있다.

B. 다시 듣고 맞는 문장을 고르시오.

4. a. ★ 그는 광부였지만 나무로 물건들을 만들었다.
   b. ☐ 그는 나무로 물건들을 만들어 돈을 벌었다.

스크립트

a. He was a miner but he made things with wood.
b. He made money by making things with wood.

Review   p. 104

1. ticket, misplaced, Take, in a few minutes
2. tour, guided, every corner, working, experience
3. account, fill, Here you go, sign
4. actor, lawyer, quit, he is happy, come true
5. happen, fell, stop

✻ 듣고 빈칸을 채우시오.

해석

1. M 승차권을 확인하겠습니다.
   W 오, 못 찾겠네요. 어디에 뒀는지 모르겠어요.
   M 천천히 하세요. 잠시 후에 다시 오겠습니다.

2. 우리 엄마는 여행 안내원이셨다. 수천 명의 사람들에게 세계 곳곳을 안내하셨다. 이제는 일을 하지 않으시지만, 일에서 얻은 경험으로 사람들에게 도움을 주신다.

3. W 예금 계좌를 만들고 싶습니다.
   M 물론입니다. 이 서류를 작성해 주시겠어요?
   W 네, 여기 있습니다.
   M 감사합니다. 이제 여기에 서명만 하시면 다 된 겁니다.

4. 나의 형은 배우이다. 그는 변호사였고 30대 후반에 일을 관두었다. 지금 그는 어린 시절의 꿈을 이루기 때문에 행복하다.

5. M 어쩌다 이렇게 됐나요?
   W 애가 놀이터에서 발을 헛디뎌서 넘어졌어요.
   M 먼저 지혈을 해야겠어요.

On Your Own   p. 105

LISTEN & WRITE

들리는 질문을 써 보세요.

스크립트

May I see your ticket?
Could I have your name, please?
How much can you spend?
What does your mother do?

표를 보여주시겠습니까?

성함이 어떻게 되십니까?

얼마나 많은 돈을 쓸 수 있습니까?

어머니의 직업은 무엇입니까?

PRONUNCIATION

/ t / vs / ʧ /

☞ 듣고 따라 해 보시오.

깡통, 꼭대기, 시간, 고양이, 그것, 매트

☞ 듣고 따라 해 보시오.

턱, 자르다, 차임, 붙잡다, 가려움, 성냥

☞ 주의 깊게 듣고 차이점을 발견해 보시오.

깡통 / 턱	꼭대기 / 자르다
시간 / 차임	고양이 / 붙잡다
그것 / 가려움	매트 / 성냥

듣고 들리는 단어에 표시하시오.

스크립트 chin, chop, time, catch, itch, mat

깡통	☐	턱	★
꼭대기	☐	자르다	★
시간	★	차임	☐
고양이	☐	붙잡다	★
그것	☐	가려움	★
매트	★	성냥	☐

Practice Test　　　　　p. 106~107

1. 1) c　　2) c　　2. 1) baseball player　　2) d
3. 1) c　　2) c　　4. 1) a　　2) c　　5. 1) a　　2) c

✻ 듣고 알맞은 답을 고르시오.

1. 사람들이 그들의 직업에 대해 이야기하고 있다. 그들의 직업은 무엇인가?

스크립트

M　Guess what my job is. I make people laugh and cry. I make them excited and scared. I become a different person in different times and places. It's fun, because I can live many different lives. I have been in dozens of movies, but I can remember every one of them.

W　I help people to plan their travel. There are a lot of things to take care of. I help them plan their trips, what to see, where to stay, and so on. I give them information about various places around the world. These days more people are going to Asia.

M　제 직업이 무엇인지 알아 맞춰 보세요. 저는 사람들을 웃기기도 하고 울리기도 합니다. 흥분시키거나 공포에 떨게 하기도 하죠. 여러 가지 시간과 장소에서 다양한 성격의 사람이 됩니다. 여러 가지 다른 삶을 살아 볼 수 있어서 재미있습니다. 지금까지 수십 개의 영화에 출연했지만, 저는 그 영화들을 하나하나 다 기억할 수 있습니다.

W　저는 사람들이 여행을 계획하는 것을 도와줍니다. 신경 쓸 것이 많이 있죠. 저는 사람들이 여행 일정, 무엇을 볼 것인가, 어디에 머물 것인가 등등을 계획하는 것을 돕습니다. 저는 사람들에게 세계 여러 곳의 정보를 줍니다. 요즘에는 점점 많은 사람들이 아시아에 가더군요.

1) 남자의 직업은 무엇인가?
　a. 화가　　b. 가수　★c. 배우　　d. 음악가

2) 여자의 직업은 무엇인가?
　a. 여행 안내원　　　　b. 비행기 조종사
★c. 여행사 직원　　　　d. 호텔 지배인

2. 두 사람이 이야기하고 있다.

스크립트

W　What do you do for a living?

M　I play baseball.

W　How long have you been playing?

M　For eight years.

W　What do you do on the team? I mean do you hit, pitch, or catch?

M　I hit. I hit lots of balls. I'm batting even in my dreams.

W　How many home runs have you hit?

M　250.

W　무슨 일을 하세요?

M　야구를 합니다.

W　얼마나 하셨습니까?

M　8년이요.

W　팀에서 어떤 걸 하세요? 그러니까 타자, 투수, 포수 중 어느 거요?

M　타자요. 볼을 많이 쳤죠. 심지어 꿈에서도 쳐요.

W　지금까지 홈런은 몇 개를 치셨나요?

M　250개요.

1. 빈칸을 채우시오.
　그는 프로 ____야구____ ____선수____ 이다.

2. 대화 내용과 일치하지 <u>않는</u> 것은?
　a. 그는 야구를 해서 돈을 번다.
　b. 그는 타자이다.
　c. 그는 10년 못 되게 이 일을 했다.
★d. 그는 일 년에 홈런을 250개 친다.

3. John은 일하고 있다.

스크립트

> W Can you show me some digital cameras, please?
> M Certainly, ma'am. Do you have any particular brand in mind?
> W I'd prefer Canon.
> M How about this one? It's the newest model.
> W It looks cool, but it's more than I can afford.
> M How much can you spend?
> W Around $200.

해석

W 디지털 카메라 좀 보여 주실래요?

M 물론이죠, 손님. 특별히 생각하고 계신 상표가 있나요?

W 캐논이 좋아요.

M 이건 어떠세요? 가장 최근 모델이에요.

W 멋지긴 하지만 제가 쓸 수 있는 것보다 비싸네요.

M 얼마나 쓰실 수 있나요?

W 200달러 정도요.

1) John의 직업은 무엇인가?
　a. 계산원　　b. 식당 종업원
★c. 점원　　d. 사진 작가

2) 대화 내용과 일치하는 것은?
　a. 손님은 비디오 카메라를 찾고 있다.
　b. 손님은 점원이 보여주고 있는 제품이 마음에 들지 않는다.
★c. 손님은 200달러 이상 지출할 수 없다.
　d. 손님은 John이 보여 준 제품이 오래된 모델이어서 좋아하지 않는다.

4. 두 사람이 이야기하고 있다.

스크립트

> M I have made cars and trucks all my life. Now, I want to see the world.
> W This package to Asia is perfect for you.
> M Oh, how long does it take? I only have three weeks.
> W It leaves Thursday and takes two weeks.
> M Perfect! And how much is the package?
> W Only $3,300.
> M _____OK. I will take it._____

해석

M 전 일생 동안 승용차와 트럭을 만들었어요. 이제 세상을 보고 싶어요.

W 아시아로 떠나는 이 패키지 상품은 아주 근사해요.

M 아, 여행 기간은 얼마나 되나요? 전 3주 밖에 시간이 없어요.

W 목요일에 출발하고 2주가 걸린답니다.

M 좋아요! 그리고 이 패키지는 가격이 얼마인가요?

W 겨우 3,300달러예요.

M _____좋아요. 이걸로 할게요._____

1) 이어질 수 있는 가장 적절한 대답은 무엇인가?
★a. 좋아요. 이걸로 할게요.
　b. 아뇨, 너무 머네요.
　c. 네, 같이 갑시다.
　d. 아뇨, 너무 오래 걸리네요.

2) 말하는 사람들은 누구인가?
　a. 여행사 직원과 목수
　b. 호텔 접수원과 공장 직원
★c. 공장 직원과 여행사 직원
　d. 가게 점원과 운전사

5. 두 사람이 이야기하고 있다.

스크립트

> W Could I have your name and ticket, please?
> M Here. It's Tim Sutton.
> W Oh, are you the Tim Sutton that made the news?
> M Yes.
> W You fell off your bike in Stage Five, and lost time.
> M Well, I had to stop the blood coming from my cuts.
> W But you won, anyway. Could I have you sign my shirt for my son?
> M Sure.

해석

W 이름과 표를 보여 주시겠습니까?

M 여기요. Tim Sutton입니다.

W 아, 당신이 바로 뉴스에 나온 그 Tim Sutton이신가요?

M 네.

W 5단계에서 오토바이에서 떨어져서 시간을 지체했었죠.

M 네, 상처에서 흐르는 피를 멈춰야만 했어요.

W 하지만 어쨌든 이기셨잖아요. 제 아들을 위해 제 셔츠에 사인해 주시겠어요?

M 그러죠.

1) 대화에 대해 사실인 것은 무엇인가?
★a. Tim은 유명하다.
　b. Tim은 여자의 이름이 필요하다.
　c. Tim은 여자의 표에 사인을 했다.
　d. Tim이 경주에서 졌다는 뉴스였다.

2) Tim Sutton이 하는 일은 무엇인가?
　a. 뉴스 앵커이다.

b. 스포츠 의류를 만든다.
★c. 프로 오토바이 경주 선수이다.
d. 의사이다.

Dictation   p. 108

1. Guess, job, become, I can live, movies, every one of them, travel, take care of, trips, information, world, people
2. for a living, playing, What do you do, I hit lots of balls, dreams, hit
3. show me, Certainly, in mind, How about, newest, It looks cool, spend
4. made, my life, how long, three weeks, takes, how much
5. name, ticket, made, fell off, bike, I had to stop, cuts, sign

UNIT 14
How was the trip?

Getting Ready   p. 109

1. 1. b 2. d 3. a 4. c
2. 1. e 2. c 3. a 4. d 5. b

1. 네모 안에서 알맞은 단어 묶음을 골라 빈칸에 기호를 쓰시오.

> a. 롤러코스터, 워터 슬라이드, 범퍼카
> b. 모래, 맑은 하늘, 유람선, 섬
> c. 박물관, 사찰, 고분, 교회, 벽화, 시내 관광
> d. 급류 타기, 모닥불, 강, 숲

1. 해변		b
2. 산		d
3. 놀이공원		a
4. 유적지		c

2. 질문을 답과 연결시키시오.

1. 여행 어땠어?   e. 아주 안 좋았어.
2. 휴가 갔다가 언제 돌아왔어?   c. 지난 주에.
3. 유럽은 좋았니?   a. 물론. 아주 좋았어.
4. 이거 여행가서 찍은 사진이야?   d. 응, 그래.
5. 어느 나라가 제일 좋았어?   b. 프랑스가 제일 좋았어.

Listening Task   p. 110~111

Listening 1	1. c	2. b	3. c	4. a
Listen Again A	1. b	2. a	3. a	
B	4. a			
Listening 2	1. c	2. a	3. a	4. a
Listen Again A	1. b	2. a	3. a	
B	4. a			

Listening 1   p. 110

그들은 어디에 있는가/다녀왔는가? 듣고 알맞은 답을 고르시오.

1. a. 놀이공원   b. 산   ★c. 해변
2. a. 놀이공원   ★b. 유적지   c. 섬
3. a. 산   b. 해변   ★c. 놀이공원
4★a. 산   b. 호수   c. 해변

스크립트

1. I love this place. The sky is blue. The water is crystal clear. The wind is light and cool. It's nice and quiet here. Let's just lie on the sand. That'll be enough for today.

2. The temples were amazing. The tombs were huge. The wall paintings were so alive. How did they do all that five thousand years ago? So what are we going to do today? Are we going to the museums? Or are we going on a city tour?

3. There are too many people here. We have to wait for everything. My little brothers like this place. They ride everything over and over: the roller coaster, water slide, and bumper cars. They're having a lot of fun, but I am really tired.

4. We enjoyed rafting on the river. It was exciting. I screamed all the way but I didn't want to get off. We didn't sleep in a hotel, but camped out in the woods. We saw stars at night and sang songs around a campfire.

해석

1. 여기가 아주 마음에 들어요. 하늘이 파래요. 물은 수정같이 맑고요. 바람은 가볍고 시원해요. 편안하고 조용한 곳이에요. 그냥 모래 위에 누워 보세요. 오늘은 그것만으로도 충분해요.

2. 사찰들은 놀라웠어요. 고분은 거대했어요. 벽화는 너무 생생했죠. 5천 년 전에 어떻게 그런 걸 다 만들었을까요? 그럼 오늘은 뭘 할까요? 미술관에 갈까요? 아니면 시내를 둘러볼까요?

3. 여긴 사람이 너무 많아요. 뭐든 다 기다려야 되네요. 제 남동생들은 여기를 좋아해요. 모두 다 여러 번 반복해서 타요. 롤러코스터, 워터 슬라이드, 범퍼카까지요. 아이들은 아주 재미있어 하지만 저는 정말 피곤해요.

4. 강에서 급류 타기를 즐겼어요. 짜릿했죠. 내내 소리를 질렀는데, 내리고 싶진 않았어요. 우리는 호텔에서 자지 않고 숲에서 야영을 했어요. 밤에 별도 보고 모닥불에 둘러앉아서 노래도 불렀어요.

Listen Again

p. 110

다시 듣고 알맞은 답을 고르시오.

1. 이 장소에 대한 설명으로 옳지 <u>않은</u> 것은?
   a. 조용하다.
   ★b. 붐빈다.
   c. 좋은 곳이다.

2. 휴가에 대한 설명으로 옳지 <u>않은</u> 것은?
   ★a. 자연 풍경을 많이 보고 있다.
   b. 문화적인 것들을 많이 보고 있다.
   c. 오래된 것들을 많이 보고 있다.

3. 이 장소에 대한 설명으로 옳지 <u>않은</u> 것은?
   ★a. 별로 혼잡하지 않다.
   b. 탈 것이 많다.
   c. 어린이들이 어른들보다 더 좋아한다.

B. 다시 듣고 가장 적절하게 요약한 것을 고르시오.

4. a. ★ 그녀는 급류 타기와 캠핑을 즐겼다.
   b. ☐ 그녀는 무서워서 배에서 내렸다.

Listening 2

p. 111

말하는 사람들은 어디에 다녀왔는가? 알맞은 답을 고르시오.

1. a. 아프리카   b. 아시아   ★c. 유럽
2. ★a. 바다   b. 숲   c. 놀이공원
3. ★a. 섬   b. 숲   c. 해변
4. ★a. 사촌 집   b. 친구 집   c. 조부모님 댁

스크립트

1.
M Caroline! When did you get back from your vacation?
W On Monday.
M How was the trip? Did you like Europe?
W Absolutely.
M What country did you like best?
W Spain. I liked the old buildings and churches there.

2.
W How was the trip?
M It was awful. At first, it was okay. The cruise was fun – I enjoyed the party on the ship. But on the second day, I got sick and couldn't eat anything. And for the next two days the weather was so bad, we couldn't go outside. We stayed in our room and played cards.
W Oh, that's too bad.

3.
M Was this a picture taken on your vacation?
W Yes. The island was far away. There were no cars, no big hotels or restaurants. The animals were so friendly: we could feed the birds, and we could even touch some turtles. They didn't run away from us.
M Sounds like you had a very special experience.
W I did.

4.
M So you visited your cousin this summer?W Yes. We hadn't seen each other in such a long time.
M How was it?
W Not so good. I had a wonderful time with my cousin. But my brother got hurt badly while he was swimming in the river. My mom was so worried that we hurried home.

해석
1. M Caroline! 휴가에서 언제 돌아왔어?
   W 월요일에.
   M 여행 어땠어? 유럽은 좋았어?
   W 물론이지.
   M 어느 나라가 제일 좋았어?
   W 스페인. 오래된 교회랑 건물들이 좋더라.

2. W 여행 어땠어?
   M 끔찍했어. 처음엔 괜찮았어. 배 타는 건 재밌었어. 배 위에서 파티도 즐겼지. 그런데 둘째 날 난 아파서 아무 것도 못 먹었어. 그 다음 이틀은 날씨가 너무 안 좋아서 밖으로 나갈 수가 없었어. 우리는 방 안에 머물면서 카드놀이를 했어.
   W 오, 정말 안됐다.

3. M 이게 휴가 가서 찍은 사진이야?
   W 응. 그 섬은 멀리 떨어져 있었어. 자동차도 없고, 큰 호텔이랑 식당도 없었어. 동물들도 아주 친근했어. 새 먹이도 좀 줬고, 거북이도 만져 볼 수 있었어. 안 도망가더라고.
   M 아주 특별한 경험을 한 것 같구나.
   W 그랬지.

4. M 그럼 너 이번 여름에 사촌 집에 다녀왔어?
   W 응. 너무 오래 안 만났었어.
   M 어땠어?
   W 그저 그랬어. 사촌하고는 아주 재미있었어. 그런데 내 남동생이 강에서 수영하다가 심하게 다쳤어. 엄마가 너무 걱정하셔서 서둘러 집에 왔어.

Listen Again   p. 111

다시 듣고 알맞은 답을 고르시오.

1. 휴가에 대한 내용과 일치하는 것은?
   a. 그녀는 하나의 나라에만 다녀왔다.
   ★b. 그녀는 옛 유물들이 좋았다.
   c. 그녀는 금요일에 돌아왔다.

2. 휴가에 대한 내용과 일치하는 것은?
   ★a. 그는 배를 타고 여행했다.
   b. 그는 여러 곳을 방문했다.
   c. 그는 아파서 방 안에 있었다.

3. 여행에 대한 설명으로 옳지 <u>않은</u> 것은?
   ★a. 그녀는 큰 호텔에 묵었다.
   b. 그녀는 자연과 가까이 있었다.
   c. 그녀는 동물을 좀 만졌다.

B. 다시 듣고 맞는 문장을 고르시오.

4. a. ★ 그녀는 남동생이 아파서 서둘러 집에 갔다.
   b. □ 그녀는 지루해서 서둘러 집에 갔다.

스크립트

> a. She hurried home because her brother was sick.
> b. She hurried home because she was bored.

Review   p. 112

1. trip, awful, sick, weather, outside
2. fun, ride, tired, wait
3. back, How, clear, light, I was happy, sand
4. city tour, church, museum, have, park
5. exciting, camped, sang songs, campfire

✻ 듣고 빈칸을 채우시오.

해석

1. W 여행 어땠어?
   M 끔찍했어. 첫날에는 아파서 아무 것도 못 먹었어. 다음 이틀간은 날씨가 너무 안 좋아서 밖으로 나갈 수가 없었어.

2. 우리 아이들이 무척 재미있어해요. 뭐든지 타고 또 타요. 그런데 저는 정말 피곤해요. 사람이 너무 많아요. 뭐든 다 기다려야 해요.

3. M 휴가에서 언제 돌아왔어?

W 화요일.
M 여행은 어땠어?
W 놀라웠어! 하늘이 파랬어. 물은 수정같이 맑았어. 바람은 부드럽고 시원했어. 모래 위에 누워 있으니 행복했어.

4. 제 말씀을 들어주세요! 오늘은 시내 관광을 합니다. 오래된 교회를 볼 거예요. 우리는 유명한 박물관을 방문할 것입니다. 그리고 시간이 충분하면, 모두가 보고 싶어 하던 불꽃놀이를 보기 위해 강변 공원에 갈 거예요.

5. M 급류타기 재미있었어?
   W 응, 신났어. 계속 소리 질렀어.
   M 호텔에서 묵었어?
   W 아니. 밖에서 야영했지. 별 보고 모닥불에 둘러앉아서 노래를 불렀어.

On Your Own   p. 113

LISTEN & WRITE

듣고 질문을 써 보세요.

스크립트

> When did you come back?
> Did you like Europe?
> What city did you like best?
> Was this picture taken on the trip?

해석
언제 돌아왔습니까?
유럽은 좋았습니까?
어떤 도시가 가장 좋았습니까?
이 사진은 여행에서 찍은 것입니까?

PRONUNCIATION

/ h / vs / f /
☞ 듣고 따라 해 보시오.
모자, 회관, 듣다, 뒤꿈치, 잡다
☞ 듣고 따라 해 보시오.
뚱뚱한, 떨어지다, 공포, 느끼다, 접다
☞ 주의 깊게 듣고 차이점을 발견해 보시오.
모자 / 뚱뚱한   회관 / 떨어지다   듣다 / 공포
뒤꿈치 / 느끼다   잡다 / 접다

✻ 단어를 듣고 들은 단어에 표시하시오.

스크립트 hat, fall, fear, heel, fold

모자	★	뚱뚱한	□
회관	□	떨어지다	★
듣다	□	공포	★

뒤꿈치 ★   느끼다 ☐
잡다 ☐   접다 ★

Practice Test   p. 114~115

1. 1) c   2) d   2. 1) c   2) b   3. 1) d   2) a
4. 1) c   2) a   5. 1) c   2) d

✿ 듣고 알맞은 답을 고르시오.

1. 사람들이 휴가 차 여행을 하는 동안 이야기하고 있다.

스크립트

M Look at those temples and tombs. They are huge.
W And look at those wall paintings. They look so alive.
M It's amazing.
W By the way, what are we doing tomorrow?
M I think we are going to the museum.
W I only hope the weather is a little cooler. It's so hot here.
M I hope there are less people in the museum. It's crowded everywhere.

해석
M 저 사찰하고 고분들 좀 봐. 거대하다.
W 그리고 저 벽화도 봐. 정말 생동감이 넘친다.
M 놀라워.
W 그런데, 우리 내일 뭐 하지?
M 미술관에 갈 것 같아.
W 나는 그냥 날씨가 조금만 더 시원했으면 좋겠어. 여기는 너무 더워.
M 나는 미술관에 사람들이 좀 적었으면 좋겠어. 어디나 너무 붐벼.

1) 이들은 지금 어디에 있는가?
   a. 놀이공원   b. 해변
★c. 유적지   d. 숲 속

2) 대화 내용과 일치하지 않는 것은?
   a. 이들은 날씨가 마음에 들지 않는다.
   b. 이들은 오래 된 사찰들은 이미 봤다.
   c. 이들은 미술관은 아직 보지 않았다.
★d. 이 여행지에는 관광객이 많지 않다.

2. 한 여자가 자신의 휴가에 대해 이야기하고 있다.

스크립트

The island was full of animals and plants. There were no such things as tall buildings or cars. We walked on the beach with birds and turtles all around. They didn't run away from us. I even touched them. Some animals looked very unusual. I felt like I was part of the place. It was a special experience.

해석
그 섬은 동물과 식물로 가득했다. 고층 빌딩이나 자동차 같은 것은 없었다. 우리는 새와 거북이와 함께 해변을 거닐었다. 동물들은 도망치지 않았다. 나는 동물들을 만져보기까지 했다. 몇몇 동물들은 아주 이상해 보였다. 내가 그곳의 일부가 된 기분이었다. 특별한 경험이었다.

1) 여자는 어디에 다녀왔는가?

2) 그녀의 휴가에 대한 설명에서 옳지 않은 것은?
   a. 여행은 아주 즐거웠다.
★b. 그녀는 특이한 자동차를 운전했다.
   c. 그녀는 거기 있는 동물들을 만질 수 있었다.
   d. 동물들은 사람을 두려워하지 않았다.

3. Jeff와 John은 John의 휴가 여행에 대해 이야기하고 있다.

스크립트

Jeff Where have you been, John?
John Many places. Big cities, small towns and countryside.
Jeff What did you enjoy most?
John It's hard to pick one thing. But I liked the hot-air balloon riding best. It was amazing. I will never forget it.
Jeff Do you have any pictures of it?
John Sure. Come on.

해석
Jeff 어디에 갔다 왔어, John?
John 여러 군데. 대도시하고 작은 동네하고 시골.
Jeff 어디가 제일 좋았어?
John 하나를 고르기는 어려운데. 그래도 열기구 타는 것이 제일 좋았어. 아주 놀라웠어. 절대 잊지 못할 거야.
Jeff 사진도 찍었어?
John 그럼. 이리 와 봐.

1) John이 가지 않은 곳은?
   a. 대도시   b. 작은 동네
   c. 시골   ★d. 해변

65

2) 여행에 대한 설명에서 옳지 <u>않은</u> 것은?

★a. 그는 시골이 가장 좋았다.

b. 그는 여러 곳에 갔다.

c. 그는 열기구를 탔다.

d. 그가 여행하는 동안 찍은 사진이 있다.

4. 남자와 여자가 만나고, 한 명은 다른 한 명이 사진을 갖고 있는 것을 본다.

스크립트

> W Welcome back, Mark!
>
> M Thanks, Jenny!
>
> W Did you like Germany?
>
> M Absolutely!
>
> W Was this picture taken on the trip?
>
> M Yes, it was! We stayed in this ancient castle for a week!
>
> W I like castles! Especially ancient ones! Gail went to England last year and took pictures. I liked the English castles in her pictures, too!

해석

W 돌아온 걸 환영해, Mark!

M 고마워, Jenny!

W 독일은 마음에 들었어?

M 물론이지!

W 이 사진은 여행에서 찍은 거야?

M 응, 맞아! 우린 일주일 동안 이 고성에서 머물렀어!

W 나도 성을 좋아하는데! 특히 고대의 성! Gail이 작년에 영국에 가서 사진을 찍었어. 난 그녀가 찍은 사진 속의 영국 성도 좋았어!

1) 대화에 대해 사실인 것은 무엇인가?

a. Gail은 올해 영국에 갔다.

b. Jenny는 영국과 독일에 갔다.

★c. Mark는 최근 독일에 갔다.

d. Jenny는 Gail과 함께 영국에 갔다.

2) 말하는 사람들의 기분은 어떠한가?

★a. 신나는 　 b. 슬픈 　 c. 화가 난 　 d. 놀란

5. 선생님이 학생들에게 이야기하고 있다.

스크립트

> W Finally, write about what historic site you liked best and why? We saw three museums, two islands, four parks, a church, and the Old City tour. What did you think about the site before you went? What about when you were back from the trip? You have one week to finish and turn it in.

해석

W 마지막으로, 어떤 유적지가 가장 좋았는지와 그 이유를 쓰세요. 우리는 박물관 세 군데, 섬 두 군데, 공원 네 군데, 교회 한 곳, 그리고 구시가를 관광했죠. 여러분이 그곳에 가기 전에는 그 장소에 대해 어떻게 생각했나요? 여행에서 돌아와서는 어땠나요? 글쓰기를 끝내고 제출할 기간을 일주일 주겠어요.

1) 말하는 사람이 듣는 사람에게 원하지 <u>않는</u> 것은 무엇인가?

a. 그 유적지에서 보기로 기대했던 것에 대해 설명하시오.

b. 그 유적지를 선택한 이유를 설명하시오.

★c. 유적지에서 보지 않은 것을 설명하시오.

d. 유적지를 하나 고르시오.

2) 말하는 사람과 듣는 사람은 어느 유적지를 관람했는가?

a. 두 곳의 교회

b. 신도시 관광

c. 공원 한 곳

★d. 세 곳의 박물관

Dictation	p. 116

1. temples, huge, alive, amazing, a little cooler, museum
2. island, walked, beach, run away, unusual, experience
3. places, towns, hard to pick, amazing, pictures, come on
4. Welcome, Did you like Germany, taken, trip, ancient, castles, took pictures
5. historic site, two islands, church, tour, back from the trip, turn it in

UNIT 15
What's on TV tonight?

Getting Ready	p. 117

1. **The reason he likes them:** exciting, excellent, touching

   The reason he dislikes them: too violent, disappointing, ridiculous

2. 1. b 　 2. a 　 3. d 　 4. c

1. 알맞은 칸에 단어들을 써 넣으시오.

너무 폭력적이어서	실망스러워서	신나서
우스워서	뛰어나서	감동적이어서

그가 좋아하는 프로그램 : 뉴스, 스포츠, 영화, 다큐멘터리

그가 싫어하는 프로그램 : 토크쇼, 퀴즈쇼, 리얼리티쇼, 음악
프로그램

좋아하는 이유 ___신나서, 뛰어나서, 감동적이어서___

싫어하는 이유 ___너무 폭력적이어서, 실망스러워서, 우스워서___

2. 질문을 답과 연결시키시오.

1. 오늘 밤에 TV에서 뭐 하니? b. 영화와 퀴즈쇼를 해.
2. 12번으로 돌려도 될까? a. 아니, 게임이 끝날 때 까지는 안 돼.
3. 어젯밤에 뉴스 봤어? d. 아니, 안 봤어. 넌 봤어?
4. 그 프로그램 언제 하지? c. 금요일에 해.

Listening Task
p. 118~119

Listening 1	1. b	2. c	3. b	4. a
Listen Again A	1. c	2. b	3. a	
B	4. a			
Listening 2	1. X	2. O	3. X	4. X
Listen Again A	1. b	2. c	3. b	
B	4. a			

Listening 1
p. 118

사람들이 어떤 종류의 프로그램에 대해 이야기하고 있는가?

1. a. 뉴스 ★b. 토크쇼 c. 버라이어티쇼
2. a. 드라마 b. 영화 ★c. 다큐멘터리
3. a. 스포츠 ★b. 리얼리티쇼 c. 게임쇼
4. ★a. 퀴즈쇼 b. 뉴스 c. 다큐멘터리

스크립트

1. The talk show is on Thursday at 3 p.m. Don't miss it this week. I'm sure it will be great. Have you seen the talk show host lately? She has lost 60 pounds! She's going to tell us all about her diet secrets on the show.

2. "The Animal Planet" this week was excellent! It was about the mammoth discovered in the ice last month. A mammoth from millions of years ago! Think about it! Isn't it amazing? This program is very useful. It's Fridays at 6:30 p.m. on Channel 20. Check it out!

3. That reality show is just embarrassing. A rich man dates twenty women and chooses one for his wife. It is ridiculous! It's like choosing a pet from a pet store. I don't understand why it's so popular. When is it? It's on NBS Friday at 11:00 p.m. Why, do you want to watch it?

4. Did you see the quiz show "The Millionaire" last night? It was exciting! A young woman won a million dollars! She was really smart and quick. But she was also very lucky. The other contestants made mistakes on really easy questions. She was probably too excited to go to sleep last night.

해석

1. 그 토크쇼는 목요일 오후 3시에 해요. 이번 주를 놓치지 마세요. 정말 굉장할 거라고 확신해요. 최근에 TV에서 그 토크쇼 진행자를 보셨어요? 살을 60파운드나 뺐어요! 그녀는 쇼에서 자신의 다이어트 비법을 모두 이야기할 거예요.

2. 이번 주 '애니멀 플래닛'은 대단했어요. 지난달에 빙하에서 발견된 매머드 이야기였어요. 수백만 년 전에 살던 매머드요! 생각해 보세요! 놀랍지 않아요? 이 프로그램은 아주 유익해요. 금요일 오후 6시 30분 20번에서 해요. 한번 보세요!

3. 리얼리티쇼는 당황스러울 뿐이에요. 돈 많은 남자가 여자 20명과 데이트를 한 다음 결혼 상대로 한 명을 골라요. 정말 말도 안 돼요! 애완동물 가게에서 애완동물을 고르는 것 같잖아요. 이게 왜 인기 있는지 모르겠어요. 언제 하냐고요? 밤 11시에 NBS에서 해요. 왜요, 보고 싶은가요?

4. 어젯밤에 '백만장자'라는 퀴즈쇼 보셨어요? 진짜 흥분됐어요! 어떤 젊은 여자가 우승해서 백만 달러를 받았어요! 그 여자는 진짜 똑똑하고 재빨랐어요. 하지만 운도 좋았죠. 다른 참가자들이 너무 쉬운 문제에서 실수를 하더라고요. 제 생각엔 그 여자는 너무 흥분해서 어젯밤에 잠도 못 잤을 것 같아요.

Listen Again
p. 118

A. 다시 듣고 틀린 것을 고르시오.

1. a. 다이어트에 대해 할 것이다.
   b. 토크쇼의 진행자에 대한 이야기일 것이다.
   ★c. 그녀 인생의 비밀에 대한 이야기일 것이다.

2. a. 이 프로그램은 유익하다.
   ★b. 거대한 고래에 대한 내용이다.
   c. 빙하에서 발견된 동물에 대한 이야기이다.

3. ★a. 선택할 애완동물이 있다.
   b. 부유한 남자와 여러 명의 여자가 있다.
   c. 인기가 많다.

B. 다시 듣고 가장 적절하게 요약한 것을 고르시오.

4. a. ★ 그 여자는 똑똑하고 운이 좋아 백만 달러를 우승 상금으로 받았다.
   b. □ 그 여자는 문제가 너무 쉬워서 백만 달러를 우승 상금으로 받았다.

Listening 2

p. 119

처음에 말하는 사람이 자기가 좋아하는 프로그램을 볼 수 있는가?
볼 수 있으면 O에, 볼 수 없으면 X라고 표시하시오.

1. ___X___   2. ___O___   3. ___X___   4. ___X___

스크립트

1.

M What's on TV tonight?

W Well, there's nothing you like. No sports, no western movies.

M How about the game show "Target"?

W It's on Thursday, not Wednesday.

M In that case, I think I'll go to bed early tonight.

2.

M Mom, I need to see the "Earth Report" for my term paper. Could you record it for me tonight?

W Why don't you do it yourself?

M It's on too late and I can't stay up until then.

W When is it?

M It's at 1:00 a.m. on NBC .

W That is late. Go to bed. I'll take care of it.

3.

W Can I change to Channel 9, Dad?

M Why, Amy?

W There's a live Beagles concert on. They're my favorite rock band.

M Sorry but no. You'll have to wait until this football game is over.

W Please, Dad! The concert will be over by then.

M Sorry, but this game is very important to me.

4.

M Is "Police Story" not on this week?

W No, the program is not on any more.

M Why did they cancel such a popular program?

W It was popular with men, but not with women. Women didn't like it because it was too violent.

M That's not fair.

해석

1. M 오늘 밤에 TV에서 뭐 하지?

   W 글쎄, 네가 좋아하는 건 아무 것도 안 해. 스포츠도 안 하고, 서부영화도 안 해.

   M 게임 쇼 '타깃'은?

   W 수요일이 아니고 그건 목요일에 해.

M 그럼 난 오늘 밤은 일찍 자는 게 낫겠어.

2. M 엄마, 저 학기말 숙제 때문에 '지구 리포트'를 봐야 해요. 오늘 밤에 녹화해 주실 수 있으세요?

   W 네가 직접 하지 그래?

   M 너무 늦게 해서 그때까지 깨어있을 수가 없어요.

   W 언제 하는데?

   M NBC에서 새벽 1시에 해요.

   W 정말 늦네. 가서 자거라, 내가 해 줄게.

3. W 9번으로 채널 돌려도 될까요, 아빠?

   M 왜 그러니, Amy?

   W Beagles가 라이브 공연을 하거든요. 제가 제일 좋아하는 록밴드예요.

   M 미안하지만 안 돼. 이 풋볼 경기가 끝날 때까지 기다리거라.

   W 제발, 아빠! 그때는 콘서트 끝나요.

   M 미안, 그래도 이건 나한테 정말 중요한 경기야.

4. M 이번 주에는 '폴리스 스토리' 안 해?

   W 안 해. 이제 아예 안 하던데.

   M 왜 그런 인기 있는 걸 그만하는 걸까?

   W 남자들한테는 인기 있지만, 여자들한테는 아니거든. 여자들은 너무 폭력적이어서 그걸 싫어했어.

   M 그건 불공평해.

Listen Again

p. 119

A. 다시 듣고 틀린 것을 고르시오.

1. a. 게임쇼는 오늘 하지 않는다.
   ★b. 오늘은 목요일이다.
   c. 남자는 오늘 밤에 TV를 보지 않을 것이다.

2. a. Jeff는 숙제 때문에 그 프로그램을 봐야 한다.
   b. 그 프로그램은 너무 늦게 한다.
   ★c. Jeff와 그의 엄마는 그 프로그램을 함께 볼 것이다.

3. a. Amy의 아빠는 풋볼 경기 보는 것을 좋아한다.
   ★b. Amy는 TV 소리를 줄이고 싶어 한다.
   c. Amy는 채널을 바꾸고 싶어한다.

B. 다시 듣고 맞는 문장을 고르시오.

4. a. ★ 그는 그 프로그램을 놓쳤다.
   b. ☐ 그는 그 프로그램이 너무 폭력적이라고 생각한다.

스크립트

a. He misses the program.
b. He thinks the program was too violent.

Review   p. 120

1. on, There're sports, movies, action
2. embarrassing, chooses, ridiculous, popular
3. quiz, it was on, Thursday, Channel
4. documentary, excellent, millions, amazing
5. on, cancel, variety show, fair

✽ 듣고 빈칸을 채우시오.

해석

1. W 오늘 밤 TV에서 뭐 해?
   M 스포츠하고 다큐멘터리를 좀 하네.
   W 그런데 영화는 안 해?
   M 어, 하는데, 네가 좋아하는 액션 영화는 안 해.

2. 이 리얼리티쇼는 황당하기만 해. 돈 많은 남자가 여자 20명과 데이트 한 다음 애인으로 한 명을 선택해. 진짜 터무니없어! 이게 왜 그렇게 인기 있는지 모르겠어.

3. M 어젯밤에 퀴즈쇼 봤어?
   W 보고 싶었는데, 언제 하는지를 몰랐어.
   M 목요일 9시, 9번에서 해.

4. 지난 주 금요일 7번에서 한 다큐멘터리는 정말 좋았어. 그냥 좋은 정도가 아니었어. 대단했어. 빙하에서 발견된 매머드가 나왔어. 수백만 년 전의 매머드야. 정말 놀라웠어!

5. W 그 퀴즈쇼는 더 이상 안 하더라.
   M 왜 그렇게 인기 있는 프로그램을 그만 하는 걸까?
   W 어린 시청자들을 더 끌기 위해 버라이어티쇼를 시작했어.
   M 내가 제일 좋아하는 프로였는데. 이건 불공평해.

On Your Own   p. 121

LISTEN & WRITE

듣고 질문을 써 보세요.

스크립트

What's on TV tonight?
Is a talk show on this Friday?

Did you see the documentary last night?
Do you watch news every day?

해석

오늘 밤 TV에서 무엇을 합니까?
이번 금요일에 토크쇼를 합니까?
어젯밤에 그 다큐멘터리를 봤습니까?
매일 뉴스를 봅니까?

PRONUNCIATION

/ æ / vs / a /
☞ 듣고 따라 해 보시오.
고양이, 모자, 부족, 지도, 검은
☞ 듣고 따라 해 보시오.
간이 침대, 뜨거운, 잠그다, 자루걸레, 막다
☞ 주의 깊게 듣고 차이점을 발견해 보시오.
고양이 / 간이 침대   모자 / 뜨거운   부족함 / 잠그다
지도 / 자루걸레   검은 / 막다

단어를 듣고 들은 단어에 표시하시오.

스크립트 cot, hat, lack, mop, block

고양이	☐	간이침대	★
모자	★	뜨거운	☐
부족함	★	잠그다	☐
지도	☐	자루걸레	★
검은	☐	막다	★

Practice Test   p. 122~123

1. 1) T	2) T	3) F	4) F	5) F	6) T 7) F
2. 1) d	2) c		3. 1) d	2) d	
4. 1) b	2) d		5. 1) a	2) d	

✽ 듣고 체크하거나 알맞은 답을 고르시오.

1. 여자가 TV 프로그램에 대해 이야기하고 있다. 듣고 T나 F에 체크하시오.

스크립트

I never miss this talk show. The guests are not only famous people but also ordinary people like you and me. But it is never disappointing. It's the show's host Natalie Jones that makes it so popular. With her, people feel at home and talk about themselves. Last week Natalie told about herself: her unhappy childhood, her marriage, and her children. It was very touching.

해석

저는 이 토크쇼를 놓친 적이 없어요. 초대 손님들이 유명한 사람들만 나오는 게 아니라 당신과 저 같은 평범한 사람들도 나오거든요. 그래도 실망스러웠던 적은 한 번도 없어요. 이 쇼를 인기 있게 만드는 것은 진행자 Natalie Jones예요. 그녀와 함께 있으면 사람들이 편안해져서 자기 이야기를 해요. 지난 주에는 Natalie가 사진에 내해 이야기했어요. 불행했던 어린 시설, 결혼, 아이늘에 대해서요. 아주 감동적이었어요.

1. 이 프로그램은 토크쇼이다. (T)
2. 쇼의 진행자는 여자이다. (T)
3. 항상 유명한 사람들이 쇼에 출연한다. (F)
4. 이 쇼는 항상 실망스럽다. (F)
5. 이 쇼는 유명한 초대 손님들 때문에 인기가 아주 많다. (F)
6. 쇼의 진행자는 사람들을 편안하게 만든다. (T)
7. 지난주에 진행자가 자신의 식이요법에 대해 이야기했다. (F)

2. Susan과 Brian은 TV 프로그램에 대해 이야기하고 있다.

스크립트

> W This show is ridiculous. I don't know why it is so popular.
> M It is a reality show. What do you expect from reality?
> W It's so violent and embarrassing.
> M I like it. It's realistic. It only shows real life. Hey, don't change the channel!

해석

W 이 쇼는 정말 터무니 없어. 이게 왜 그렇게 인기인지 모르겠어.

M 리얼리티쇼잖아. 현실에서 뭘 바라나?

W 너무 폭력적이고 당황스러워.

M 난 좋은데. 사실적이잖아. 진짜 삶만 보여줘. 이봐, 채널 돌리지 마!

1. 이 쇼는 _____ 이다.
   a. 드라마 b. 버라이어티쇼 c. 다큐멘터리 ★d. 리얼리티쇼

2. 대화 내용과 일치하는 것은?
   a. 여자는 쇼가 너무 사실적이어서 싫어한다.
   b. 남자는 쇼가 폭력적이기 때문에 좋아한다.
   ★c. 이 쇼는 아주 인기가 많다.
   d. 남자는 채널을 돌릴 것이다.

3. Jeff는 어머니와 이야기하고 있다.

스크립트

> M Mom, where is the quiz show?
> W I guess it's on WBC, Channel 12.
> M It's at 6:30, right?
> W I think so. But why? You don't watch it very often.
> M One of my teachers will appear on the show. He is really smart. I think he will beat the other two contestants easily.
> W Stop the channel there. It's on Channel 11, not 12.

해석

M 엄마, 퀴즈쇼는 어디서 해요?

W 12번 WBC에서 하는 것 같던데.

M 6시 30분, 맞죠?

W 그런 것 같아. 그런데 왜? 그렇게 자주 안 보잖아.

M 선생님 한 분이 그 쇼에 나올 거예요. 그 선생님은 정말 아는 게 많으세요. 그 선생님이 다른 두 경쟁자를 쉽게 이길 것 같아요.

W 채널 바꾸지 마. 12번이 아니라 11번에서 해.

1) 프로그램에 대해 일치하지 않는 것은?
   a. 퀴즈 프로그램이다.
   b. 11번에서 한다.
   c. 6시 30분에 한다.
   ★d. Jeff가 가장 좋아하는 프로그램이다.

2) 대화 내용과 일치하는 것은?
   a. Jeff의 친구가 프로그램에 출연할 것이다.
   b. 두 명의 참가자가 경쟁한다.
   c. Jeff는 이 쇼를 매우 자주 본다.
   ★d. Jeff는 그의 선생님이 이길 거라고 확신한다.

4. Mike가 Karen에게 이야기하고 있다.

스크립트

> M Did you see the documentary Friday night?
> W No, I didn't. Did you?
> M Yes, it was about baseball.
> W Too bad! My husband plays on a team.
> M Oh, it was so popular that it's being shown, again.
> W What day is it on?
> M It's on Tuesday at 10.
> W I'll tell my husband! Thanks!

해석

M 금요일 밤에 다큐멘터리 봤어?

W 아니, 못 봤어. 넌 봤어?

M 봤어, 야구에 관한 거였어.

W 이런! 내 남편은 팀에서 야구를 해.

M 아, 그 프로그램이 아주 인기가 많아서 다시 방송해 준대.

W 그게 언제야?

M 목요일 10시야.

W 남편에게 말해 줘야겠어! 고마워!

1) 말하는 사람들은 무엇에 대해 이야기하고 있는가?
   a. 몇 명의 야구 선수   ★b. TV 다큐멘터리
   c. 여자의 남편   d. 야구 경기

2) 대화에 대해 사실이 아닌 것은 무엇인가?
   a. 여자는 다큐멘터리 보는 것을 놓쳤다.
   b. 다큐멘터리는 목요일에 다시 방송될 것이다.
   c. 여자의 남편은 야구를 한다.
   ★d. 여자의 남편은 야구를 좋아하지 않는다.

5. 한 소녀가 아버지와 이야기하고 있다.

스크립트

W Where is my favorite TV show, tonight?
M Which one? "The Animal Lover"?
W Yes. Is it not on this week? Have they cancelled the program?
M I think they did.
W Why? It's a very touching but useful show about real animals and the people who care for them.
M Right. I remember sometimes you cried for the hurt or sick animals.

해석
W 오늘 밤 제가 가장 좋아하는 TV쇼가 어느 채널에서 하죠?
M 어떤 것? '애니멀 러버' 말이니?
W 네. 이번 주엔 방송 안 하나요? 프로그램이 취소됐나요?
M 취소된 것 같구나.
W 왜요? 실제 동물과 그들을 돌보는 사람들에 대한 감동적이고 유용한 프로그램인데요.
M 그래. 다치거나 병든 동물들 때문에 네가 가끔 울던 것이 기억나는구나.

1) 소녀가 가장 좋아하는 TV쇼는   .
★a. 주간 리얼리티쇼이다.   b. 월간 다큐멘터리이다.
   c. 주간 퀴즈쇼이다.   d. 월간 토크쇼이다.

2) 대화 내용과 일치하지 않는 것은 무엇인가?
   a. 그 쇼는 동물에 관한 것이다.
   b. 그 쇼는 이번 주에 하지 않는다.
   c. 그 쇼는 취소되었다.
★d. 그 쇼는 연인들에 관한 것이다.

Dictation   p. 124

1. talk show, disappointing, popular, people feel at home, children, touching
2. ridiculous, reality, violent, It's realistic, channel
3. quiz, it's on, very often, will appear, He is really smart, It's on
4. Friday night, baseball, husband, team, popular, Tuesday, Thanks
5. favorite, Which one, cancelled, useful, care for, sick animals

UNIT 16
I don't think so.

Getting Ready   p. 125

1. 1. A   2. A   3. D   4. A   5. A
   6. A   7. D   8. A   9. D   10. D
2. 1. b   2. e   3. d   4. a   5. c   6. f

1. 동의하는 표현이면 'A', 동의하지 않는 표현이면 'D'를 쓰시오.

1. 그런 것 같아.	A
2. 나도 그렇게 생각해.	A
3. 난 그렇지 않은 것 같은데.	D
4. 나도 그래.	A
5. 나도 안 그래.	A
6. 좋은 생각인데.	A
7. 그건 별로 좋은 생각이 아닌 것 같아.	D
8. 나도 그래.	A
9. 글쎄, 잘 모르겠는데.	D
10. 난 너에게 동의하지 않아.	D

2. 표현을 응답과 연결시키시오.

1. 난 개를 좋아하지 않아.   b. 나도 싫어해.
2. 나는 그가 보고 싶을 거야.   e. 나도, 그는 좋은 사람이야.
3. 이번 금요일 날 모이자.   d. 좋은 생각이야.
4. 그 영화 재미있어.   a. 나도 그래. 대단했어.
5. 난 긴장돼.   c. 나도 그래.
6. 그는 그녀와 결혼해야 할 것 같아.
   f. 난 그렇게 생각하지 않아. 그녀는 너무 어려.

Listening Task   p. 126~127

Listening 1	1. Bad news	2. Bad mews
	3. Good news	4. Good news
Listen Again A	1. a 2. c	3. c
B	4. a	
Listening 2	1. Disagree	2. Disagree
	3. Agree	4. Disagree
Listen Again A	1. c 2. a	3. c
B	4. a	

Listening 1   p. 126

좋은 소식인가, 좋지 않은 소식인가? 하나에 표시하시오.

1. 좋은 소식 _____   좋지 않은 소식 ____★____
2. 좋은 소식 _____   좋지 않은 소식 ____★____

3. 좋은 소식 ___★___   좋지 않은 소식 _____

4. 좋은 소식 ___★___   좋지 않은 소식 _____

스크립트

1.

W You know what? Jerry got dumped.

M By whom? Caroline?

W Yes. Now Caroline is seeing another boy she met on the Internet.

M Poor Jerry! He must be heartbroken. I feel so bad for him.

W Me, too.

2.

M Did you hear Carl is going to move?

W No. When? Where?

M His father has got a new job in Texas and they are moving next month.

W That's too bad. I'm going to miss him.

M So am I.

3.

W Guess what. Alex won a scholarship!

M He did? Now he can go to university.

W And he doesn't have to work so hard after school.

M I think we should celebrate with him.

W Let's get together this Friday.

M I don't think that's a good idea. Friday is his busiest day.

4.

W You know Janet has a new sister, don't you?

M No. Did her mother have a baby?

W No, it's not that. She's got a little puppy and she calls it her sister.

M She must be happy. My mom doesn't like animals, so I can't have a pet.

W Me, neither.

해석

1. W 그거 알아? Jerry가 차였대.

  M 누구한테? Caroline?

  W 응. Caroline은 지금 인터넷에서 사귄 다른 남자를 만나고 있어.

  M 불쌍한 Jerry! 슬픔에 빠져 있겠지. 진짜 마음이 안 좋다.

  W 나도 그래.

2. M Carl이 이사 간다는 소식 들었어?

  W 아니. 언제? 어디로?

  M 그의 아빠가 텍사스에서 새 직장을 구하셔서 다음 달에 이사를 간대.

W 유감이야. 그가 보고싶을 거야.

M 나도.

3. W 있잖아, Alex가 장학금을 탔대!

  M 그래? 이제 대학에 갈 수 있겠네.

  W 그리고 학교 끝나고 힘들게 일할 필요도 없어.

  M 우리가 그를 축하해줘야 할 것 같아.

  W 이번 주 금요일에 모이자.

  M 그건 별로인 것 같아. 금요일은 그가 가장 바쁜 날이잖아.

4. W Janet에게 여동생 생긴 거 알아?

  M 몰랐어. 어머니께서 아기 낳으셨대?

  W 아니, 그게 아냐. 그녀에게 아기 강아지가 생겼는데 그녀가 동생이라고 불러.

  M 좋겠다. 우리 엄마는 동물을 싫어하셔서 난 애완동물을 못 길러.

  W 나도 마찬가지야.

Listen Again   p. 126

A. 다시 듣고 알맞은 답을 고르시오.

1. 대화 내용과 일치하는 것은?

  ★a. 둘 다 친구에 대해 같은 마음이다.

  b. Jerry는 지금 매우 행복하다.

  c. Caroline은 지금 기분이 좋지 않다.

2. 대화 내용과 일치하는 것은?

  a. Carl은 Texas에 일자리를 얻었다.

  b. 이사는 다음 주에 할 것이다.

  ★c. 둘 다 이 소식에 유감스러워 하고 있다.

3. 대화 내용과 일치하지 <u>않는</u> 것은?

  a. Alex는 방과 후에 열심히 일했다.

  b. Alex는 대학에 갈 돈이 필요했다.

  ★c. 둘 다 금요일이 축하하기에 적당한 날이라고 생각한다.

B. 다시 듣고 가장 적절하게 요약한 것을 고르시오.

4. a. ☒ Janet은 새끼 강아지가 생겼다.

  b. ☐ Janet의 어머니가 아기를 낳았다.

Listening 2   p. 127

서로 동의하는가, 동의하지 않는가? 하나에 표시하시오.

1. 동의한다 _____   동의하지 않는다 ___★___

2. 동의한다 _____   동의하지 않는다 ___★___

3. 동의한다 ___★___   동의하지 않는다 _____

4. 동의한다 _____   동의하지 않는다 ___★___

1.

M Did you see *The Runaway*?

W No, not yet. But I heard that movie is good.

M Everybody says that, but I didn't think so. Harry Ford is too old for the part. You know he is in his sixties!

W True, he is not young but he's still good. And he is very funny. That's why people still love him.

2.

M I think I'll buy a used car.

W I don't think that's a good idea.

M It's cheaper. I don't have much money.

W I know. But you will end up spending more money repairing it.

M Thanks for your advice but I've already made up my mind.

3.

W Do you watch the "Guiding Post" on MBS?

M Yes, every day. I love that soap opera.

W Who do you think Susan will marry? I hope she marries Bill.

M So do I. John is richer and more handsome, but he won't make a good husband.

W That's exactly what I think.

4.

M The Dodgers should change their pitcher.

W I don't think so. He is just nervous. He will be okay soon.

M No. He is different today. He is slow. He's in bad condition.

W I don't agree with you.

해석

1. M "도망자" 봤어?

   W 아니, 아직. 그 영화가 좋다는 말은 들었어.

   M 다들 그렇다고 하는데, 난 아닌 것 같아. Harry Ford는 그 역할을 하기엔 너무 늙었어. 그는 60대잖아!

   W 그래, 젊진 않지만 아직 꽤 괜찮잖아. 그리고 그는 정말 재미있어. 그러니까 사람들이 아직도 좋아하지.

2. M 나 중고차를 살까 해.

   W 별로일 것 같은데.

   M 더 싸잖아. 나는 돈이 별로 없어.

   W 알아. 하지만 결국 수리하는 데 더 돈을 많이 쓰게 될 거야.

   M 충고는 고맙지만 이미 결정했어.

3. W 너 MBS에서 하는 "가이딩 포스트" 봐?

   M 응, 매일. 난 그 드라마 정말 좋아해.

   W Susan이 누구랑 결혼할 거라고 생각해? 난 Bill하고 했으면 좋겠어.

   M 나도. John이 돈도 더 많고 잘생겼지만, 좋은 남편은 못 될 거야.

   W 내 생각이랑 똑같네.

4. M 다저스는 투수를 바꿔야 해.

   W 아니야. 저 투수는 그냥 긴장한 거야. 곧 괜찮아 질 거야.

   M 아니. 오늘은 좀 달라. 느려. 컨디션이 안 좋은 것 같아.

   W 난 그렇게 생각하지 않아.

Listen Again   p. 127

A. 다시 듣고 알맞은 답을 고르시오.

1. 대화 내용과 일치하는 것은?

   a. 둘 다 그 배우가 더 이상 멋지지 않다고 생각한다.

   b. 그 배우는 50대이다.

   ★c. 둘 다 그 배우가 더 이상 젊지 않다고 생각한다.

2. 대화 내용과 일치하는 것은?

   ★a. 둘 다 중고차가 더 싸다는 데 동의한다.

   b. 둘 다 중고차를 사면 돈이 절약될 거라고 생각한다.

   c. 남자는 중고차를 사는 것에 대한 생각을 바꿀 것이다.

3. 대화 내용과 일치하지 않는 것은?

   a. 그들은 남자가 좋은 남편이 되기 위해 부자일 필요는 없다고 생각한다.

   b. 둘 다 여자 등장인물이 Bill과 결혼하기를 바란다.

   ★c. John은 부자이지만 잘생기지 않았다.

B. 다시 듣고 맞는 문장을 고르시오.

4. a. ★ 남자는 다저스가 투수를 바꿔야 한다고 생각한다.

   b. ☐ 여자는 그들이 투수를 바꾸는 것에 찬성한다.

스크립트

a. The man thinks the Dodgers should change their pitcher.

b. The woman agrees that the Dodgers should change their pitcher.

Review   p. 128

1. used, idea, so, repair
2. hear, miss, too
3. got, must, I can't have a pet, Neither
4. hope, bad condition, agree
5. actor, know, think, I don't think, become

✷ 듣고 빈칸을 채우시오.

해석

1. M 나 중고차를 사려고 해.
   W 별로 좋은 생각인 것 같지는 않은데.
   M 하지만 돈을 절약할 수 있잖아.
   W 난 그렇게 생각하지 않아. 수리하는 데 비용이 더 들 거야.

2. W Max가 이사 간다는 소식 들었어?
   M 응. 그가 정말 보고 싶을 거야.
   W 나도.

3. M Pam에게 귀엽고 작은 강아지가 생겼어.
   W 정말 좋겠다. 나는 애완동물을 못 키워. 우리 엄마가 못 키우게 하셔.
   M 우리 엄마도 그래.

4. W 걱정하지 마. 그는 곧 더 잘 할 거야.
   M 그러기를 바라. 그런데 그는 오늘 상태가 안 좋은 것 같아.
   W 그렇지 않은 것 같은데.

5. W 난 그 배우가 마음에 안 들어. 경찰을 하기에는 몸집이 너무 작아.
   M 글쎄, 나는 잘 모르겠어.
   W 그렇게 생각하지 않니?
   M 응, 경찰이 되기 위해 몸집이 클 필요는 없을 것 같아.

On Your Own
p. 129

LISTEN & WRITE

듣고 질문을 써 보세요.

스크립트

Do you need to study harder?
We don't need to study English Grammar any more. What do you think?

해석
당신은 더 열심히 공부해야 합니까?
우리는 더 이상 영어 문법을 공부하지 않아도 됩니다. 어떻게 생각하십니까?

PRONUNCIATION

/ a / vs / < /

☞ 듣고 따라 해 보시오.
   경찰, 인형, 부두, 잠그다, 충격

☞ 듣고 따라 해 보시오.
   컵, 무딘, 오리, 행운, 껍데기

☞ 주의 깊게 듣고 차이점을 발견해 보시오.

   경찰 / 컵   인형 / 무딘
   부두 / 오리   잠그다 / 행운
   충격 / 껍데기

✷ 단어를 듣고 들은 단어에 표시하시오.

스크립트 cop, dull, dock, lock, shuck

경찰	★	컵	☐
인형	☐	무딘	★
부두	★	오리	☐
잠그다	★	행운	☐
충격	☐	껍데기	★

Practice Test
p. 130~131

1. 1) c   2) d   2. 1) a   3. 1) a   2) a
4. 1) a   5. 1) d   2) d

✷ 듣고 알맞은 답을 고르시오.

1. Susan이 친구와 이야기하고 있다.

스크립트

W Kevin says he's going to quit school.
M Is he? What's the problem?
W He said he is going to make money.
M I don't think that's a good idea.
W Me, neither. I tried to change his mind, but I couldn't.
M Why does he need money so badly?
W I don't know. Maybe he is going to start a business.
M I think he is still too young for that.

해석
W Kevin이 학교를 그만둘 거래.
M 그래? 뭐가 문제래?
W 돈을 벌 거라고 말했어.
M 별로 좋은 생각 같지는 않은데.
W 나도 별로인 것 같아. 설득하려고는 해 봤는데, 안 되더라.
M 왜 그렇게 절실하게 돈이 필요할까?
W 모르겠어. 아마 사업을 시작하려나 봐.
M 그러기에는 아직 너무 어린 것 같은데.

1) 이어질 응답으로 어울리지 않는 것은?
   a. 나도 그래.   b. 맞아.
   ★c. 나도 그렇지 않은 것 같아. d. 나도 그렇게 생각해.

2) 대화 내용과 일치하지 않는 것은?
   a. 그들의 친구에 대해 이야기하고 있다.
   b. 친구는 학교를 그만두려고 한다.
   c. 친구는 돈을 벌고 싶어 한다.
   ★d. 그들은 친구가 학교를 그만둬야 한다는 데 동의한다.

2. 엄마가 아들과 이야기하고 있다.

스크립트

M　Mom, I'm going to be a millionaire.
W　That would be nice.
M　I think I can make a million dollars in one year.
W　Well... I don't know about that.
M　But I'll try hard.

해석

M　엄마, 저는 백만장자가 될 거예요.
W　그거 좋겠는데.
M　1년만에 백만 달러를 벌 수 있을 것 같아요.
W　글쎄... 난 잘 모르겠구나.
M　그래도 전 열심히 해 볼 거예요.

1) 이어질 응답으로 가장 알맞은 것을 고르시오.

★a. 좋은 생각이야.　　　　b. 나도 그래.
　c. 난 그렇게 하지 않을 것 같아. d. 난 거기에 동의하지 않아.

3. Jeff와 Maria가 이야기하고 있다.

스크립트

Jeff　I read the book and it was just great. If you haven't read it yet, read it. You'll love it.
Maria　I did, but I couldn't finish it. I fell asleep in a few minutes.
Jeff　I can't believe it. How can you go to sleep while reading such an exciting book? It is long but it is an interesting book.
Maria　I know it's a famous book. But it's boring to me. I don't like fantasy.
Jeff　You're so different from me!

해석

Jeff　나 그 책 읽었는데 정말 대단해. 아직 안 읽었으면 읽어 봐. 네 마음에 들 거야.
Maria　읽으려고 했는데, 다 못 읽었어. 몇 분 만에 잠이 들었어.
Jeff　믿을 수 없어. 어떻게 그런 신나는 책을 읽으면서 잠이 들 수가 있어? 길긴 하지만 재미있는 책이야.
Maria　유명한 책이라는 건 알아. 그런데 나한텐 지루해. 난 공상물은 안 좋아해.
Jeff　너는 나랑 너무 다르구나!

1) 책에 대한 내용과 일치하지 않는 것은?

★a. 역사책이다.　　　　b. 공상 소설이다.
　c. 내용이 긴 책이다.　d. 유명한 책이다.

2) 대화 내용과 일치하지 않는 것은?

★a. Maria는 그 책이 흥미진진하다는 것에 동의한다.
　b. Maria는 그 책이 유명하다는 것에 동의한다.
　c. Maria는 공상물은 좋아하지 않는다.
　d. Jeff는 그 책을 읽는 중에는 절대 잠이 들지 않는다.

4. Paul과 Jean은 가장 친한 친구이다.

스크립트

Paul　Let's get together this Wednesday.
Jean　Sounds like a good idea.

Paul　Hey, look at this!
Jean　Oh, that movie is good.
Paul　I think so, too. It's excellent for learning about Korea.
Jean　Well, I don't know about that. It's just an adventure movie.
Paul　Maybe we should pick something else.

해석

Paul　이번 주 수요일에 모이자.
Jean　좋은 생각이야.
Paul　이봐, 이것 좀 봐.
Jean　아, 그 영화 재밌겠는걸.
Paul　그런 것 같아. 한국을 배우기 위한 최고의 영화야.
Jean　음, 그런 건 모르겠어. 그저 모험 영화야.
Paul　다른 영화를 골라야겠네.

1) 대화 내용과 일치하지 않는 것은?

★a. 그들은 함께 한국에 대해 배울 것이다.
　b. 그들은 한국 영화를 가지고 있다.
　c. 그들의 모임은 수요일이다.
　d. 그들은 다른 영화를 고를 것이다.

5. 다음은 Jane의 일기이다.

스크립트

My mom and I usually agree on things, but yesterday we didn't. I think I should marry Tony. My mom doesn't think so. She thinks I am too young. I don't agree with her, so we had a big fight. I finally agreed with my mom that I have to tell him good-bye for now. I'll miss him, but I understand.

해석

엄마와 나는 보통 마음이 맞지만, 어제는 아니었다. 나는 Tony와 결혼해야 한다고 생각한다. 엄마는 그렇게 생각하지 않으신다. 엄마는 내가 너무 어리다고 생각하신다. 내가 엄마 생각에 찬성하지 않아서 우리는 크게 싸우고 말았다. 결국 나는 이제 그와 헤어져야 한다는 엄마의 의견을 따른다. 나는 Tony를 그리워하

헤어져야 한다는 엄마의 의견을 따른다. 나는 Tony를 그리워하겠지만, 이해한다.

1) 말하는 사람의 기분은 어떠한가?
   a. 놀란　　　　　　b. 불쾌한
   c. 무서운　　　★d. 실망한

2) 다음 중 소녀에 대해 일치하는 것은 무엇인가?
   a. 그녀는 엄마와 마음이 맞지 않곤 했었다.
   b. 그녀는 Tony의 생각에 동의하지 않는다.
   c. 그녀는 Tony를 더 이상 사랑하지 않는다.
   ★d. 그녀는 Tony와 결혼하지 않을 것이다.

Dictation　　　　　　　　　　p. 132

1. going to quit, What's the problem, make money, neither, so badly, I don't know, too young
2. I'm going to, nice, in one year, about that, I'll try
3. great, You'll love it, finish, I can't believe it, interesting, I know, boring to me, different from
4. Sounds like, learning about, something else
5. agree, yesterday, doesn't think so, too young, we had a big fight, I'll miss him

Memo

Memo

Memo

Memo